The Impact of Mindfulness Meditation Programs on Performance-Related Outcomes

Implications for the U.S. Army

KIMBERLY A. HEPNER, ERIKA LITVIN BLOOM, SYDNE NEWBERRY, JESSICA L. SOUSA, KAREN CHAN OSILLA, MARIKA BOOTH, ARMENDA BIALAS, CAROLYN M. RUTTER

Prepared for the United States Army
Approved for public release; distribution unlimited

For more information on this publication, visit **www.rand.org/t/RRA1522-1**.

About RAND

The RAND Corporation is a research organization that develops solutions to public policy challenges to help make communities throughout the world safer and more secure, healthier and more prosperous. RAND is nonprofit, nonpartisan, and committed to the public interest. To learn more about RAND, visit www.rand.org.

Research Integrity

Our mission to help improve policy and decisionmaking through research and analysis is enabled through our core values of quality and objectivity and our unwavering commitment to the highest level of integrity and ethical behavior. To help ensure our research and analysis are rigorous, objective, and nonpartisan, we subject our research publications to a robust and exacting quality-assurance process; avoid both the appearance and reality of financial and other conflicts of interest through staff training, project screening, and a policy of mandatory disclosure; and pursue transparency in our research engagements through our commitment to the open publication of our research findings and recommendations, disclosure of the source of funding of published research, and policies to ensure intellectual independence. For more information, visit www.rand.org/about/research-integrity.

RAND's publications do not necessarily reflect the opinions of its research clients and sponsors.

About This Report

This report documents research and analysis conducted as part of a project entitled *Mindfulness in the U.S. Army: Identifying Best Practices*, sponsored by U.S. Army G-1, Personnel. The purpose of the project was to identify best practices in mindfulness programs for soldiers and their adult family members.

This research was conducted within RAND Arroyo Center's Personnel, Training, and Health Program. RAND Arroyo Center, part of the RAND Corporation, is a federally funded research and development center (FFRDC) sponsored by the United States Army.

RAND operates under a "Federal-Wide Assurance" (FWA00003425) and complies with the *Code of Federal Regulations for the Protection of Human Subjects Under United States Law* (45 CFR 46), also known as "the Common Rule," as well as with the implementation guidance set forth in Department of Defense (DoD) Instruction 3216.02. As applicable, this compliance includes reviews and approvals by RAND's Institutional Review Board (the Human Subjects Protection Committee) and by the U.S. Army. The views of sources utilized in this study are solely their own and do not represent the official policy or position of DoD or the U.S. Government.

Acknowledgments

We gratefully acknowledge the support of Jenna Newman, social science advisor in the Army Resilience Directorate. We are also grateful for the consultation provided by Patricia Herman, Aneesa Motala, Sean Robson, and Matt Walsh of RAND, who provided input on the development of the systematic review protocol, execution of the systematic review, and analyses. In addition, we thank Jody Larkin and Orlando Penetrante in RAND Knowledge Services for conducting the database searches for the systematic review. We appreciate the team who participated in the systematic review, including RAND's Rephael Houston, Sarita Lee, Rosemary Li, and Nabeel Qureshi. We thank Martha Timmer for conducting additional data synthesis. Furthermore, we thank Lauren Skrabala for revisions to the report and Hilary Peterson for report preparation. Finally, we appreciate the valuable insights we received from Sean Grant of RAND and J. Greg Serpa of the U.S. Department of Veteran Affairs. We addressed their constructive critiques as part of RAND's rigorous quality assurance process to improve the quality of this report.

Summary

Meditation is the act of focusing one's attention and awareness on a particular subject or experience (Walsh and Shapiro, 2006). *Mindfulness meditation* is a specific form of meditation practice that involves paying attention, on purpose, to the present moment without judgment (Kabat-Zinn, 2012). Regular mindfulness practice is intended to help reduce attachment to thoughts and emotions that cause distress, foster compassion and well-being, and promote individual agency in decisionmaking (Ludwig and Kabat-Zinn, 2008). Numerous mindfulness-based programs have been developed and studied, but most research has focused on two types of programs: mindfulness-based stress reduction and mindfulness-based cognitive therapy. Among those in the U.S. military, there has been growing interest in the potential benefits of mindfulness meditation, such as promoting attention and concentration, emotion regulation, impulse control, decision-making, morale, productivity, and other outcomes associated with better readiness and resilience of individual service members and units.

Mindfulness meditation programs may have a role in supporting service member readiness. *Readiness*, "the ability of military forces to fight and meet the demands of assigned missions," is vital to the success of the U.S. armed forces (U.S. Department of Defense, 2017, p. GL-10). Readiness is shaped by team cohesion and individual soldier training, discipline, and fitness (U.S. Army, 2019b). *Resilience* typically refers to the ability to grow and adapt over time in response to challenges (U.S. Army, 2019a). This ability is shaped by a variety of factors, including individual- and unit-level characteristics. Individual readiness is associated with soldier discipline, training, and preparedness, but individual resilience seems to be associated with personality traits, such as emotional stability, sociability, and conscientiousness (Friborg et al., 2005).

Although studies have suggested that mindfulness-based interventions might be effective in enhancing military readiness and resilience, this has not been rigorously evaluated. This report fills that gap by presenting results from a systematic review of the research on mindfulness meditation as it pertains to outcomes of interest to the U.S. military in general and the U.S. Army specifically. At the Army's request, we conducted a systematic review and meta-analyses of published literature on mindfulness programs, with a focus on outcomes relevant to soldier readiness and resilience in nonclinical adults. We supplemented our systematic review by examining how mindfulness meditation could support stress management and exploring characteristics of selected mindfulness programs. The goal was to develop recommendations for mindfulness meditation programs for soldiers, should the Army choose to implement such programs in the future.

Methods

Any systematic literature review must be guided by one or more research questions. In collaboration with the Army, we developed a single overriding question that captured 13 outcomes that are potentially relevant to soldiers' readiness and performance and that are priorities for the Army. We also generated two subquestions that focused on whether the effects of mindfulness programs differ between military and civilian populations (1a) and by program components (1b). See Box S.1.

We screened 5,900 unique publications and ultimately identified 104 articles, representing 106 studies, that met the inclusion and exclusion criteria for our systematic review. We followed guidelines for conducting high-quality systematic reviews. We assessed the quality of each study, the quality of the body of evidence for each outcome, and potential publication bias. Whenever possible, we grouped similar studies based on characteristics that might affect the estimated effectiveness of mindfulness, including the type of comparison group used in the study and whether the intervention was a mindfulness program or an analogue. When

> **BOX S.1**
> **Key Question Guiding the Systematic Review**
>
> Key Question 1: What is the effect of mindfulness programs on attention/concentration; decisionmaking; emotion regulation; impulse control/impulsivity; and work-related outcomes pertaining to absenteeism, accidents, communication skills, interpersonal conflict, morale, productivity, social support, teamwork, and turnover among nonclinical adults (both civilian and military populations)?
>
> - Key Question 1a: Do the effects of mindfulness programs differ for military versus civilian populations?
> - Key Question 1b: Do the effects of mindfulness programs differ by program characteristics, such as the type of mindfulness practice (e.g., mindfulness-based stress reduction), exposure (e.g., length or intensity of the program), or delivery format (e.g., in person, online, mobile app)?

sufficient studies were available for a given outcome, we conducted a meta-analysis to pool results and generate an estimated effect size. Guided by content-area experts and previous meta-analyses, we classified the attention and emotion regulation outcomes into multiple suboutcomes and did separate meta-analyses on each suboutcome.[1]

The quality of the existing literature limited our ability to draw strong conclusions about the effect of mindfulness programs for our target outcomes. Most studies in the systematic review were of poor overall quality with small numbers of participants, and most outcomes of interest to the Army were reported by only a small number of studies. Few of the studies focused on military populations, and although we included only studies of military-age populations, program effects—and, thus, best practices—might differ between civilian and military populations. Most studies assessed outcomes immediately after the intervention, and few studies included longer-term follow-up assessments. This limited our ability to identify the potential sustained effects of mindfulness programs.

The Army also aims to support the resilience of soldiers' family members, so we supplemented our systematic review with a brief review of recent (published between 2015 and May 2021) systematic reviews examining the effects of mindfulness meditation on three high-priority outcomes that are relevant to both soldiers and their adult family members: stress, parenting, and relationship problems.

Implementing Mindfulness Meditation Programs in the Army

If Army leaders opt to expand the implementation of mindfulness programs, they must consider best practices in order to help ensure the programs' success. Mindfulness meditation programs vary considerably in their characteristics, such as length and timing, individual or group format, and whether they include virtual delivery. This variability makes it challenging for the Army to know which program (or programs) to implement and how. Unfortunately, the existing literature does not provide clear guidance on best practices for implementing mindfulness meditation programs. To fill this gap, we supplemented our systematic review by exploring the characteristics of four mindfulness programs: mindfulness-based stress reduction, mindfulness-based cognitive therapy, mindfulness-based mind fitness training, and mindfulness-based

---

[1] In this report, we refer to the *attention/concentration* outcome as simply *attention*. The impulse control/impulsivity outcome reflects both a positive outcome (impulse control) and a negative outcome (impulsivity). In this report, we refer to the *impulse control/impulsivity* outcome as simply *impulsivity*, except where impulse control was specifically evaluated.

attention training; the latter two were developed specifically for service members. We used descriptions from the program developers to compare key characteristics of these programs that the Army might consider when implementing its own mindfulness meditation programs for soldiers. It will be important for the Army to consider factors that make service members and military settings unique, and the success of mindfulness meditation programs could hinge on, for example, when they are delivered (e.g., while soldiers are on duty versus off duty) and the degree of commander involvement.

Key Findings

We found beneficial effects of mindfulness programs for some aspects of attention and emotion regulation, along with impulsivity and work-related morale and social support, but no apparent benefit for productivity. The strength of the evidence was generally low, and the strength of the best evidence was only moderate. We identified too few studies to conduct meta-analyses for decisionmaking, work-related communication skills, and work-related teamwork, and there were no studies on work-related absenteeism, accidents, interpersonal conflict, or turnover. Table S.1 summarizes the high-level findings from our systematic review.

Mindfulness May Improve Some Aspects of Attention and Emotion Regulation, Impulsivity, and Work-Related Morale and Social Support

Our analyses indicated that mindfulness may improve accuracy on attention tests that involve resolving conflicts or solving problems (executive attention) but not reaction time or self-perception of attention. Regarding emotion regulation, we found that mindfulness may increase the use of a specific adaptive emotion regulation strategy (reappraisal), decrease the use of a specific maladaptive emotion regulation strategy (suppression), and reduce the extent to which negative emotions slow down reaction time on attention tests (emotional interference). Our analyses did not suggest that mindfulness improves general emotion regulation ability or that it decreases negative mood intensity. Our analyses suggested that mindfulness may have a small beneficial effect on impulsivity, and the strength of evidence for this finding was moderate. Furthermore, our analyses showed a small beneficial effect of mindfulness on morale, and our confidence in this conclusion was also moderate. For social support, our analyses showed a medium beneficial effect, but the strength of this evidence was low.

The Available Evidence Does Not Suggest That Mindfulness Improves Other Outcomes of Interest to the Army

Across the 13 target outcomes in our systematic review, there was inadequate evidence to suggest that mindfulness had an effect on eight of the outcomes; however, future research could strengthen the evidence for these outcomes. Our analyses indicated that mindfulness programs did not have a significant impact on productivity. For three outcomes (decisionmaking, communication skills, and teamwork), we identified relevant studies but were not able to conduct pooled analyses. Finally, we did not find any relevant studies for four target outcomes (absenteeism, accidents, interpersonal conflict, and turnover).

Mindfulness Programs Reduce Stress and May Reduce Parental Stress, Which Could Benefit Army Families

Numerous systematic reviews suggest that mindfulness programs can be effective in reducing stress in non-clinical populations. Our supplementary review of recent systematic reviews indicated that mindfulness

TABLE S.1

Overview of Findings from the Systematic Review

Outcome	Effect of Mindfulness Programs	Strength of the Evidence	Number of Studies
Attention			
Executive attention accuracy (resolving conflicts or solving problems)	Potential small beneficial effect	Moderate	23 studies
Self-perception of attention and reaction time	No effect	Very low to moderate[a]	4–25 studies (per suboutcome)
Decisionmaking	Unknown	Very low	Too few studies to conduct pooled analyses
Emotion regulation			
Reappraisal, suppression, and emotional interference	Potential small to medium beneficial effect	Low	Fewer than 5 studies (per suboutcome)
General emotion regulation and change in negative mood	No effect	Very low to low[a]	Fewer than 5 studies (per suboutcome)
Impulsivity	Potential small beneficial effect	Moderate	Fewer than 5 studies
Work-related outcomes			
Absenteeism, accidents, interpersonal conflict, and turnover	Unknown	Very low	No studies
Communication skills and teamwork	Unknown	Very low	Too few studies to conduct pooled analyses
Morale	Potential small beneficial effect	Moderate	Fewer than 5 studies
Productivity	No effect	Low	Fewer than 5 studies
Social support	Potential medium beneficial effect	Low	Fewer than 5 studies

NOTE: Shaded rows indicate outcomes for which there was evidence of a potential effect of mindfulness programs, although, in many cases, the strength of evidence was low.

[a] These ranges reflect grades for different suboutcomes. Each individual suboutcome had a grade of very low, low, or moderate.

programs significantly decreased self-reported stress, were associated with some modest improvements in systolic blood pressure and heart rate, and may promote small to medium improvements on other select physiological measures of job stress (e.g., cortisol levels, heart rate variability) (Querstret et al., 2020; Pascoe et al., 2017; Heckenberg et al., 2018). Taken together, the studies provide robust support for the positive impact of mindfulness on general stress reduction. Studies of parenting stress suggest that mindfulness programs could benefit both parent and child outcomes. One systematic review of studies on mindful parenting programs indicated small to moderate improvements in parenting stress and symptoms associated with externalizing disorders in children (Townshend et al., 2016). Another identified a link between improvements in parental stress and child and youth outcomes, even when only the parents participated in a mindfulness program (Burgdorf, Szabó, and Abbott, 2019). However, none of these studies focused on military populations, and they often had small samples or were of low quality.

More Research Is Needed to Identify Best Practices for Implementing Mindfulness Programs in the Military

Although there is evidence to support the efficacy of mindfulness programs to reduce stress and anxiety (Chiesa, 2009; Khoury et al., 2015; Sharma and Rush, 2014; Fjorback et al., 2011), the Army will need to consider several factors before implementing such programs. However, the research literature on mindfulness programs in real-world military settings is scant, and clear guidance about best practices is not yet available. We identified three categories of program characteristics for the Army to consider: program goal, target audience, and program structure and design. Mindfulness-based mind fitness training and mindfulness-based attention training have been used with military populations, but research support for these programs is more limited than it is for mindfulness-based stress reduction. With further study, it is possible that these programs will provide greater clarity on best practices for mindfulness meditation program implementation in military contexts.

We identified possible considerations for implementing mindfulness programs targeting military populations. First, it may be important to consider scheduling constraints and other logistical challenges that service members face, particularly when selecting the program structure, duration, and modality. Second, it may be helpful to design programs with the hierarchical structure of the military in mind. Finally, it may be beneficial to consider the importance of the trainer. Lessons learned from resilience training programs suggest that military personnel might find programs delivered by a fellow service member more acceptable and relevant (Roski et al., 2019). However, more research is needed to establish standards for trainer competencies and determine how the quality of the trainer might affect outcomes for mindfulness program participants (Crane et al., 2012; Ruijgrok-Lupton, Crane, and Dorjee, 2018; Khoury et al., 2013).

Recommendations

After considering our findings, we identified two recommendations to inform the Army's decisionmaking process regarding mindfulness meditation programs for soldiers.

Recommendation 1. Conduct High-Quality Evaluations of Mindfulness Meditation with Soldiers

Our systematic review suggests that mindfulness meditation could have an impact on a variety of outcomes related to soldier performance, including aspects of attention, emotion regulation, impulsivity, and work-related morale and social support. But, because of the generally small effect sizes that we identified and the low levels of evidence for these effects, there is not strong support for implementing mindfulness meditation programs Army-wide at this time. However, we did identify robust evidence that such programs have a medium-sized effect on reducing stress among civilian populations. It is possible that the Army will choose to implement mindfulness programs to support stress management and that such programs could have additional benefits on other performance-related outcomes, such as morale, social support, and emotion regulation. Even small effects could be beneficial when implemented across a large proportion of the force.

However, we recommend that the Army conduct high-quality evaluations of mindfulness meditation before pursuing large-scale implementation. Such evaluations could help fill the evidence gap related to the impact of mindfulness meditation in military populations, identify best practices for implementation, and clarify the effects on individual and unit readiness and resilience. We identified seven studies that were funded by the U.S. Army or the Department of Defense and that met our inclusion criteria (all evaluating mindfulness-based mind fitness training or mindfulness-based attention training), and, for all seven, we identified major concerns with the quality of the design or implementation that could have biased the results.

This report provides explicit recommendations for designing studies of the rigorous quality needed to ensure that programs are effective and feasible before attempting large-scale implementation.

Recommendation 2. Assess the Impact of Mindfulness Meditation on Military Families

Although we found robust evidence that mindfulness meditation reduces general stress and promising evidence that it could reduce parental stress, we did not identify any systematic reviews addressing relationship problems or other aspects of parenting. Further research is needed to rigorously assess the impact of mindfulness meditation on military families—with a focus on outcomes that are relevant to this population, such as relationship problems, parenting, and child outcomes. Additional studies or pilot evaluations of these interventions would provide additional guidance on whether they should be made more widely available. Decreasing stress and improving the well-being of military families is a high priority for the Army Resilience Directorate and the Department of Defense overall, and programs that enhance the well-being and resilience of families can have a significant impact on military readiness.

Contents

Available at www.rand.org/t/RRA1522-1

Figures and Tables

Figures

Tables

CHAPTER ONE

Introduction

The U.S. Army and the U.S. Department of Defense (DoD) implement various programs to enhance the readiness and resilience of military service members. Mindfulness meditation is a specific form of meditation practice in which an individual pays attention, on purpose, to the present moment without judgment (Kabat-Zinn, 2012). Designed to foster increased capacity for self-regulation and moment-to-moment awareness with openness and curiosity, mindfulness programs may have promise for improving outcomes related to soldier readiness and resilience (Eberth and Sedlmeier, 2012). Research suggests that mindfulness programs are associated with decreased stress and increased well-being, both among individuals with specific clinical diagnoses (e.g., anxiety, depression) and in nonclinical (healthy) populations (Chiesa and Serretti, 2010; Khoury et al., 2013; Khoury et al., 2015). Yet, it remains unclear how mindfulness programs might affect a variety of other outcomes relevant for nonclinical soldiers, such as emotion regulation, attention, and morale. If mindfulness were to demonstrate beneficial effects on outcomes related to readiness and resilience, identifying best practices for implementing mindfulness in military settings would be important. At the Army's request, RAND Arroyo Center researchers conducted a systematic review and meta-analysis of published literature on mindfulness programs, with a focus on outcomes relevant to nonclinical soldiers. We supplemented our systematic review with an overview of how mindfulness meditation could support stress management and an exploration of characteristics of selected mindfulness programs. The goal was to develop recommendations for mindfulness programs for soldiers, should the Army choose to implement such programs in the future.

In this chapter, we provide a brief introduction to mindfulness meditation, summarize the results of previous systematic literature reviews and meta-analyses, outline our key research questions, and introduce considerations for whether and how best to implement mindfulness meditation programs in the U.S. Army.

Mindfulness Meditation

In this section, we provide an overview of mindfulness meditation and the existing literature on the effects of practicing mindfulness. *Meditation* is the act of focusing one's attention and awareness on a particular subject or experience (Walsh and Shapiro, 2006). As noted earlier, *mindfulness meditation* is a type of meditation in which an individual focuses their attention, on purpose, to the present moment without judgement (Kabat-Zinn, 2012). Mindfulness meditation practice may involve focused attention on bodily sensations, aspects of the external environment (e.g., sound), thoughts or emotions, or other dimensions of the human experience. Regular mindfulness practice is intended to reduce attachment to thoughts and emotions that can cause distress, to foster compassion and well-being, and to promote individual agency in decisionmaking (Ludwig and Kabat-Zinn, 2008). There has been a growing interest in mindfulness-based programs to aid management of physical and mental health conditions and to promote general well-being in nonclinical populations. Multiple cross-sectional imaging studies suggest that the brains of people who practice mindfulness meditation regularly are different from those of nonmeditators, although this finding has yet to be replicated in randomized controlled research designs and thus may be attributable to population differences between meditators and nonmeditators (Tang, Hölzel, and Posner, 2015). That these differences have been found in multiple parts of the brain suggests that the changes associated with regular mindfulness practice may not be specific to a single pathway or structure in the brain (Tang, Hölzel, and Posner, 2015).

Numerous mindfulness-based programs have been developed and studied, but most research and community dissemination efforts have focused on two types of programs: mindfulness-based stress reduction (MBSR) and mindfulness-based cognitive therapy (MBCT).

- MBSR was originally developed in the early 1970s as an eight-week course for individuals experiencing chronic illness, stress, or pain (Kabat-Zinn, 2011). Since then, it has been refined and tested in other populations and settings. It is now typically delivered as a series of eight weekly 2.5-hour group meetings, but other formats, including online courses, are available. MBSR includes instruction in breathing awareness and techniques, mindful eating, yoga, and meditation practices, such as body scan (Adhikari, Kothari, and Khadka, 2018; Dreeben, Mamberg, and Salmon, 2013) and loving kindness (Hofmann et al., 2015; Salzberg, 2011).[1] (For an example curriculum, see Kabat-Zinn, 2017.)
- MBCT is an adaptation of MBSR that incorporates elements of cognitive behavioral therapy (Kuyken et al., 2008). It was developed as a relapse prevention program for individuals with recurrent major depressive disorder (Segal, Teasdale, and Williams, 2002). But, like MBSR, MBCT has since been tested in other populations and settings and in various formats other than weekly group meetings, including online delivery (see, for example, Khoury et al., 2013; Be Mindful, undated). MBCT adopts the same eight-week workshop structure used by MBSR (Dimidjian and Segal, 2015) and is typically delivered by an instructor in weekly 2-hour group sessions. Between sessions, participants complete daily homework assignments, such as practicing mindfulness meditation and performing cognitive therapy skill exercises (Ruths et al., 2013).

Although MBSR and MBCT are the most well-studied mindfulness programs, many others have been developed and tested in research studies. These programs are quite diverse in their content, format, and delivery mode (e.g., group versus individual sessions, in-person versus virtual), duration (e.g., number and length of sessions), and setting. A common unifier across most programs is the inclusion of guided mindfulness meditation in some form, either during the initial training sessions or through assigned home practice between sessions. Guided meditation is a practice in which a trainer or teacher leads an individual through a meditation session in real time or through an audio recording. Adaptations of MBSR that have been developed for service members include mindfulness-based mind fitness training (MMFT) (Stanley et al., 2011) and mindfulness-based attention training (MBAT) (Jha, Zanesco, Denkova, Morrison, et al., 2020).

Most mindfulness programs have multiple elements, and researchers continue to study which of these elements contribute the most to program effectiveness and *how* exactly mindfulness works. Analogue studies are one method that has the potential to increase understanding of how mindfulness works. An *analogue study*, typically conducted in a laboratory setting, involves administering a very brief mindfulness analogue exercise (e.g., a single 15-minute guided meditation) followed by an immediate assessment of outcomes, such as changes in mood or attention. The mindfulness exercises tested in analogue studies are not intended to be

---

[1] Body scan meditation is derived from Buddhism and involves focusing full attention on the body, systematically scanning from head to toe to observe any sensations in a mindful and accepting manner (Adhikari, Kothari, and Khadka, 2018). The version of the body scan meditation used in MBSR also encourages individuals to maintain open, nonjudgmental attention on each part of the body as they meditate (Dreeben, Mamberg, Salmon, 2013). Loving-kindness meditation, also derived from Buddhism, emphasizes the interconnectedness of human beings (Salzberg, 2011) and encourages compassion toward the self and others (Hofmann, Grossman, Hinton, 2011).

complete mindfulness programs and are not expected to have long-term effects. Although analogue studies may deliver unique insights that may ultimately inform the development and implementation of mindfulness programs delivered in real-world settings, we are unaware of any specific examples of studies that have provided such insights. Analogue studies have significant limitations and must be interpreted with caution. In particular, developing mindfulness skills requires training and practice time. Therefore, the immediate effects of passive listening to a recording of a brief mindfulness meditation exercise, as is common in analogue studies, may not reflect the effects of active mindfulness practice, particularly when administered to participants with no previous meditation experience.

Relevance of Mindfulness Meditation for Army Personnel

Mindfulness meditation programs may have a role in supporting service member readiness. *Readiness*, "the ability of military forces to fight and meet the demands of assigned missions," is vital to the success of the U.S. armed forces (DoD, 2017, p. GL-10). Readiness is shaped by team cohesion and individual soldier training, discipline, and fitness (U.S. Army, 2019b). *Resilience* typically refers to the ability of a person or entity to grow and adapt over time in response to challenges (U.S. Army, 2019a). This ability is shaped by a variety of different factors, including individual- and unit-level characteristics. Individual readiness is associated with soldier discipline, training, and preparedness, but individual resilience seems to be associated with personality traits, such as emotional stability, sociability, and conscientiousness (Friborg et al., 2005).

Various Army programs incorporate mindfulness principles to support and enhance soldier and unit readiness, including during basic combat training (Adler et al., 2015). For example, mindfulness principles are incorporated into the programs designed to increase resilience and optimize performance, including the Master Resilience Training Course run by the Army's Comprehensive Soldier and Family Fitness program (Harms et al., 2013). Customized training for soldiers and their families is also available through Army Ready and Resilient Performance centers (U.S. Army, undated-b; U.S. Army, undated-c). Such programs were designed to improve outcomes that contribute to military readiness, including emotion regulation, attention, decisionmaking, and physical performance (Harms et al., 2013). Studies have suggested that mindfulness-based interventions might have promise in these areas, but these findings need to be rigorously evaluated, and best practices for disseminating and implementing mindfulness-based practice within the Army need to be identified.

Systematic Review and Meta-Analysis

The first step in developing evidence-based recommendations and guidance is an examination of the relevant evidence. A systematic review ensures that *all* potentially relevant evidence—not just evidence that might support one position or another—is identified and evaluated. Systematic evidence reviews are planned, documented, and conducted transparently in accordance with rigorous standards and methods (Higgins et al., 2021). First, researchers pose one or more key questions that they hope to answer. They then identify all published research articles addressing those key questions, applying clear inclusion and exclusion criteria to the search to ensure that it captures the most-relevant evidence. The reasons for excluding a particular study or article must be documented, and inclusion and exclusion criteria must be applied transparently and uniformly. When several studies examine similar interventions or outcomes, a meta-analysis may be performed to develop an overall, or *pooled*, estimate of treatment effect. In addition to primary analyses, sensitivity analysis may be performed to assess the robustness of findings based on assumptions made, such as decisions about which study results are combined. Systematic reviews also use standard tools to assess the quality of each study outcome, weigh the overall strength of evidence for each conclusion, and document the conclusions and the processes used to arrive at them.

Prior Systematic Reviews of Mindfulness Meditation

Systematic reviews have been used to estimate the effectiveness of mindfulness meditation on the treatment or management of a wide variety of conditions, as well as on the development or improvement of various skills or abilities. Systematic reviews have indicated that mindfulness programs reduce anxiety and stress in both clinical (i.e., individuals with a specific diagnosis) and nonclinical or healthy populations (Chiesa and Serretti, 2009; Khoury et al., 2015; Sharma and Rush, 2014; Fjorback et al., 2011). Mindfulness-based interventions have been shown to be moderately effective for treating depression and anxiety, although the mechanisms underlying this effect are unclear (Hofmann et al., 2010; van der Velden et al., 2015; Alsubaie et al., 2017). Systematic reviews also have suggested that, in clinical populations, mindfulness meditation is effective at reducing insomnia (Wang et al., 2019), posttraumatic stress disorder (Hilton, Maher, et al., 2017), and chronic illness (Crowe et al., 2016). There is promising research indicating that mindfulness programs might be effective in treating chronic pain conditions, hypertension, and substance use disorders, although the results have been variable and more research is needed (Hilton, Hempel, et al., 2017; Anheyer et al., 2017; Solano López, 2018; Grant et al., 2017; Li et al., 2017). MBSR, in particular, has demonstrated effectiveness as a supportive treatment for pain, anxiety, and depression in patients with cancer (Zhang, Zhao, and Zheng, 2019).

In nonclinical populations, systematic reviews have indicated that mindfulness programs are moderately effective in reducing stress and improving other aspects of health and well-being (Chiesa and Serretti, 2009; Khoury et al., 2015). Improvements in psychological well-being are a common finding (Zhang, Zhao, and Zheng, 2019; Ngamkham, Holden, and Smith, 2019), as are improvements in physiological and psychological measures of stress (Sharma and Rush, 2014). Workplace mindfulness training programs have been shown to be effective at reducing burnout and improving the psychological health and well-being of employees (Bartlett et al., 2019). Some systematic reviews have suggested that mindfulness-based interventions have promise for improving outcomes related to readiness and resilience in nonclinical military populations (Deuster and Schoomaker, 2015; Jha, Morrison, et al., 2017; Zanesco et al., 2019), although these studies have focused mainly on the effects of MBSR and other mindfulness programs on stress and burnout (Chiesa and Serretti, 2009; Eberth and Sedlmeier, 2012; Khoury et al., 2015; Sharma and Rush, 2014).

The strength of conclusions reached in systematic reviews of mindfulness programs were limited, in large part, by the quality of the existing literature. Many studies of mindfulness programs have had small sample sizes, had weak study designs, or did not use rigorous assessment measures, although the quality of these studies has improved over time (Creswell, 2017; Goldberg et al., 2017). In recent systematic reviews focused on nonclinical adult populations, most studies addressed the effect of mindfulness programs on stress, burnout, or psychological well-being. At the outset of this project, there were no systematic reviews of the effects of mindfulness programs on many performance-related outcomes relevant to nonclinical military populations.

Systematic Review Approach in This Report

In collaboration with the project's sponsor, Army Resilience Directorate (a directorate within U.S. Army G-1, Personnel), we developed a key question that guided our systematic review (see Box 1.1). This process ensured that the key question—and the selected outcomes—would be particularly relevant to the Army and soldier performance. The scope of our systematic review was quite broad: We identified 13 outcomes of interest. The selection of the key question, the target outcomes, and the methodological approach for the review and meta-analyses are discussed in greater detail in Chapter Two and Appendix A. Briefly, we adhered to well-

BOX 1.1
Key Question Guiding the Systematic Review

Key Question 1: What is the effect of mindfulness programs on attention/concentration; decisionmaking; emotion regulation; impulse control/impulsivity; and work-related outcomes pertaining to absenteeism, accidents, communication skills, interpersonal conflict, morale, productivity, social support, teamwork, and turnover among nonclinical adults (both civilian and military populations)?

- Key Question 1a: Do the effects of mindfulness programs differ for military versus civilian populations?
- Key Question 1b: Do the effects of mindfulness programs differ by program characteristics, such as the type of mindfulness practice (e.g., MBSR, MBCT), exposure (e.g., length or intensity of the program), or delivery format (e.g., in person, online, mobile app)?

standardized guidance in conducting a high-quality systematic quantitative and qualitative review and meta-analyses (Higgins et al., 2021; Agency for Healthcare Research and Quality [AHRQ], 2014). When we were able to identify three or more studies that were sufficiently similar in design and measured the same outcome, we performed meta-analyses. For studies whose outcomes could not be included in a pooled analysis, we describe the findings narratively. Additional methodological details are provided in the next chapter.

Our review included 13 outcomes that were relevant to soldier performance, but the Army also aims to support the resilience of family members. Therefore, we supplemented our systematic review with a search for recent systematic reviews (published between 2015 and May 2021) examining the effects of mindfulness meditation on three high-priority outcomes that are relevant to both soldiers and their adult family members: stress, parenting, and relationship problems.

Implementing Mindfulness Meditation Programs in the Army

Through the systematic review and meta-analyses presented in this report and our examination of the effects of mindfulness meditation programs on several key outcomes, we aim to inform the Army's decisionmaking process regarding the implementation of such programs for soldiers. If Army leaders opt to expand the implementation of mindfulness programs, they must consider best practices in order to help ensure the programs' success. Mindfulness meditation programs vary considerably in their characteristics, such as length and timing, individual or group format, and whether the program includes a virtual component. There are even variations within a given type of program. For example, a systematic review indicated that the number of hours for an MBSR program can vary from six to 28, although MBSR developers recommend 31 hours of instruction (Santorelli et al., 2017). Different versions of a program often result from adapting a standard program to use with a specific population, to achieve a specific target outcome, or to improve feasibility and acceptability. This variability makes it challenging for organizations, such as the Army, to know which program to implement and how.

Unfortunately, the existing literature does not provide clear guidance on best practices for implementing mindfulness meditation programs. To fill this gap, we supplemented our systematic review by describing the characteristics of four mindfulness programs (MBSR, MBCT, MMFT, and MBAT) using program descriptions from the developers. We used these descriptions to explore the aspects of the programs that the Army might consider when implementing its own mindfulness meditation programs for soldiers. We also highlight studies from our systematic review that adapted these target programs and describe their variability (e.g., number of sessions and program hours, individual versus group format) to illustrate options for how the

Army could implement these four types of mindfulness programs. Finally, we highlight additional factors that the Army could consider in adapting mindfulness programs for a military setting. In that assessment, we explore factors that are unique to the military and could affect the success of program implementation, such as where programs are housed, when they are delivered (e.g., while personnel are on duty versus off duty), and the degree to which commanders are involved.

Organization of This Report

In the remainder of this report, we (1) provide the findings of a systematic review and meta-analyses of the effect of mindfulness meditation on outcomes that relate to the readiness of Army soldiers and (2) consider factors important for program implementation. We do not provide an overview of mindfulness meditation programs currently delivered by the Army. Rather, we examine the evidence on mindfulness meditation for numerous outcomes related to soldier performance and provide guidance on considerations for implementing mindfulness programs in the Army.

Chapter Two provides an overview of study methods. Chapter Three presents an overview of the studies included in the systematic review. In Chapter Four, we provide estimates of the effects of mindfulness meditation on each of the 13 target outcomes included in our systematic review. In Chapter Five, we supplement our systematic review with an overview of recent systematic reviews evaluating the effects of mindfulness interventions on two outcomes relevant to military families (general stress and parenting stress). Chapter Six describes characteristics of selected mindfulness meditation programs and explores considerations for implementing these programs in the military. Finally, Chapter Seven summarizes our findings and offers recommendations regarding mindfulness meditation programs for soldiers.

Additional details are provided in several appendixes. Appendixes A and B provide methodological details on our systematic review protocol and a summary of the strength of evidence by outcome, respectively. Detailed findings for our systematic review are presented in Appendixes C–F.

In six additional appendixes available online at www.rand.org/t/RRA1522-1, we provide additional detail on our study methods:

- Appendix G presents the full details of our literature search strategy, including databases searched, search terms, and time periods covered for our systematic review.
- Appendix H presents a complete evidence table for the 106 studies included in our systematic review.
- Appendix I catalogs the outcome measures and the number of studies that used each measure in the systematic review.
- Appendix J provides a detailed assessment of the quality of each study included in the systematic review.
- Appendix K presents results of our analysis to detect publication bias, which did not indicate evidence of publication bias in the studies included in our systematic review.
- Appendix L includes technical details of our supplemental meta-analysis of data presented in an existing systematic review of the effects of mindfulness meditation on stress.

CHAPTER TWO

Methods

In this chapter, we briefly describe the methods used to conduct the systematic review and meta-analyses. Detailed information about our protocol appears in Appendix A. Subsequently, we describe our methods for a supplementary review of recent systematic reviews on mindfulness meditation and three additional outcomes relevant to soldiers and their families (general stress, parenting, and relationship problems). Finally, we describe our methods for characterizing four selected mindfulness programs.

Systematic Review

We conducted a systematic review and meta-analyses to assess the effects of mindfulness meditation on 13 outcomes relevant to readiness and resilience among nonclinical military populations. Our approach to the evidence review was based on the *Methods Guide for Effectiveness and Comparative Effectiveness Reviews* (AHRQ, 2014) and the *Cochrane Handbook for Systematic Reviews of Interventions* (Higgins et al., 2021). Our approach to reporting the results follows Preferred Reporting Items for Systematic Reviews and Meta-Analyses (PRISMA) guidelines (AHRQ, 2014; Page et al., 2021). Our systematic review is also registered with the International Prospective Register of Systematic Reviews, or PROSPERO, database (2021 CRD42021227957).

Key Question and Outcomes of Interest

We developed the overall key question of the effect of mindfulness meditation on outcomes related to readiness and resilience in nonclinical (healthy) adults and refined this question in discussions with the sponsor (see Box 2.1). We included two subquestions that focused on assessing whether the effects of mindfulness programs differ between military and civilian populations (1a) and whether the effect of mindfulness medi-

---

BOX 2.1
Key Question Guiding the Systematic Review

Key Question 1: What is the effect of mindfulness programs on attention/concentration; decisionmaking; emotion regulation; impulse control/impulsivity; and work-related outcomes pertaining to absenteeism, accidents, communication skills, interpersonal conflict, morale, productivity, social support, teamwork, and turnover among nonclinical adults (both civilian and military populations)?

- Key Question 1a: Do the effects of mindfulness programs differ for military versus civilian populations?
- Key Question 1b: Do the effects of mindfulness programs differ by program characteristics, such as the type of mindfulness practice (e.g., MBSR, MBCT), exposure (e.g., length or intensity of the program), or delivery format (e.g., in person, online, mobile app)?

tation differs by program components (1b). Refinements to the overall key question in collaboration with the sponsor largely focused on selecting the target outcomes of interest. Ultimately, we included 13 outcomes that are potentially relevant to soldiers' readiness and performance. We also consulted with RAND subject-matter experts, drawing on additional expertise related to the measurement of performance (especially as it relates to military operational specialties) and mindfulness meditation. We developed definitions for each outcome (see Table 2.1).

We aimed for all of the outcomes to be relevant to soldier readiness and performance, but we also wanted to draw on relevant civilian literature. Thus, several of the outcomes are specifically work-related (e.g., work-related interpersonal conflict). Our attention outcome includes concentration as a component of attention. Throughout this report, we refer to *attention/concentration* as simply *attention*. In addition, our impulse control/impulsivity outcome reflects both a positive outcome (impulse control) and a negative outcome (impulsivity). In this report, we refer to the *impulse control/impulsivity* outcome as simply *impulsivity*, except where impulse control was specifically evaluated.

TABLE 2.1

Definition of Outcomes Included in the Systematic Review

Outcome	Definition
Attention	An individual's general ability or capacity to pay attention, indexed by self-perception or by speed or accuracy when completing a simple task
Decisionmaking	Accuracy or appropriateness (e.g., based on a framework of morality or other relevant considerations) of an individual's decisions, judgments, or reasoning
Emotion regulation	Degree to which individuals can regulate or control their emotions (general emotion regulation ability); frequency or tendency to use a specific strategy to express their emotions
Impulsivity	The tendency of an individual to react without full consideration of the negative consequences of their behavior, indexed by self-perception or performance on a task
Work-related absenteeism	Total amount or percentage of time absent from work
Work-related accidents	Number or frequency of incidents described as accidents
Work-related communication skills	An employee's perception of the quality of their communication with coworkers
Work-related interpersonal conflict	An employee's perception of the quality of their relationships with coworkers (e.g., how frequently they experience disagreements or other hostile interactions that induce negative emotions)
Work-related morale	An individual's perceived level of satisfaction with, attitudes toward, or feelings about their job
Work-related productivity	Quantity of work produced or quantity of output
Work-related social support	An employee's perception of how frequently or to what extent they provide social support to their colleagues, or their colleagues provide social support to them, or an individual's perception of their overall work environment with regard to social support (i.e., the degree to which employees provide social support to each other)
Work-related teamwork	How often or the degree to which an employee works together with or helps other employees complete their work
Work-related turnover	The percentage of employees who left the organization within a specified period

Search Strategy and Sources

We developed our search strategy in collaboration with a RAND reference librarian and by consulting recently published reviews of mindfulness interventions. Appendix G, which accompanies this report online, provides a complete account of our search strategy. In brief, we searched ten electronic databases for articles on randomized controlled trials (RCTs) and observational studies with a control group that were published between January 1, 2000, and August 31, 2020. We also searched ClinicalTrials.gov, a registry of both publicly and privately funded trials, to identify RCTs that enrolled nonclinical adult participants. In addition, we coordinated with the Army to identify Army- and DoD-sponsored mindfulness research. We contacted the authors of those studies for additional information as needed. Finally, we mined the reference lists of relevant systematic reviews as a supplemental search to ensure that we had identified all relevant studies.

Eligibility Criteria

To be included in our review, studies needed to meet predefined criteria. Inclusion and exclusion criteria for the review were developed using the PICOTSS (participants, intervention, comparator, outcome, timing, setting, and study design) framework. Table 2.2 provides a brief description of study eligibility criteria for each element of the PICOTSS framework. Appendix A discusses the inclusion and exclusion criteria in greater detail.

Inclusion Screening

To manage the literature search, we used Distiller Systematic Review software (DistillerSR), a web-based software for systematic reviews that includes tools for screening, full-text review, and management of extracted results. Two members of the research team independently screened titles and abstracts against specified inclusion and exclusion criteria. Prior to formally screening the titles and abstracts, the two screeners conducted a pilot test to ensure consistent application of review criteria; the pilot test included screening a randomly selected set of titles and abstracts, comparing the results, and discussing points of disagreement to resolve major decisional differences. Documents selected for inclusion by either screener were promoted to the next stage of review for full text screening.

Articles selected for full-text screening were uploaded into DistillerSR and screened independently by the two research team members, who used the software to document their decisions. Full-text screening was used to determine whether articles should be excluded or retained for outcome extraction based on the PICOTSS inclusion and exclusion criteria. Reviewers met regularly to resolve and reconcile disagreements in review decisions. If consensus could not be reached, the decision was mediated by the principal investigator. Documents identified through reference-mining underwent separate title and abstract screening and full-text screening by a single screener, and a second screener performed periodic random concurrence checks. We documented screening and final inclusion decisions in a PRISMA flow diagram, which is presented in Chapter Three (Figure 3.1).

Data Extraction

We developed a standardized form in DistillerSR to independently extract study-level data from each eligible study. Detailed instructions and rules were developed and continually reviewed and clarified as needed for use during the data-extraction process. Before we implemented the data-extraction forms in DistillerSR, independent reviewers tested the forms on multiple randomly selected eligible publications and made modifications for clarity. To ensure consistency of extraction, reviewers completed data-extraction training by independently extracting and reconciling data for several additional studies using the finalized data-extraction

TABLE 2.2

Overview of Inclusion and Exclusion Criteria

PICOTSS Category	Description
Participants	Considered for inclusion: Studies of adults (18 years or older) with no clinical diagnosis and in which the study population's mean age was less than 45
Intervention	Considered for inclusion: Studies that assessed the effects of a mindfulness program or intervention, including MBSR, MBCT, mindfulness meditation, Vipassana, Zazen, Zen, Shambhala, focused-attention meditation, or mindfulness training
	Excluded: Studies that assessed the effects of yoga, tai chi, qigong, transcendental meditation, or mind-body interventions that did not include a mindfulness meditative component (e.g., diaphragmatic breathing, chanting meditation)
Comparator	Considered for inclusion: Studies that included a waitlist control, no treatment control, or other active or passive control condition
	Excluded: Studies with control groups that received an intervention in such a way that the mindfulness intervention could not be assessed in isolation
Outcome	Considered for inclusion: Studies that reported one or more of the following outcomes, measured via self-report (i.e., questionnaire, survey, or interview), observer rating, or completion of a task: • attention • decisionmaking • emotion regulation • impulsivity • work-related absenteeism, accidents, communication skills, interpersonal conflict, morale, productivity, social support, teamwork, or turnover
	Excluded: Studies that assessed physiological or neurobiological outcomes
Timing	Studies were not limited by the duration of the mindfulness intervention or program or by the timing of the follow-up period(s)
Setting	Studies were not limited by setting
Study design	Considered for inclusion: Studies that were multiple-arm RCTs or non-randomized studies (i.e., non-randomized trials with a comparison group)
	Excluded: Single-arm (uncontrolled) trials, case reports, case series, retrospective observational studies, narrative reviews, and cross-sectional studies
Other limiters	Considered for inclusion: Studies published as full-text peer-reviewed articles or reports in English-language publications
	Excluded: Dissertations, meeting abstracts, commentaries, perspectives, letters, and other opinion pieces

forms. Data were then extracted from each included study by two independent reviewers. Any discrepancies were resolved through discussion.

Information extracted from individual studies included details from the following domains: study characteristics (e.g., study design, unit of randomization, setting), participant characteristics, intervention, comparator, and outcome. If more than one publication appeared to report on the same study, reviewers compared the descriptions of participants to ensure that data from the same study population were included in our analysis only once. Reviewers contacted the authors of several publications to request additional clarification. Outcome data (e.g., mean outcomes, sample sizes, and standard deviations) were extracted from publications by one or two members of the study team and confirmed by the statistical analyst.

Individual Study Quality

Reviewers independently assessed individual study quality (also referred to as *risk of bias* or *internal validity*) for each of the included studies. We reconciled any discrepancies during regular team meetings. We assessed study quality for RCTs using a slightly modified version of the U.S. Preventive Services Task Force assessment tool (Higgins et al., 2011; U.S. Preventive Services Task Force, 2017), which included 11 items across six domains characterizing various aspects of quality (see Table A.3); the tool also provided examples of low, unclear, and high risk. For each trial in our study, we categorized study quality as poor, fair, or good.

Study quality for trials in which participants were not randomly assigned to groups was assessed using the Newcastle-Ottawa assessment tool for non-randomized studies (Wells et al., 2019). The Newcastle-Ottawa tool includes eight items (see Table A.3) and provides operational definitions for low, moderate, and high risk of bias. This tool does not include an overall study quality rating. Therefore, we did not rate overall study quality for non-randomized trials; these studies were not included in meta-analyses and were not considered when we drew our conclusions.

Data Synthesis

We pooled studies only if (1) there were at least three RCTs that reported an effect size or reported data that allowed us to calculate an effect size and (2) all of the following criteria were met:

1. The studies implemented the same type of intervention (mindfulness program or analogue).
2. They had the same type of comparison group (passive or active).
3. They had the same type of outcome measured at the same point in time (e.g., post-intervention, three months post-intervention, or six months post-intervention).

We required three RCTs so that we could assess between-study variation. Non-randomized studies were not included in any pooled analyses. Subject-matter experts reviewed the outcome measures in each study and provided recommendations regarding which measures in each of our 13 outcome categories assessed similar concepts and therefore could be pooled. When a study had multiple intervention groups, multiple comparison groups, or multiple outcomes of the same type and timepoint, we used a hierarchy of considerations to select which group(s) or outcome to include in the pooled analysis. Additional details about our decision hierarchy for selecting interventions, comparison groups, and outcomes are provided in Appendix A. We narratively describe the study findings for non-randomized studies and other studies that could not be included in pooled analyses.

Analyses

We used effect sizes to compare outcomes in intervention groups with outcomes in the comparison group. For continuous outcomes, the effect size was calculated as the Hedges' g standardized mean difference (SMD), which is equal to the difference in mean outcomes between the intervention and comparison groups divided by the pooled standard deviation of the outcome (Hedges, 1981). General guidelines for interpreting the magnitude of the SMD suggest that 0.2 is a small effect, 0.5 is a medium effect, and 0.8 is a large effect (Faraone, 2008). For categorical outcomes, the effect size was calculated as an odds ratio.

As noted, we pooled RCT results separately based on characteristics that were expected to affect the estimated effectiveness of mindfulness, including the type of comparison group used in the study (active or passive) and whether the intervention was a mindfulness program or an analogue. For each outcome of interest, we used the Hartung-Knapp random-effects method to pool results across studies to obtain a single estimated effect of mindfulness when at least three similar RCTs examined the outcome (Van Aert and

Jackson, 2019), referred to as the SMD. When possible, we used sensitivity analyses to assess the robustness of pooled estimates to the set of studies included in the meta-analyses. Sensitivity analyses examined how much the estimated (pooled) effect of mindfulness changed when we excluded studies that were outliers. Further details about analytic methods are provided in Appendix A.

Key Questions 1a and 1b focused on whether the effects of mindfulness programs differed by population (civilians versus military personnel), by population subgroups, or by specific intervention characteristics of interest. We assessed these differences to the extent possible based on the availability of results from comparable studies.

Strength of Evidence

For each outcome for which we were able to draw a conclusion based on a pooled analysis, we assessed the overall strength of the body of evidence underlying the conclusion using a modification of the Grading of Recommendations Assessment, Development, and Evaluation (GRADE) approach (Balshem et al., 2011; Guyatt et al., 2011; AHRQ, 2014). The AHRQ modification of the GRADE approach assesses the strength of evidence across four domains:

1. study quality: based on study design and limitations; assessed as poor, fair, or good[1]
2. directness: the degree to which the assessed outcome represented the true outcome of interest; alternatively, in the case of subgroup analyses, whether comparisons of interest were made within the same study or only indirectly via meta-regression
3. consistency: similarity of effect direction and size across studies
4. precision: degree of certainty around an estimate and the statistical power of the test.

An additional metric that constitutes a fifth domain in the GRADE approach is reporting or publication bias. Reporting bias is present if there is evidence that reported outcomes were not prespecified by the study protocol or that outcomes specified in the protocol were not reported; reporting bias may also result from evidence that studies that obtained negative or statistically insignificant findings may not have been published. We assessed and reported publication bias separately (see the next section and Appendix A) but did not consider it in determining the quality of evidence (AHRQ, 2014). The assessments were conducted by three experienced team members. We report the strength of evidence for each conclusion using the following scale:

- *High* indicates high confidence that the estimated effect reflects the true effect. Further research is unlikely to change the estimates or our confidence in the estimates.
- *Moderate* indicates moderate confidence that the estimated effect reflects the true effect. Further research may change the estimates and our confidence in the estimates.
- *Low* indicates low confidence that the estimated effect reflects the true effect. Further research is likely to change estimates and our confidence in the estimates.
- *Very low* indicates that evidence is either unavailable or does not permit a conclusion to be drawn.

The conclusions and the results of the GRADE assessments for each conclusion are presented in a strength-of-evidence table in Appendix B. If data were insufficient to support a conclusion for a particular subquestion of interest, we indicate the reason (e.g., too few studies, inconsistency of findings).

---

[1] In the U.S. Preventive Services Task Force assessment tool, this first domain is called *study limitations.*

Publication Bias

Publication bias refers to the tendency of studies to be published only if findings are statistically significant. This can cause problems when pooling findings across studies and can bias pooled estimates toward finding a difference between the intervention and control groups. Formal evaluation of publication bias requires a relatively large number of pooled studies.

Funnel plots are created when pooled results include ten or more studies (Sterne et al., 2011). When there are few studies, publication bias can be evaluated informally, by looking at the relationship among sample size, publication year, and the significance of study findings. Evidence of publication bias may exist if older and smaller studies are more likely than newer and larger studies to report statistically significant findings. We did not find any evidence of publication bias for the studies included in our analyses. Detailed description of analyses examining publication bias are provided in Appendix K, available online.

Supplementary Review of Mindfulness Meditation and Stress

The focus of our systematic review and meta-analyses was on 13 outcomes related to soldier performance, which we selected in collaboration with the project sponsor. Yet decreasing stress and improving the well-being of adult family members are high priories for the Army Resilience Directorate in its efforts to support individual and unit readiness and resilience (U.S. Army, undated-a). Although we did not include stress among the outcomes in our systematic review, we conducted a supplemental search of recent systematic reviews on mindfulness programs for general stress, parenting, and relationship problems in nonclinical adult populations. The purpose of this supplemental review was to assess available literature on these additional outcomes that are of interest for soldiers and their adult family members. We selected these outcomes in collaboration with the study sponsor. This supplemental search was separate from our systematic review described earlier.

For this supplemental review, we searched the Google Scholar, PubMed, and PsycINFO databases for peer-reviewed systematic reviews published between 2015 and May 2021. Two reviewers assessed full-text articles that were screened for inclusion during title and abstract review, and then those reviewers reached consensus on which reviews to include. We excluded articles that evaluated studies with narrow samples (e.g., medical students) or non-stress outcomes (e.g., mental health), as well as older publications when newer reviews were available. We used AMSTAR 2 (A MeaSurement Tool to Assess Systematic Reviews, 2nd version) to assess the quality of review articles (Shea et al., 2017). In addition, we described examples of innovative mindfulness programs drawn from several recent systematic reviews of brief or technology-enabled interventions focused on stress reduction. Findings are presented in Chapter Five. Although we sought to summarize systematic reviews evaluating the effects of mindfulness programs on relationship outcomes, our search yielded no recent relevant reviews. Therefore, our discussion of findings focuses on general stress and parenting stress.

Characteristics of Selected Mindfulness Meditation Programs

Mindfulness meditation programs share a common goal of supporting participants in ongoing mindfulness practice, but these programs can vary widely. Given the emerging state of the literature on some mindfulness meditation programs, determining best practices for implementing these programs—particularly with soldiers—remains challenging. In Chapter Six, we describe and compare four mindfulness programs: MBSR, MBCT, MMFT, and MBAT. We first describe a suggested framework for distilling the important characteristics of these programs. To develop this framework, we searched the Google Scholar, PubMed, and PsycINFO databases for articles describing best practices for describing and implementing mindfulness programs and then pooled the types of program characteristics that we thought would be most useful for the Army to consider prior to implementation (e.g., program goal, target audience, program duration, modality). Second, we use the framework to describe the characteristics of interest for the four previously mentioned mindfulness programs using materials from the program developers. We selected MBSR and MBCT because we considered them to be more-established mindfulness programs, and we selected MMFT and MBAT because they have been evaluated in military populations. Third, we describe the characteristics of the programs as they were evaluated in studies included in our systematic review. Last, we describe a separate effort to conduct a literature search on best practices for implementing mindfulness programs with military populations, and we summarize the key findings for the Army to consider. For this effort, we searched the Google Scholar, PubMed, and PsycINFO databases for relevant articles on mindfulness programs conducted with military populations and best practices for implementing programs in military settings.

CHAPTER THREE

Results of the Systematic Review

This chapter presents an overview of the results of the systematic review. We describe the results of the literature search, characteristics of the included studies, and the study quality of included studies.

Results of the Search

Figure 3.1 presents a PRISMA flow diagram documenting the results of our search. We identified 3,414 citations through searches of electronic databases (using the search terms listed in Appendix G, available online) and 2,486 from additional sources (2,442 from reference-mining existing systematic reviews, 40 directly from the authors of DoD-funded research, and four that provided additional information needed on included articles). After removing duplicates, we screened 5,900 titles and abstracts and obtained the full text for 915 articles identified as potentially eligible for inclusion by one or both of two independent reviewers.

A total of 811 articles were excluded at the full-text review stage because they did not meet our study's inclusion criteria. Reasons for exclusion included

- enrolling a population that had a clinical diagnosis, that included individuals who were under 18 years old, or whose average age was over 45
- implementing an intervention in which mindfulness meditation was not the focus or a multicomponent intervention that made it impossible to isolate the role of mindfulness meditation
- having a comparison group that did not allow us to isolate the effects of mindfulness
- not reporting on an outcome of interest
- having a study design that was single-arm or cross-sectional or that used a retrospective cohort.

We also excluded meeting minutes, commentaries, and letters to the editor. A list of the 811 publications excluded at the full-text stage with the reasons for exclusion is available upon request. A total of 104 articles, representing 106 studies, met the inclusion criteria. Bibliographic details for all included articles are presented in a separate section of the References list at the end of this report.

Table 3.1 provides an overview, by key question, of the number of included studies that examine each of our 13 outcomes, including the number of studies that we were able to include in meta-analyses. We describe the results of our meta-analyses in Chapter Four and provide detailed analyses in Appendixes C–F. We identified the most studies for attention and emotion regulation, which allowed us to conduct several meta-analyses for those outcomes. A small number of studies were identified for four outcomes (impulsivity, morale, productivity, and social support), which was sufficient to support meta-analyses for each of those outcomes. We identified too few studies on decisionmaking, communication skills, and teamwork to conduct meta-analyses, so we present these studies descriptively. We did not identify any studies for four outcomes (absenteeism, accidents, interpersonal conflict, and turnover).

FIGURE 3.1

PRISMA Flow Diagram of Search Results

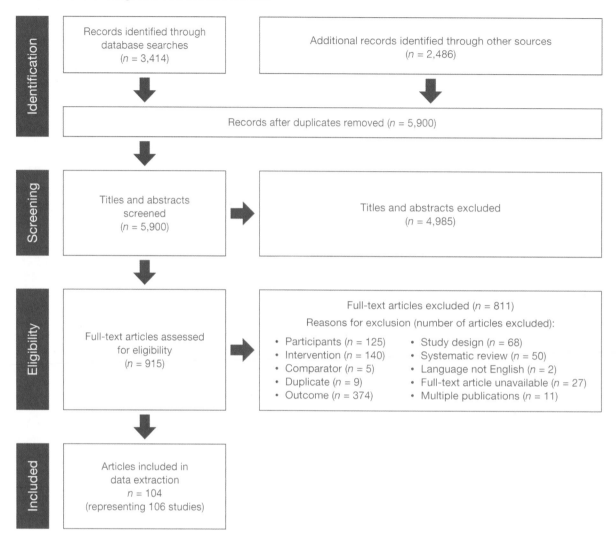

The included studies allowed us to address Key Question 1 only for short-term (i.e., post-intervention) outcomes. There were not enough studies available for pooling in any outcome category that included outcomes measured during a longer-term follow-up period after the mindfulness program ended.

The included studies did not provide sufficient evidence to address Key Question 1a or 1b. Only seven studies—all of which focused on attention outcomes only—involved participants who were military personnel, and there was not a sufficient number of studies in any category (e.g., mindfulness versus analogue, active versus passive comparison groups) to compare attention outcomes for military versus civilian populations. Additionally, there was an insufficient number of studies, or the studies' intervention designs were too variable within any of the pooled analyses, to evaluate whether the effects of mindfulness differed by intervention characteristics.

TABLE 3.1

Evidence Base for Key Questions

Key Question	Number of Studies Included in the Systematic Review[a]	Number of Studies included in Meta-Analyses
Key Question 1. What is the effect of mindfulness programs on _____ among nonclinical adults (both civilian and military populations)?		
Attention	64	43
Decisionmaking	3	0
Emotion regulation	26	15
Impulsivity	6	3
Work-related absenteeism	0	0
Work-related accidents	0	0
Work-related communication skills	1	0
Work-related interpersonal conflict	0	0
Work-related morale	9	4
Work-related productivity	4	3
Work-related social support	5	3
Work-related teamwork	2	0
Work-related turnover	0	0
Key Question 1a: Do the effects of mindfulness programs differ for military versus civilian populations?	Unable to evaluate	
Key Question 1b: Do the effects of mindfulness programs differ by program characteristics, such as the type of mindfulness practice (e.g., MBSR, MBCT), exposure (e.g., length or intensity of the program), or delivery format (e.g., in person, online, mobile app)?	Unable to evaluate	

[a] Studies could have reported on multiple outcomes of interest, so this column totals more than the 106 included studies.

Description of Included Studies

We extracted data from 104 articles that reported results from 106 studies. The study characteristics are described briefly here. The evidence table summarizing study details, participants, interventions, and outcomes can be found in Appendix H, which accompanies this report online.

Participants

Studies in our systematic review enrolled an average of 133.5 (standard deviation [SD]: 235.6) participants. The smallest study had 18 participants, and the largest had just under 2,300. Seventy-five percent of studies had fewer than 150 participants. The majority of participants were female (mean: 59.5 percent female; SD: 23.4), and the average age of participants was 28.3 (SD: 8.2). Only 6.6 percent of studies ($n = 7$) included a military population. A large percentage of studies enrolled university students (43.4 percent) and general populations of community-dwelling adults (27.4 percent). Fewer studies specifically enrolled working adults (e.g., employees of a particular organization) (15.1 percent) or health care workers or first responders (7.5 percent). Nearly half of studies required that enrolled participants did not have any prior experience with meditation (46.2 percent). An equal share of studies (46.2 percent) did not report any requirement pertaining to prior meditation experience. Few studies *required* prior meditation experience (2.8 percent) or enrolled a mix of participants (e.g., divided participants into groups based on prior meditation experience) (4.7 percent).

Intervention

Across 104 articles reporting results from 106 studies, 121 mindfulness meditation interventions were evaluated. Interventions were categorized into two general types. The first type comprised complete mindfulness meditation training programs, referred to as mindfulness programs or studies, that were designed to have a long-term impact on participants. These programs usually combined multiple elements (e.g., didactic instruction, mindfulness exercises, home practice) and were delivered over a series of sessions or a period of weeks. The other type of intervention comprised mindfulness analogues. As described earlier, analogues are very brief, typically single-session interventions (e.g., a single 15-minute guided meditation) delivered virtually (e.g., participants listen to an audio recording) in a laboratory, followed by an immediate assessment of outcomes. Analogues are not expected to have a long-term impact on participants and instead are used to evaluate *how* mindfulness works to inform the development of mindfulness programs. For example, an analogue study might assess the immediate effects of a brief mindfulness meditation on risk-taking behavior to indicate how mindfulness affects impulsivity. We analyzed mindfulness programs separately from analogues.

Figure 3.2 shows the breakdown of the types of interventions evaluated, including MBSR, MBCT, general (or unnamed) mindfulness meditation and training programs, analogues, and other interventions. MMFT, MBAT, and smartphone applications (e.g., Headspace) are examples of programs classified as "other." MMFT was evaluated in five studies, and MBAT was evaluated in four studies.

FIGURE 3.2
Types of Mindfulness Interventions Evaluated in Included Studies

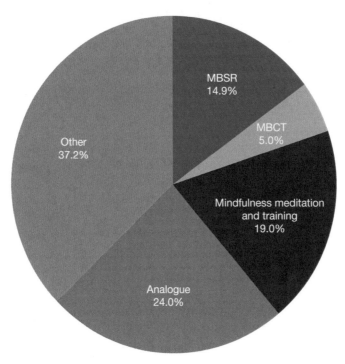

NOTE: The chart reports the percentage breakdown of the 121 mindfulness interventions evaluated in the studies included in our systematic review. Because of rounding, numbers might not sum exactly to 100.

Mindfulness Programs

Across the 121 interventions evaluated, 92 were mindfulness programs (i.e., not analogues). More than half of these mindfulness programs were conducted in person with a trainer, such as in a classroom, at a worksite, or at a retreat center (65.2 percent). Few programs were virtual and led by a trainer with real-time participation, which we refer to as *virtual synchronous* (3.3 percent). Some programs were virtual with no real-time participation, which we refer to as *virtual asynchronous* (18.5 percent), and others involved a mix of virtual and in-person participation (13.0 percent). A small percentage of mindfulness programs were entirely app-based (8.8 percent) or integrated a smartphone application with another delivery format (5.4 percent). Programs varied in their duration, both in the number or length of sessions and in the number of weeks from start to finish (Table 3.2).

Most mindfulness programs were delivered over multiple sessions (81.5 percent), but some were self-paced, online, or app-based (14.1 percent). Very few were conducted in a single session (4.4 percent). More than half were conducted in a group setting (58.7 percent), while a smaller number were individual (21.7 percent) or a mix of individual and group delivery (19.6 percent). Figure 3.3 shows the breakdown of these characteristics by program type.

TABLE 3.2

Duration Characteristics of Mindfulness Programs

Characteristic	Mean	SD
Number of sessions	11.5	14.1
Total program hours	12.8	13.8
Program duration, in weeks	6.5	5.5
Home practice hours	28.1	54.9

NOTE: *n* = 92 mindfulness programs.

FIGURE 3.3

Delivery Timing of Mindfulness Programs, by Program Type

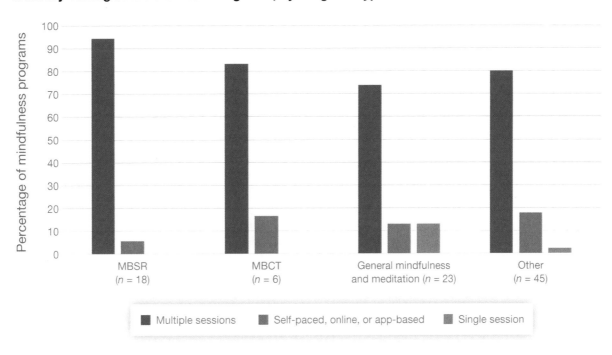

Some mindfulness programs suggested daily homework (e.g., engaging in independent mindfulness practice) (20.6 percent), and some required it (41.3 percent). For example, participants could be asked to log their practice times, sometimes in workbooks provided by the research leader. In the case of app-based interventions, some apps had remote monitoring functions. Other programs specifically did not require home practice (19.6 percent), and information about practice requirements was missing or not mentioned for the remainder (18.5 percent). Most mindfulness programs were standardized (97.8 percent) or ensured that each participant or group received an intervention presented in a standardized way rather than individualized to the participant. However, a few studies were unclear on whether the program was standardized in this way (2.2 percent). Relatedly, several mindfulness programs included a participant workbook or handouts (10.9 percent). Trainer preparation varied; some trainers had attended a mindfulness training workshop, others engaged in regular home practice of mindfulness meditation, and still others had undergone extensive training and certification in delivering MBSR or another type of mindfulness program. Trainer-to-participant ratio, when reported, also varied across studies, although this ratio was often not reported in the studies. Most programs did not offer any follow-up support or encouragement after the program ended (97.8 percent).

Analogues

In contrast to mindfulness programs, most analogues (n = 29 interventions) were delivered through a virtual asynchronous modality (72.4 percent), while the rest were virtual synchronous (10.3 percent) or in-person (17.2 percent). Many of these virtual analogues consisted of an audio recording that participants listened to while they were physically in a research laboratory at a university. No analogues were delivered through a mix of in-person and virtual sessions. Among the analogues, less than one-fifth (17.2 percent) were entirely app-based, and none was app-based and integrated with another component. The majority were conducted in a single session (86.2 percent), although several were delivered over multiple sessions (13.8 percent). None had any stated requirements for homework or home practice, and all were standardized. Analogues were typically conducted individually (86.2 percent); however, several were delivered to groups of participants (10.3 percent), and one was offered as a mix of individual and group sessions (3.5 percent). Because analogue interventions are not expected to affect long-term outcomes, none offered follow-up support or encouragement after the intervention.

Comparator

Comparison groups could be categorized as passive (e.g., no intervention) or active (e.g., other type of intervention). Passive comparison groups included assignment to a waitlist for the mindfulness program (23.4 percent) or nothing (18.2 percent). More than half of the included studies used an active comparison group (58.4 percent). Physical activities, classroom instruction on related topics, and music listening are each an example of an active comparison group.

Outcome

As noted earlier (see Table 3.1), we identified numerous studies reporting data for one or more of our target outcomes. We grouped the outcome measures into two categories: (1) self-report measures that were elicited face to face, on paper, or through an online survey questionnaire (e.g., using questions with Likert scale responses) and (2) performance measures, which were most often assessed using a computerized interface. The outcome measures used in our included studies can be found in Appendix I, which is available online.

Timing

Nearly all studies (99 percent) assessed outcomes at baseline and immediately after the end of the intervention. However, a few studies included additional longer-term follow-up: Only 14 percent of studies had follow-up times that ranged from four weeks to 12 months.

Setting

Settings varied widely across studies; about one-third examined interventions that were delivered virtually, and one-fifth focused on interventions delivered in school settings (Figure 3.4). The virtual setting category includes all interventions administered via an audio recording, online interface, or smartphone application, meaning that the participant was not physically in the presence of another individual during the intervention. Thus, within the virtual category, some interventions were delivered remotely (e.g., participant was at home) and others were delivered in a specific location (e.g., a research laboratory at a university). Nearly 7 percent of the studies in our systematic review were conducted in a military setting. Almost half were conducted in North America (46.2 percent), and fewer were conducted in Europe (26.4 percent), Asia (16.0 percent), Australia (5.7 percent), or South America (5.7 percent).

FIGURE 3.4
Settings of Included Studies

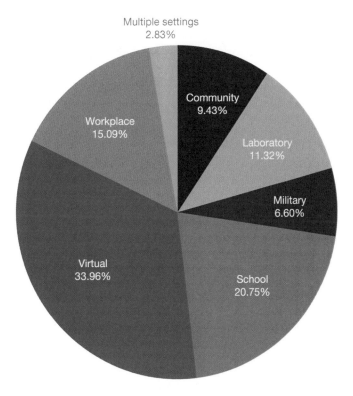

NOTE: The chart reports the percentage breakdown of the settings for the 106 studies included in our systematic review. The *multiple settings* category includes combinations of community/school and workplace/virtual.

Study Design

Most of the included studies were RCTs (87.7 percent). The remaining 12.3 percent were non-randomized trials in which at least one mindfulness program was compared with a control or comparison group, but the groups were not randomly assigned.

Study Quality for Individual Included Studies

Our systematic review comprised 93 RCTs and 13 non-randomized trials. As described in Chapter Two and in Appendix A, we used different quality assessment tools for each of the two study designs.

Study Quality for Randomized Controlled Trials

The U.S. Preventive Services Task Force (2017) tool for assessing individual study quality rates a study on multiple criteria:

- how the participants were randomized (*random sequence generation [selection bias]*)
- whether participants or study staff were aware of or could predict the condition to which participants had been assigned (*allocation concealment*)
- whether participants or study staff were aware of which intervention the participant received (*blinding of participants and personnel*)
- whether study staff who measured outcomes were aware of which intervention the participant received (*blinding of outcome assessment*)
- how much outcome data were missing (i.e., drop-outs) or collected but not reported (*incomplete outcome data* and *selective reporting of outcome data*).

Other criteria address problems with randomization (e.g., Did any participants randomized to the comparison group receive the intervention instead?), outcome measurement (e.g., Were the measures reliable and valid?), definitions of interventions (e.g., Were the measures clear?), and analysis (e.g., Was the analysis done appropriately?).

We used this assessment tool to evaluate RCTs, and it allowed us to assign an overall quality score to each study. The overall rating was determined by the combination of ratings for the individual criteria. However, one particular criterion—use of intent-to-treat analysis (see the next paragraph)—had a strong influence on the overall rating: If a study was rated poor on that criterion, the overall rating would be poor even if all other criteria were rated as high.

Most of the RCTs that met our inclusion criteria—70 of 93—had poor study quality overall. The most common reason that a study was rated as poor quality is that results were not analyzed for all participants enrolled (incomplete outcome data). Analyzing results for all study enrollees—called *intent-to-treat analysis*—is a requirement for a rating of good quality. Instead, these poor-quality studies included only study completers in their results. Ten studies met the criteria for good quality, and 13 met the criteria for fair quality. Few publications described studies' randomization procedures or procedures for allocation concealment. Almost no studies reported on blinding participants to their assigned intervention or blinding those who assessed outcomes to intervention assignment. And only 26 studies reported having registered or published a study protocol—the only sure way to determine that the study outcomes were prespecified. Study-level quality ratings are provided in Appendix J, which accompanies this report online.

Study Quality for Non-Randomized Studies

We used the Newcastle-Ottawa tool to assess the quality of observational studies. The tool focuses on the similarity (representativeness) of the cohorts to the population of interest, the similarity of the cohorts to each other (for our purposes, the mindfulness intervention group and the control group), ascertainment that participants accessed or attended the program, ascertainment of the comparability of outcome measures prior to the study, controls for potential confounders of concern (such as gender, age, or prior experience), blinding of outcome assessors, appropriateness of follow-up times, and intent-to-treat analysis. This assessment tool does not automatically assign an overall quality score to each study, and—because we did not include the non-randomized studies in our meta-analyses—we did not assign overall scores for such studies.

The fact that these trials assigned participants to groups using a non-random process automatically lowered the quality of the studies; however, because of other items used to assess quality, the studies tended to be fair in quality. Most studies (11 of 13) included highly selective populations (such as soldiers or health care personnel) rather than a broad population. Only two studies matched participants on age, gender, and prior meditation experience, and five studies matched participants on two characteristics. Eight of the 13 studies included all enrolled participants in analyses. Study-level quality ratings are provided in Appendix J, available online.

Summary

Our literature search process identified 5,900 unique study titles of potential interest (through database searches, reference-mining of systematic reviews, and studies suggested by other experts). From those, we identified 106 studies reported in 104 publications that met our inclusion criteria: 93 RCTs and 13 non-randomized studies (a small number of studies would have met our inclusion criteria but reported no usable data).

Studies tended to be small, enrolling an average of 134 participants, and most enrolled more women than men. The average age of participants was 28 years. Nearly half of the studies enrolled college students, and only 7 percent ($n = 7$) included a military population. Nearly half of the studies were conducted in North America.

Across the 106 studies, 121 mindfulness meditation interventions were assessed. We divided the studies into two types: (1) those that tested the effects of a complete mindfulness meditation program, typically delivered over multiple sessions and designed to have a long-term impact on participants, and (2) those that tested the effects of a brief mindfulness analogue intervention (e.g., a 15-minute audio recording of a mindfulness meditation exercise) that was not expected to have long-term effects. More than half of the studies included an active comparison group, such as exercise or education.

Most of the studies reported on one of two outcomes: attention or emotion regulation. Only a small number of studies reported on decisionmaking; impulsivity; or work-related communication skills, morale, productivity, social support, and teamwork. We did not identify any studies for four outcomes (work-related absenteeism, accidents, interpersonal conflict, and turnover). Most studies measured outcomes only at the end of the intervention programs and did not include any longer-term follow-up with participants.

Study settings varied: About one-third of the studies were conducted virtually, and the remainder were conducted in person. About one-fifth were conducted in person at schools, and 15 percent were conducted in workplaces. Finally, more than 90 percent of the included studies were RCTs, and the remainder were non-randomized trials.

Most included studies were of poor quality. RCTs rarely described methods for randomization or concealment of allocation, many failed to analyze results for all participants, and implementation of participant- and assessor-blinding was almost never reported. Non-randomized studies usually enrolled highly select populations and usually failed to consider potentially important confounding factors in the analyses.

CHAPTER FOUR

Effects of Mindfulness Meditation on Target Outcomes

In this chapter, we summarize the results of our findings regarding the effect of mindfulness on each of the nine target outcomes for which we identified at least one study that met our inclusion criteria. We first present findings for attention and emotion regulation, each of which comprised multiple outcomes targeted to different aspects of the broader outcome. Then, we present findings for four outcomes for which we found very few studies but were able to conduct meta-analyses (impulsivity, work-related morale, work-related productivity, and work-related social support). Finally, we present a brief overview of three outcomes for which we identified studies but were unable to combine them to conduct pooled analyses (decisionmaking, work-related communication skills, and work-related teamwork). As noted earlier, we did not identify any studies for four work-related outcomes (absenteeism, accidents, interpersonal conflict, and turnover). Tables 4.1–4.3 summarize the findings and conclusions for the outcomes for which we were able to conduct pooled analyses, along with an assessment of the strength of the evidence using GRADE ratings. We provide an overview of each outcome and GRADE rating in Appendix B. Details of the studies included in each pooled analysis, complete results from the pooled analyses, and narrative reviews of the studies that could *not* be included in the pooled analyses are provided in Appendixes C–F. Box 4.1 highlights key findings from this chapter.

BOX 4.1

Key Findings: Effects of Mindfulness Meditation on Target Outcomes

- Mindfulness may improve some aspects of attention, emotion regulation, impulsivity, and work-related morale and social support.
- Available evidence suggests that mindfulness does not improve work-related productivity, but the quality of this evidence is low, and more studies are needed to improve confidence in this conclusion.
- There were not enough studies to evaluate whether mindfulness had an effect on decisionmaking, work-related communication skills, or work-related teamwork.

Effects of Mindfulness on Attention

Attention is a basic cognitive process that influences almost everything people do (i.e., behavior) and experience (i.e., emotions and physical sensations) (Posner and Rothbart, 2007). In the broadest sense, the word *attention* encompasses individuals' conscious awareness of their environment and how and when they react to stimuli in their environment. In research studies, attention has been measured by an individual's self-perception (i.e., a rating scale of how well they were paying attention during a specific period or how good their attention is in general) or by their performance on a paper and pencil or a computerized attention test measuring, for example, reaction time and accuracy. In these performance tasks, an individual must respond as rapidly as possible—or withhold responses—to designated target stimuli. Attention is critically important for service members, who face life-threatening circumstances and must maintain focus to conduct military operations (Kosni et al., 2018).

There has been significant interest in quantifying the extent of attention deficits associated with various medical and psychiatric conditions that are common among service members—for example, traumatic brain injury (Mathias and Wheaton, 2007), depression (Wang, Zhou, and Zhu, 2020), and anxiety (Shi, Sharpe, and Abbott, 2019)—as well as in determining whether mindfulness and other psychological and behavioral interventions are associated with improvements in attention. Given that *attention* is a very broad term and has been measured in a multitude of ways, previous meta-analyses in which attention was a primary outcome of interest have typically grouped attention outcomes into two categories: reaction time (speed of response) and accuracy (e.g., number of errors, proportion of correct responses). Attention has also been categorized by domain or type of attention (e.g., visual, auditory). However, these analyses lack consistency in the number of attention domains and which outcomes are assigned to each. For example, some meta-analyses have included as few as two domains: *simple* attention tests with only one type of stimulus (e.g., simple reaction time task) and *complex* attention tests with multiple types of stimuli (Lim and Dinges, 2010). Others have included as many as six domains, including some of the following: processing or psychomotor speed, auditory attention, visuospatial attention, attention span, selective attention, divided attention, sustained attention, and attentional control (Mathias and Wheaton, 2007; Wang, Zhou, and Zhu, 2020).

After reviewing the attention outcomes in our included studies and consulting with subject-matter experts, we selected an influential model of attention to guide our meta-analysis strategy. The model proposes three networks of attention (Posner and Rothbart, 2007):

- *Alerting attention* refers to maintaining an alert and ready-to-respond state in which the individual is constantly monitoring the environment for target stimuli (Fan et al., 2002).
- *Orienting attention* refers to shifting one's attention to a specific target stimulus (Fan et al., 2002).
- *Executive attention* involves more-complex cognitive processes, including resolving conflicts and solving problems.

Each of these networks has been associated with the activation of different brain structures and neurotransmitters.

We first categorized the attention studies into two types based on how the attention outcome was measured: (1) outcomes measured by self-assessment or self-perception, which involved participants using a rating scale of overall attentional ability or capacity, either generally or during a specific period, and (2) outcomes measured by performance testing, which included administering tests of alerting attention reaction time or accuracy, orienting attention reaction time or accuracy, or executive attention reaction time or accuracy. We conducted a separate meta-analysis for each of these seven categories (self-perception plus the six types of performance measures) whenever we identified a sufficient number of studies for pooling. Most of the performance-related outcomes were categorized as executive attention reaction time or executive attention accuracy. The remainder of this section summarizes the findings regarding the effects of mindfulness meditation on attention. The strength of evidence and conclusion for each suboutcome are summarized in Table 4.1. The full results of the pooled analyses and narrative syntheses, along with study details, are provided in Appendix C.

TABLE 4.1

Results from Pooled Analyses of the Effects of Mindfulness on Attention

Attention Outcome	Intervention, Comparison Type	Pooled Effect Size (95% CI), Number of Pooled Studies, Number of Participants in the Sample	Study Quality	Strength of Evidence and Conclusion	Reason for Downgrading or Upgrading
Self-perception of attention	Mindfulness, passive	SMD = 0.17 (95% CI = −0.30, 0.64), 4 studies, n = 200	Poor	Moderate overall strength of evidence for **no effect**	Conclusions based on each meta-analysis were graded low for relatively poor study quality and imprecision, but overall strength of evidence was upgraded for consistency within and across study types and for directness.
	Mindfulness, active	SMD = 0.05 (95% CI = −0.26, 0.37), 5 studies, n = 264	Fair		
	Analogue, active	SMD = 0.15 (95% CI = −0.06, 0.36), 4 studies, n = 306	Poor–fair		
Alerting attention reaction time	Mindfulness, passive	SMD = 0.05 (95% CI = −0.26, 0.37), 4 studies, n = 177	Poor	Very low strength of evidence for **no effect**	Strength of evidence was downgraded for poor study quality, indirectness, and imprecision.
Orienting attention reaction time	Mindfulness, passive	SMD = 0.11 (95% CI = −0.22, 0.44), 5 studies, n = 201	Poor	Moderate overall strength of evidence for **no effect**	Conclusions based on each meta-analysis were graded low for relatively poor study quality and imprecision, but overall strength of evidence was upgraded for directness and for consistency within and across study types.
	Mindfulness, active	SMD = 0.13 (95% CI = −0.23, 0.48), 5 studies, n = 263	Poor		
Executive attention reaction time	Mindfulness, passive	SMD = 0.18 (95% CI = −0.13, 0.48), 11 studies, n = 503	Poor	Very low overall strength of evidence for **no effect**	Conclusions based on each meta-analysis were graded low for relatively poor study quality, indirectness, inconsistency, and imprecision; overall strength of evidence remained very low because of a lack of consistency within and across study types.
	Mindfulness, active	SMD = 0.36 (95% CI = 0.11, 0.62), 8 studies, n = 263[a]	Poor		
	Analogue, active	SMD = 0.18 (95% CI = −0.19, 0.54), 6 studies, n = 338	Poor		
Executive attention accuracy	Mindfulness, passive	SMD = 0.37 (95% CI = −0.16, 0.58), 10 studies, n = 582	Poor	Moderate overall strength of evidence for a **beneficial effect**	Two conclusions based on individual meta-analyses were rated low, and one was rated moderate. Overall strength of evidence was upgraded for relative consistency across study types.
	Mindfulness, active	SMD = 0.30 (95% CI = 0.06, 0.54), 9 studies, n = 272[a]	Poor		
	Analogue, active	SMD = 0.00 (95% CI = −0.28, 0.28), 6 studies, n = 272	Poor		

NOTE: CI = confidence interval.

[a] This SMD value reflects the results with the outlier study removed, as described in the text.

Self-Perception of Attention

We conducted three meta-analyses for self-perception of attention: mindfulness studies with passive (four studies) and active (five studies) comparison groups, respectively, and analogue studies with active comparison groups (four studies) (Tables C.1–C.3 in Appendix C). None of the three meta-analyses indicated a beneficial effect of mindfulness on self-perception of attention (SMDs = 0.01–0.17; Figures C.2–C.4). The strength of the evidence supporting a lack of benefit of mindfulness for self-perception of attention was moderate (Table 4.1). Only one RCT, which involved military personnel who received MMFT, showed a beneficial effect of mindfulness. Of four non-randomized studies, which could not be included in meta-analyses, only one showed a beneficial effect.

Alerting Attention and Orienting Attention

A single meta-analysis for alerting attention reaction time outcomes included four mindfulness studies with passive comparison groups. The pooled result did not indicate a beneficial effect of mindfulness on alerting attention reaction time (SMD = 0.05; 95% CI = 0.26, 0.37; I^2 = 14.2%[1]) (Table 4.1, Table C.4, and Figure C.5).

We had a sufficient number of studies to conduct two meta-analyses for orienting attention reaction time outcomes in mindfulness studies with passive (five studies) and active (five studies) comparison groups, respectively. Neither pooled result indicated a beneficial effect of mindfulness on orienting attention reaction time (SMDs = 0.11–0.13) (Tables C.5–C.6; Figures C.6 –C.7). The strength of the evidence supporting this conclusion was moderate (Table 4.1). Two studies could not be included in a pooled analysis—an analogue RCT (Lai, MacNeil, and Frewen, 2015) and a non-randomized study (Ching et al., 2015)—and neither study found a beneficial effect of the intervention on orienting attention reaction time.

Executive Attention

We conducted meta-analyses on two aspects of executive attention: reaction time and accuracy.

We conducted three meta-analyses for executive attention reaction time outcomes in mindfulness studies with passive (11 studies) and active (nine studies) comparison groups, respectively, and in analogue studies with active comparison groups (six studies). None of these three pooled results indicated a beneficial effect of mindfulness on executive attention reaction time (SMDs = 0.18–0.25) (Tables C.7–C.9; Figures C.8–C.11). We identified one outlier in the analysis for mindfulness studies with active comparison groups that had a very large effect size favoring mindfulness. When we reran this analysis with the outlier removed (eight studies), the result did show a beneficial effect of mindfulness on executive attention reaction time (SMD = 0.36; 95% CI = 0.11, 0.62; I^2 = 41.7%) (Figure C.10). When we consider all these analyses together, we conclude that mindfulness does not have a beneficial effect on executive attention reaction time, but the strength of the evidence supporting this conclusion was very low. Two analogue RCTs with passive comparison groups and six non-randomized studies that could not be included in pooled analyses also reported an executive attention reaction time outcome; results were mixed.

We conducted three meta-analyses for executive attention accuracy outcomes in mindfulness studies with passive and active comparison groups (ten studies each), respectively, and analogue studies with active comparison groups (six studies). We identified one extreme outlier in the analysis for mindfulness studies with active comparison groups; the effect size in this study strongly favored mindfulness, and its confidence intervals were completely outside the confidence interval of the pooled result. Both pooled results for mindfulness studies (with the outlier removed in the active comparison groups analysis; nine studies) indicated a beneficial effect of mindfulness on executive attention accuracy (SMDs = 0.30–0.37) (Tables C.10–C.12).

---

[1] I^2 indicates the study's calculated heterogeneity.

In contrast, the pooled result for the analogue studies with active comparison groups did not indicate a beneficial effect of mindfulness on executive attention accuracy (SMD = 0.00; 95% CI = –0.28, 0.28; I^2 = 35.9%) (Figures C.12–C.15). When all these analyses are considered together, we conclude that mindfulness programs, but not analogue interventions, had beneficial effects on executive attention accuracy. The strength of the evidence supporting this conclusion was moderate (Table 4.1).

Effects of Mindfulness on Emotion Regulation

Difficulty in regulating emotions has been identified as a primary risk factor in the development and maintenance of psychiatric disorders, including mood and anxiety disorders, eating disorders, substance use disorders, and personality disorders (Sloan et al., 2017). In contrast, effective emotion regulation is associated with positive health and behavioral outcomes, including in job satisfaction and performance (John and Gross, 2004; Madrid, 2020). As a result, many types of interventions, including mindfulness programs, that target clinical populations or nonclinical populations incorporate some form of training in emotion regulation skills.

Emotion regulation has proven difficult to define and assess. We used two influential models of emotion regulation to guide our meta-analysis strategy. One model proposes that emotion regulation involves four components: "(a) awareness and understanding of emotions; (b) acceptance of emotions; (c) the ability to engage in goal-directed behavior, and refrain from impulsive behavior, when experiencing negative emotions; and (d) access to emotion regulation strategies perceived as effective" (Gratz and Roemer, 2004, p. 43). The Difficulties in Emotion Regulation Scale is a widely used self-report questionnaire that was developed to correspond to this model. The total score may be interpreted to reflect overall general emotion regulation ability.

Another model conceptualizes emotion regulation as the processes (i.e., strategies) that people use to regulate or control their emotions (Gross, 1998). Later work has focused on six primary strategies. Three are considered adaptive (i.e., positive): acceptance, problem-solving, and reappraisal. Three are considered maladaptive (i.e., negative or harmful): rumination, suppression, and avoidance (Aldao, Nolen-Hoeksema, and Schweizer, 2010). *Acceptance*, which is explicitly targeted by mindfulness programs and is a key component of mindfulness meditation, refers to the act of accepting the emotions that one is experiencing exactly as they are, without attempts to judge them or change them (Aldao, Nolen-Hoeksema, and Schweizer, 2010). *Reappraisal* (i.e., reassessment) is an effort to view a situation from a different perspective that changes the emotional consequences of that situation (Gross and John, 2003). In contrast, *avoidance* and *suppression* refer to deliberate attempts to avoid experiencing negative emotions or to stop oneself from experiencing or expressing them, respectively, whereas *rumination* involves thinking continuously about upsetting or worrying thoughts that cause negative emotions. Highlighting the importance of the relationship between emotion regulation and mindfulness, a 2019 study indicated that increased use of reappraisal and decreased use of rumination may account for the positive effects of mindfulness meditation on depression and anxiety (Parmentier et al., 2019).

We identified 26 studies (18 mindfulness programs, eight analogues) that included an emotion regulation outcome, and we separated the studies into two categories: those that used self-report measures and those that measured emotion regulation indirectly in response to a negative stimulus or as interference with attention (referred to as *emotional interference with attention* or simply *emotional interference*). From there, we categorized self-report measures of emotion regulation into the following two types based on the two models described here, and we conducted separate meta-analyses of each type:

1. general emotional regulation ability (Difficulties in Emotion Regulation Scale or a similar questionnaire that asked individuals how well they were able to regulate their emotions or how much difficulty they had in regulating their emotions)

2. frequency or extent of use of specific types of adaptive and maladaptive emotion regulation strategies; reappraisal (adaptive) and suppression (maladaptive) were the two outcomes for which there were sufficient studies to conduct meta-analyses.

If a study included more than one outcome in a given category that could be included in a pooled analysis, we selected the outcome that was most similar to the other outcomes included in that pooled analysis.

One indirect measure assesses a change in self-reported negative mood intensity after receiving a mindfulness analogue intervention in combination with a mood induction that occurred immediately before or after the analogue intervention. A *mood induction* is a research procedure or task administered in an experimental context (typically, a laboratory setting) that is intended to induce a specific emotion or mood. For example, a common mood induction technique is to expose participants to images or videos or ask them to perform a task intended to elicit negative emotions, such as sadness or anxiety (Lench, Flores, and Bench, 2011). In these studies, a smaller increase or larger decrease in negative mood intensity following the mood induction was assumed to be evidence of more-successful emotion regulation.

Finally, in studies assessing *emotional interference* with attention, participants completed a simple attention test that contained distracting emotional content (e.g., pictures or words intended to elicit negative emotions). Better performance (i.e., faster reaction time, fewer errors, or both) was assumed to be evidence of more-successful emotion regulation (i.e., less interference). As we did with the change in mood intensity measure, we considered these tests of emotional interference to be an indirect measure of emotion regulation because they were administered in an experimental laboratory context rather than a real-world context, and participants were not asked to rate their perceived susceptibility to emotional interference. The strength of evidence and conclusion for each suboutcome are summarized in Table 4.2. The full results of the pooled analyses and narrative syntheses, along with study details, are provided in Appendix D.

General Emotion Regulation Ability

We conducted a meta-analysis of four RCTs of mindfulness programs with passive control groups. This pooled analysis showed no effect of mindfulness on general emotion regulation ability (SMD = 0.11; 95% CI = −0.25, 0.47; I^2 = 57.8%) (Table D.1 and Figure D.1 in Appendix D). The strength of the evidence supporting this conclusion was low (Table 4.2). One analogue RCT with an active control group could not be included in the meta-analysis (Watford and Stafford, 2015). This analogue study did not show a significant effect of the mindfulness analogue on "state" (i.e., in that moment) general emotion regulation ability.

Use of Reappraisal and Suppression

We conducted a meta-analysis of four RCTs of mindfulness programs with passive control groups that reported both the use of reappraisal and the use of suppression as outcomes (four studies each) (Table D.2). Our pooled analyses indicated evidence of beneficial effects of mindfulness on increasing use of reappraisal (SMD = 0.27; 95% CI = 0.02, 0.52; I^2 = 75.9%) (Figure D.2) and on decreasing use of suppression (SMD = 0.17; 95% CI = 0.00, 0.33; I^2 = 49.6%) (Figure D.3). The strength of the evidence supporting these conclusions was low. The same four studies were included in each pooled analysis; study quality was good in one study, poor in two studies, and fair in one study.

Change in Negative Mood Intensity

We conducted one meta-analysis of three analogue studies with active comparison groups that reported on change in negative mood intensity following a mood induction (Table D.3). This analysis did not indicate evi-

TABLE 4.2

Results from Pooled Analyses of the Effects of Mindfulness on Emotion Regulation

Emotion Regulation Outcome	Intervention, Comparison Type	Pooled Effect Size (95% CI), Number of Pooled Studies, Number of Participants in the Sample	Study Quality	Strength of Evidence and Conclusion	Reason for Downgrading or Upgrading
General emotion regulation ability	Mindfulness, passive	SMD = 0.11 (95% CI = −0.25, 0.47), 4 studies, n = 628	Poor	Low strength of evidence for **no effect**	Strength of evidence was downgraded for inconsistency and imprecision.
Reappraisal	Mindfulness, passive	SMD = 0.27 (95% CI = 0.02, 0.52), 4 studies, n = 630	Poor	Low strength of evidence for a **beneficial effect**	Strength of evidence was downgraded for poor study quality and inconsistency.
Suppression	Mindfulness, passive	SMD = 0.17 (95% CI = 0.00, 0.33), 4 studies, n = 630	Poor	Low strength of evidence for a **beneficial effect**	Strength of evidence was downgraded for poor study quality and inconsistency.
Change in negative mood intensity	Analogue, active	SMD = 0.18 (95% CI = −0.17, 0.53), 3 studies, n = 244	Poor	Very low strength of evidence for **no effect**	Strength of evidence was downgraded for poor study quality, indirectness, inconsistency, and imprecision.
Emotional interference	Mindfulness, active	SMD = 0.61 (95% CI = 0.31, 0.92), 4 studies, n = 174	Poor	Low strength of evidence for a **beneficial effect**	Strength of evidence was downgraded for poor study quality and indirectness.

dence to support a difference between the mindfulness and comparison groups in change in negative mood intensity (SMD = 0.18; 95% CI = −0.17, 0.53; I^2 = 45.1%) (Figure D.4). The strength of the evidence supporting this conclusion was very low (Table 4.2).

Emotional Interference

We conducted a meta-analysis of four RCTs of mindfulness programs with active comparison groups in which participants completed various computerized attention tests with emotional content (Table D.4 in Appendix D). These attention tasks included

- an "affective" number-counting Stroop task in which participants had to count how many numbers they saw on the screen; on *congruent* trials, the numbers matched (e.g., the screen displayed two 2s), and on *incongruent* trials, they did not match (e.g., the screen displayed four 5s) (Allen et al., 2012)
- a visual discrimination task in which the participant had to indicate whether the orientation of two bars was the same or different (Menezes et al., 2013)
- an auditory discrimination task in which the participant had to indicate whether a tone was high or low pitched (Ortner, Kilner and Zelazo, 2007)
- a "dot probe" task in which participants had to indicate the location of a dot on the screen (Wu et al., 2019).

In all four tasks, each trial also included an image on the screen that was intended to be distracting and induce negative emotions. Our pooled analysis indicated evidence of a beneficial effect of mindfulness on reducing emotional interference (SMD = 0.61; 95% CI = 0.31, 0.92; I^2 = 1.8%) (Figure D.5). The strength of the evidence supporting this conclusion was low (Table 4.2).

Effects of Mindfulness on Impulsivity, Morale, Productivity, and Social Support

In this section, we present findings from meta-analyses of four outcomes for which there were a very limited number of studies but from which we were still able to estimate the effect of mindfulness. The strength of evidence and conclusion for these outcomes are summarized in Table 4.3. The full results of the pooled analyses and narrative syntheses are provided in Appendix E, along with study details.

Impulsivity

Impulsivity is broadly defined as the tendency of an individual to react without full consideration of potential negative consequences (Chamorro et al., 2012). Impulsivity includes failing to delay or withhold a response when there is a reason to delay or withhold the response (e.g., the behavior is risky). In contrast, *self-control*, which is also referred to as *impulse control* or *response inhibition*, has been characterized as the ability to withhold or delay a response when there is an immediate or short-term benefit to responding but a long-term cost. The ability to exercise self-control is important to cognitive readiness and decisionmaking (Grier, 2012). The depletion of self-control capacity can lead to increased risk-taking or risky behavior, which are closely associated with impulsivity (Herman, Critchley, and Duka, 2018; Freeman and Muraven, 2010). Impulsivity is associated with increased risk of substance use and mental health disorders, participation in risky and violent behavior, and suicide (Chamorro et al., 2012; Hausman et al., 2020; Rogers, Kelley, and McKinney, 2021). For soldiers, impulse control is important for supporting operational and strategic military readiness (Grier, 2012). Impulsivity can be assessed using self-report measures that ask people to rate how impulsive they are or by using task-based performance assessments (e.g., assessments of delay-discounting or the tendency to

TABLE 4.3

Results from Pooled Analyses of the Effects of Mindfulness on Impulsivity, Morale, Productivity, and Social Support

Outcome	Intervention, Comparison Type	Pooled Effect Size (95% CI), Number of Pooled Studies, Number of Participants in the Sample	Study Quality	Strength of Evidence and Conclusion	Reason for Downgrading or Upgrading
Impulsivity	Mindfulness, passive	SMD = 0.31 (95% CI = 0.10, 0.52), 3 studies, n = 397	Good	Moderate strength of evidence for a **beneficial effect**	Strength of evidence was downgraded for overall study quality.
Work-related morale	Mindfulness, passive	SMD = 0.33 (95% CI = 0.07, 0.58), 4 studies, n = 244	Poor	Moderate strength of evidence for a **beneficial effect**	Strength of evidence was downgraded for poor study quality.
Work-related productivity	Mindfulness, passive	SMD = 0.08 (95% CI = −0.20, 0.35), 3 studies, n = 228	Fair	Low strength of evidence for **no effect**	Strength of evidence was downgraded two levels for overall study quality and indirectness (use of different outcome measures).
Work-related social support	Mindfulness, passive	SMD = 0.54 (95% CI = 0.08, 1.00), 3 studies, n = 343	Poor	Low strength of evidence for a **beneficial effect**	Strength of evidence downgraded two levels for overall study quality and imprecision.

choose smaller rewards that are available immediately over larger rewards that will become available at a future time) (Odum, 2011; Patton, Stanford, and Barratt, 1995; Rung and Madden, 2018).

We identified five studies that examined an impulsivity outcome (Table E.1 in Appendix E). We were able to conduct a pooled analysis of three of the five studies, all of which tested mindfulness programs versus passive comparison groups and used self-reported measures of impulsivity. This pooled analysis showed a beneficial effect of mindfulness on reducing impulsivity (SMD = 0.31; 95% CI = 0.10, 0.52; I^2 = 9.1%) (Figure E.1). The strength of the evidence supporting this conclusion was moderate (Table 4.3).

Work-Related Morale

Work-related morale is an individual's perceived level of satisfaction, attitudes toward, or feelings about their job. Numerous factors are understood to influence work-related morale, including (1) individual factors, such as personality and temperament, and (2) workplace characteristics, such as leadership, teamwork, social connection, and rewards (e.g., increased pay for good performance) and punishments (e.g., verbal warnings or reprimand) (Brief and Weiss, 2002). Morale, in turn, is associated with work performance, absenteeism, and occupational health and safety (Pflanz and Ogle, 2006; Singh and Jain, 2013). For service members, alignment with the mission and values of the military is thought to be important for overall job satisfaction (DiRenzo, Tosti-Kharas, and Powley, 2022; Gutierrez et al., 2021).

We identified eight studies—six RCTs and two non-randomized studies—that assessed the impact of a mindfulness program on morale (Table E.2). We were able to conduct a meta-analysis that included four of the six RCTs, all of which had passive (waitlist) comparison groups. The result indicated a significant beneficial effect of mindfulness on morale (SMD = 0.33; 95% CI = 0.07, 0.58; I^2 = 1.1%, suggesting low heterogeneity) (Figure E.2). The strength of this evidence was moderate (Table 4.3). The two RCTs that could not be included in the pooled analysis (because of the way outcomes were measured; see Appendix E), as well as both non-randomized studies, also showed evidence of beneficial effects of mindfulness on morale.

Work-Related Productivity

We defined *work-related productivity* as the quantity of output or work produced. Productivity at work is generally associated with happiness or life satisfaction, and chronic illness and stress place workers at risk of decreased work-related productivity (Alavinia, Molenaar, and Burdorf, 2009; Zelenski, Murphy, and Jenkins, 2008). Individual productivity is also important to the overall performance and effectiveness of a team, company, or workforce (Beaton et al., 2009). Soldier job satisfaction, morale, and quality of life may therefore be related to both individual and unit productivity (Jnitova, Elsawah, and Ryan, 2017).

We identified four studies that assessed productivity as an outcome, and we were able to pool three studies that compared a mindfulness program with a passive comparison group (the fourth study compared a virtual program with an active intervention) (Table E.3). The result showed a nonsignificant pooled effect size (SMD = 0.08; 95% CI = –0.20, 0.35; I^2 = 4.8%), indicating that these mindfulness programs had no observable effect on work-related productivity (Figure E.3). The strength of this evidence was low (Table 4.3).

Work-Related Social Support

Work-related social support refers to an employee's perception of how frequently or how much they provide social support to their colleagues or that their colleagues provide to them. It also can refer to an individual's perception of the social support in the overall work environment (i.e., the degree to which employees provide social support to each other). Workplace social support is associated with job satisfaction and retention and can take the form of peer support, task support, coaching, or mentoring (Harris, Winskowski, and Engdahl,

2007). In the military, social support is associated with improved performance and sense of belonging, and research has suggested that social support can buffer against post-deployment mental health symptoms (Smith et al., 2013; Russell et al., 2016; Overdale and Gardner, 2012).

We identified five RCTs that assessed the effects of mindfulness programs on measures of work-related social support (Table E.4). A meta-analysis that included three of the studies, all with passive comparison groups, indicated a significant beneficial effect of mindfulness on work-related social support (SMD = 0.54; 95% CI = 0.08, 1.00; I^2 = 70.0%, suggesting considerable heterogeneity) (Figure E.4). The strength of this evidence was low (Table 4.3).

Effects of Mindfulness on Decisionmaking, Communication Skills, and Teamwork

In this section, we provide a brief overview of findings related to three outcomes for which there was not an adequate number of studies to conduct pooled analyses.

Decisionmaking

One aspect of job performance for which the potential effect of mindfulness meditation has generated interest is *decisionmaking*, or the accuracy or appropriateness (e.g., based on a framework of morality or other relevant considerations) of an individual's decisions, judgments, or reasoning. Mindfulness might affect decisionmaking by improving the ability to quickly determine and focus on the relevant factors that need to be considered in making a decision. Decisionmaking ability is influenced by personality, age, life experience, and health status (Strough, Parker, and Bruine de Bruin, 2015). The speed and success with which soldiers make decisions is of critical importance for the Army, yet service members face significant cognitive demands and stressors that complicate critical thinking (Grier, 2012). Most military accidents are caused by errors in judgment, decisionmaking, and other aspects of cognitive performance (Thomas and Russo, 2007), so sound decisionmaking is also important for the safety of military personnel.

Although measures of decisionmaking are varied and can be context-specific, many are either self-reported or task-based performance measures (Bruine de Bruin, Parker, and Fischhoff, 2007; Weller et al., 2018). We identified two studies that met our inclusion criteria and assessed the impact of mindfulness meditation on decisionmaking (Table F.1 in Appendix F). Both studies used performance-based outcomes. Results were mixed: One study showed a beneficial effect of mindfulness but for only one of three aspects of decisionmaking evaluated. The other study did not indicate any significant effect. Based on the findings of these two highly heterogeneous studies with respect to interventions and outcome measures, the evidence for an effect of mindfulness meditation on decisionmaking is insufficient to draw a conclusion.

Work-Related Communication Skills

One work-related outcome that may be influenced by mindfulness meditation is *communication skills*, or an employee's perception of the quality of their communication with coworkers. Such skills are vital for effective job performance and are typically assessed using self-report measures (Waldeck et al., 2012; Okoro, Washington, and Thomas, 2017; McCroskey and McCroskey, 1988). Strong interpersonal communication is particularly important in the military, where clear verbal communication can shape teamwork, command climate, and operational success (Sookermany, 2012).

We identified one study that met our inclusion criteria and assessed the effects of mindfulness meditation on communication skills compared with the effects of communication skills training (Table F.2). Using a self-reported measure, this study indicated no difference in the effect of mindfulness compared with the effect of communication skills training on workplace communication skills. Both interventions improved communication skills comparably, and the improvements were sustained three and six months later. Considering the findings of this one study, the evidence for the effect of mindfulness meditation on workplace-related communication skills is insufficient to draw a conclusion.

Work-Related Teamwork

Mindfulness could potentially impact work-related performance, including teamwork. Within civilian settings, *teamwork* can be defined as how often or to what degree an employee works together with or helps other employees complete their work. Teamwork is important to overall work performance and requires communication, coordination, mutual respect, and other factors (Valentine, Nembhard, and Edmondson, 2015). In military settings, effective teamwork is critical to readiness, unit cohesion, and mission success. Teamwork skills are taught as part of basic combat training to prepare soldiers to work together to overcome threats and challenges (Brunyé et al., 2020; Grier, 2012). Self-report survey measures are common methods of assessment and typically ask the participants to report on their own behavior or that of their team members (Valentine, Nembhard, and Edmondson, 2015).

We identified only one study that assessed the effects of mindfulness (an analogue intervention versus an active comparison group) on a measure of teamwork (Table F.3). That study did not indicate a significant difference between groups on teamwork. Considering this single RCT, the evidence is insufficient to draw a conclusion about the effect of mindfulness on work-related teamwork.

Summary

In this chapter, we described the findings from our analyses of outcomes for which we identified any studies that met our inclusion criteria: attention; decisionmaking; emotion regulation; impulsivity; and work-related morale, productivity, social support, communication skills, and teamwork. Analyses for attention and emotion regulation included multiple categories of outcome measures.

We found beneficial effects of mindfulness programs for one type of attention outcome—executive accuracy—but not for others, and the strength of the evidence was moderate. The evidence supporting a lack of beneficial effect on some outcomes was modest. Likewise, mindfulness showed beneficial effects on several types of emotion regulation outcomes—increasing the use of reappraisal and decreasing emotional interference and the use of suppression to regulate emotions—but the strength of evidence was low for these conclusions.

Only one pooled analysis could be conducted for each of the following outcomes: impulsivity, work-related morale, work-related productivity, and work-related social support. We observed beneficial effects on measures of impulsivity, work-related morale, and work-related social support. The strength of the evidence supporting these conclusions was moderate for impulsivity and morale and was low for social support.

Finally, we identified an insufficient number of studies to allow pooled analysis for decisionmaking, work-related communication skills, and work-related teamwork. Therefore, we could not draw conclusions about the effects of mindfulness programs on these outcomes.

CHAPTER FIVE

Effects of Mindfulness Meditation on Stress

Stress significantly affects personnel readiness and is associated with increased risk for post-deployment alcohol use disorder, depression, generalized anxiety disorder, post-traumatic stress disorder, and suicide among soldiers (Campbell-Sills et al., 2018; Bandoli et al., 2017; Black et al., 2011). And because military service exposes soldiers to unique occupational and combat-related stressors (Hourani, Williams, and Kress, 2006; Pflanz and Ogle, 2006; Judkins and Bradley, 2017), military-related stress can affect the well-being of those soldiers' adult family members and children (Gewirtz, DeGarmo, and Zamir, 2018). Military families experience stress during deployments, which may require separation, relocation, or changes in family structure (Everson, Darling, and Herzog, 2013). Parenting stress, in particular, is associated with poorer psychological well-being and increased risk of problems with internalizing (e.g., feeling nervous, sad, anxious, withdrawn) and externalizing (e.g., aggression, conduct problems, delinquency) for children (Burgdorf, Szabó, and Abbott, 2019; Lavee, Sharlin, and Katz, 1996; Huth-Bocks and Hughes, 2008). Children experience greater rates of stress when a parent deploys, and they may be at increased risk of developing mental health conditions, compared with children whose parents do not deploy (Mansfield et al., 2011; Lester and Flake, 2013). Military parents may experience varying stress, depending on the number and ages of their children, the number of parents deployed, and the nature of shifts in responsibilities required during cycles of deployment (Lester and Flake, 2013; Russo and Fallon, 2015). Reducing stress for military families could improve personnel readiness and further increase resilience among family members. Just as the deployment- and combat-related stressors experienced by soldiers can influence the well-being of their family members, stress-related outcomes and family member well-being can affect the health and well-being of soldiers (Harms et al., 2013).

In recognition of the Army Resilience Directorate's interest in supporting Army families and the growing number of research studies on the effects of mindfulness interventions on stress, we briefly highlight the burgeoning evidence on how mindfulness programs could help soldiers and their families. The content of this chapter supplements our systematic review findings with an overview of stress-related reviews; we did not conduct a new systematic review of the effects of mindfulness meditation programs on stress. We originally sought to summarize systematic reviews evaluating the effect of mindfulness programs on relationship outcomes, but our search yielded no recent relevant reviews. There are reviews on the prosocial effects of meditation (Kreplin, Farias, and Brazil, 2018), but we deemed them out of scope. Thus, we summarize peer-reviewed meta-analyses and systematic review articles published between 2015 and May 2021 that evaluated the effect of mindfulness interventions on stress among nonclinical general adult and parenting samples. These review articles may provide meaningful implications and new directions for how mindfulness interventions may help support soldiers and their family members in managing stress and parenting. Box 5.1 highlights selected key findings.

In each section of this chapter, we describe the studies addressed in the literature reviews, including their intervention characteristics and effect sizes. We also highlight innovative studies that might be of interest to the Army, and we provide an overview of the implications of their findings for soldiers and adult family members.

> **BOX 5.1**
>
> **Key Findings: Effects of Mindfulness Meditation on Stress**
>
> - The effect of mindfulness programs on general stress reduction is well supported.
> - The literature evaluating the effects of mindfulness programs on parenting stress is limited, but available evidence provides preliminary support for its effects on improving both parenting stress and child outcomes.

Effects of Mindfulness on General Stress

We searched the literature for systematic reviews that were published between 2015 and May 2021 and that evaluated the effects of mindfulness on stress in nonclinical populations. This search resulted in 53 review articles. We then screened titles and abstracts to ensure that the articles focused on a mindfulness meditation program tested in nonclinical samples for the effects on reducing stress. From there, we conducted full-text review of 29 articles and ultimately determined that two reviews provided the most-recent, comprehensive summaries of two aspects of stress. The first review focused on self-reported stress outcomes, and the second focused on physiological measures of stress. In addition, we supplemented our synthesis of the evidence from these two reviews with four review articles describing innovative mindfulness programs (e.g., technology, online interventions, and brief mindfulness interventions), which we briefly highlight in this chapter.

The first systematic review included 49 MBSR and MBCT studies published between 2006 and February 2019 in nonclinical samples (Querstret et al., 2020). We assessed the quality of the review using the AMSTAR 2 tool: The review employed adequate review methodology (e.g., searches of multiple databases, duplicate review of studies, and study quality assessment) and a published protocol; however, the authors did not assess included studies for possible reporting bias and did not assess the overall strength of evidence of included studies. Of the 49 studies included in the review, 30 studies (24 MBSR, six MBCT) included self-reported measures of stress outcomes, and the other studies focused on other indices of well-being and psychological health. Of the 30 studies, 25 evaluated mindfulness interventions in face-to-face groups (range: four to eight sessions; mode: 8), and five studies evaluated self-help interventions (four online, one book; range: four to eight sessions; mode: 8). Most studies (24) reported that more than half of their participants were female. Studies were conducted with samples of students (nine studies), working adults (14 studies), and other communities (seven studies). No studies were conducted with military samples.

Overall, the results of these included studies suggested that mindfulness meditation programs were associated with significant reductions in self-reported stress (Querstret et al., 2020). Of the 30 studies, 17 (16 of which were RCTs) compared a mindfulness meditation program with an active or waitlist control condition, and 13 studies had no control condition. Consistent with the methods in our systematic review, we examined the effect sizes of the subset of studies in which RCTs were conducted. Of these 16 studies, 13 evaluated MBSR and three evaluated MBCT programs. Our analyses of these subsets of studies indicated a medium-sized significant pooled random effects estimate (SMD = 0.56; 95% CI = 0.37, 0.75; I^2 = 64.1%, suggesting high heterogeneity); overall strength of evidence was not assessed. The forest plot showing the effects for individual studies is shown in Appendix L, which accompanies this report online. This finding indicates that mindfulness programs had a significant beneficial effect on stress reduction. These results suggest that mindfulness programs could have an important effect on self-reported stress. For soldiers, reduced stress and increased mindfulness-based skills may help improve health, well-being, quality of life, and resiliency and may help sustain those improvements.

Stress can be measured through self-report and through physiological measurement (i.e., measurement of how bodily systems are functioning). Acute (or severe) stress causes the body to release stress hormones (epinephrine and cortisol) that activate the sympathetic nervous system to allow for a quick fight-or-flight response (American Psychological Association, 2018). The ability to fight or flee quickly is adaptive and critical to the ability of soldiers to respond to dangerous threats, but chronic (or long-term) stress can cause illness (McEwen and Stellar, 1993) or threaten cognitive functioning (Juster, McEwen, and Lupien, 2010), thereby harming personnel readiness (Nindl et al., 2013). Physiological indicators of stress include increased blood pressure, cortisol (Juster, McEwen, and Lupien, 2010), and heart rate variability (Kim et al., 2018).

Because of this unique characteristic of stress, we briefly describe one systematic review from our search that summarized the effects of meditation programs on physiological markers of stress (Pascoe et al., 2017). This meta-analysis reviewed 45 RCTs published through December 2016 evaluating physiological outcomes (e.g., cortisol, blood pressure, heart rate, lipids, and peripheral cytokine expression). Of the 45 studies included in the review, 28 evaluated mindfulness-based meditation programs (i.e., MBSR, MBCT, mindfulness meditation, and other types of mindfulness programs). Overall, these 28 studies suggested that mindfulness-based meditation interventions may be associated with a reduction in some physiological indicators of stress. Although most studies indicated no effect of mindfulness-based programs relative to active control on most indicators, some studies showed that mindfulness-based programs were associated with reductions in systolic blood pressure and decreased heart rate (Pascoe et al., 2017). We assessed the quality of this review using the AMSTAR 2 tool: The reviewers used duplicate screening and abstraction, assessed individual study quality, and assessed the strength of evidence but did not report their inclusion or exclusion criteria and searched a limited number of databases. Similar findings have been found in workplace mindfulness programs, with medium-sized effects on select physiological variables associated with job stress (Heckenberg et al., 2018). To the extent that stress can be reduced in physiological ways, these reductions have been significantly related to improved work performance, job stress, and medical conditions (including cardiovascular disease).

Finally, in the process of reviewing the literature, we found three additional systematic reviews that were more narrowly focused on technological innovations and briefer evaluations of mindfulness programs. The first was a meta-analysis of programs delivered via the internet or a smartphone application (Victorson et al., 2020). The authors reviewed 38 studies, 18 of which targeted stress reduction and indicated medium effect sizes for reducing self-reported stress (Hedges' $g = -0.47$, a measure of effect size). Interestingly, the presence of a person providing support moderated the effects of the mindfulness programs, and the results indicated greater stress reduction in studies that did not include human support, suggesting that independent use of mindfulness programs may be effective (Victorson et al., 2020). The positive effect of these online programs is supported in another review showing a large effect of online MBSR programs (with and without human support) in reducing self-reported stress (Jayewardene et al., 2017). Finally, because intervention intensity is an important factor in implementation, we also highlight a 2017 systematic review evaluating brief mindfulness intervention studies (< 4 hours) in reducing stress among health professionals (Gilmartin et al., 2017). This review included 14 studies, and nine of them indicated improvements in provider stress. The authors concluded that the brevity of these interventions may have increased access to mindfulness interventions for health professionals who may not otherwise have had time to participate during the workday and that the inclusion of take-home practice may have increased mindfulness uptake post-training.

Effects of Mindfulness on Parenting Stress

The research on mindfulness-based parenting programs is new and growing. For example, a 2016 systematic review evaluated how mindfulness may be associated with reduced parenting stress and aid in the prevention of childhood mental health disorders (Townshend et al., 2016). We searched the literature for systematic reviews that focused on the effects of mindfulness programs in nonclinical populations for reducing parenting stress and that were published between 2015 and May 2021. We found 20 review articles, and we reviewed their titles and abstracts. Of the 20 articles, four underwent full-text review, and we ultimately determined that two articles were appropriate for summarizing in detail. The first was a systematic review of seven RCTs evaluating the effects of mindful parenting programs on youth and parenting outcomes (Townshend et al., 2016). The mindfulness-based parenting programs reviewed were delivered in group format for about six to eight weeks, and the evaluated outcomes included internalizing and externalizing disorders, emotion regulation, relationship quality, parenting stress, and resilience among family members (i.e., youth between 2.5 and 14 years and parents). This review summarized individual studies and, because of the small number and poor quality of the studies, did not pool effect sizes for analysis. Findings from this review suggested small to moderate improvements on parenting stress, parenting emotional awareness, and symptoms associated with childhood externalizing disorders, although the poor quality of the studies and the small number of rigorous trials indicated that the evidence was weak and in need of future evaluation. We assessed the quality of the review using the AMSTAR 2 tool: The description of the searches was incomplete, but screening, data extraction, and qualitative assessment were careful, and the rationale was provided for assessing the strength of evidence as insufficient.

The second article was a systematic review and meta-analysis of 18 single-group studies and six RCTs examining the effects of mindfulness on youth outcomes and parenting stress (Burgdorf, Szabó, and Abbott, 2019). Our AMSTAR 2 assessment showed a sound review methodology (e.g., searches of multiple databases, rigorous study quality assessment), although the authors did not consistently employ dual screening and abstraction, register their protocol, or assess the overall strength of evidence. Interventions included MBSR, MBCT, and mindful parenting groups; a mother/baby group; and parenting groups with separate youth or adolescent mindfulness groups. Single-group studies indicated a small effect size ($g = 0.34$) immediately after the intervention and a moderate effect size ($g = 0.53$) two months later on decreased parenting stress. The controlled trials were similar in indicating a moderate effect size ($g = 0.44$) for mindfulness parenting interventions compared with a control condition.

Youth outcomes were collected in 17 studies that also indicated moderate effect sizes on such behaviors as internalizing ($g = 0.33$), externalizing ($g = 0.39$), and cognitive outcomes (e.g., executive function; $g = 0.40$) at two-month follow-up. Patterns in increased effect sizes at follow-up compared with patterns immediately post-intervention were also observed among youth outcomes. Interestingly, reductions in parenting stress significantly predicted improvements in youth externalizing and cognitive outcomes, suggesting that reduced parenting stress has an important impact on youth outcomes. Of note, these authors found that the benefits that parents experienced from these interventions were similarly influential on children and adolescent outcomes, whether youth attended the intervention or not and regardless of the intervention's duration. Although the evidence is still growing, these results provide preliminary evidence of the dyadic benefit that mindfulness-based parenting programs have on both parents and youth. These findings are particularly important for military families who face unique stressors related to relocation, deployment, and reintegration.

Summary

Stress is significantly associated with physical and mental health consequences and significantly influences readiness and resiliency during high-stress times. Stress can affect military families as well. Parents, in general, face significant amounts of stress associated with child-rearing and providing for their families. Military parents face unique stressors associated with frequent moves, reintegration when their soldier returns from deployment, and the effects of being located apart from other family or sources of support. In this chapter, we described recent reviews that we identified that examined the effects of mindfulness programs on general and parenting stress. An important body of research supports the effects of mindfulness programs on reducing general stress in nonclinical adult samples. Importantly, these reviews were conducted with nonmilitary populations, so more research is needed to demonstrate through systematic reviews that mindfulness programs are equally effective for reducing general and parenting stress in military populations. Several reviews consistently found reductions in stress across a variety of mindfulness programs, including those that are briefer and self-guided and that use technology. Thus, these results imply that the effects of mindfulness interventions on stress outcomes are robust, and these interventions are adaptable to varying modalities.

There is a smaller yet growing literature showing promising effects of mindfulness-based parenting programs on reducing parenting stress and youth outcomes. These studies suggest the dyadic and interactional effects of reduced parenting stress on improved youth outcomes. These results emphasize the importance of intervening with parents to reduce downstream consequences in family well-being and psychological outcomes.

CHAPTER SIX

Characteristics of Selected Mindfulness Programs

A primary goal of mindfulness programs is to teach participants to begin an ongoing mindfulness practice, but programs can vary widely. As described in Chapter Three, we included several programs in our systematic review, including MBSR, MBCT, MMFT, and MBAT (which we refer to as the *named* programs), as well as general (unnamed) mindfulness programs. Given the emerging state of the literature on mindfulness meditation programs, determining best practices for implementing these programs—particularly with soldiers—remains challenging. One strategy for exploring best practices is to examine program characteristics for mindfulness programs using materials from the program developers. Thus, in this chapter, we describe the program characteristics of those four named mindfulness programs and highlight commonalities and differences.

We first describe a suggested framework for understanding important characteristics of these programs. Second, we summarize the best practices of the four named mindfulness programs' characteristics that were identified in our systematic review. We selected MBSR and MBCT because they were more-established programs, and we selected MMFT and MBAT because they have been evaluated in military populations. We also provide an overview of the characteristics of these programs, according to the studies included in our systematic review, noting that there have been several adaptations to these programs in available literature. Finally, we describe factors that the Army might consider when adapting mindfulness meditation programs for soldiers and their families.

> **BOX 6.1**
> **Key Findings: Characteristics of Selected Mindfulness Programs**
>
> - Mindfulness programs can vary widely, and the literature on best practices for program implementation—particularly with military populations—is still developing.
> - Characteristics to consider when implementing mindfulness meditation programs include the program's goal, target audience, structure, and details.
> - Although MMFT and MBAT have been tested in military populations, MBSR and MBCT programs have a stronger evidence base.

Framework for Understanding Program Characteristics

Although there is a great deal of research to support the efficacy of mindfulness programs for stress and anxiety (Chiesa, 2009; Khoury et al., 2015; Sharma and Rush, 2014; Fjorback et al., 2011), real-world implementation of these programs requires several considerations, such as which program to implement and whether or how it should be adapted to ensure program effectiveness. Depending on the program's goal and target

43

audience, its structure and design features could look different. Thus, it is important to have a framework for understanding which aspects of the programs should be considered.

In our brief literature search of existing mindfulness program implementation frameworks, several articles offered implementation frameworks, theories, or commentary relevant to our search. These articles described the theoretical underpinnings or objectives of mindfulness programs; the structural or design characteristics (e.g., length, delivery format, home practice requirements, trainer qualifications); strategies for adapting standardized programs; and the mindfulness techniques, activities, and practices emphasized in each program (e.g., body scan, sitting meditation, yoga) (Chiesa and Malinowski, 2011; Crane et al., 2017; Emerson et al., 2020; Moore et al., 2015; Michie, van Stralen, and West, 2011; Pilla et al., 2020). Several articles also discussed factors to consider in evaluating mindfulness programs (e.g., study design, outcome measures, time points of evaluation) (Chiesa and Malinowski, 2011; Crane and Hecht, 2018; Pilla et al., 2020).

Using this literature, we developed a preliminary framework that summarized the program characteristics important to consider when implementing mindfulness programs (Table 6.1). The first category is *program goal*, which was emphasized in the Meditation-Based Intervention Design checklist as an important characteristic to narrow in on the program's aim or purpose (e.g., to decrease stress) (Pilla et al., 2020). Understanding the program's goal allows facilitators to identify a target behavior to change, tailor program content, measure changes in outcomes, and choose a program that has been shown to improve that outcome. The second characteristic of our framework is *target audience* or population (Pilla et al., 2020). Tailoring the program to a particular audience may be particularly helpful in increasing trainee acceptability and buy-in (Brintz et al., 2020; Crane et al., 2017). For example, knowing that the program is directed toward soldiers could help guide program adjustments that account for factors unique to soldiers' experiences and the demands of their job (e.g., family relocation, deployment stressors). Finally, an essential characteristic of mindfulness programs is to understand the *program structure and design*. The Meditation-Based Intervention Design checklist includes such program details as the program's time frame, including the total length or duration and session frequency (e.g., 24 program hours across eight weeks); the modality in which the pro-

TABLE 6.1

Overview of the Framework for Mindfulness Program Characteristics

Category	Type	Options
Program goal	Target outcome	• Behavioral focus (e.g., stress reduction, impulsivity, emotion regulation)
Target audience	Target population	• Clinical, nonclinical • Older adults, adults, youth, children
	Military population	• Military (active duty, National Guard, reserve), other military or veterans (military retirees, veterans), military spouses or families, non-military populations
Program structure and design	Format	• Individual, group, mixed
	Delivery mode	• In-person, virtual asynchronous, virtual synchronous, mix of virtual asynchronous and synchronous, mix of in-person and virtual
	Length	• Total program hours • Program duration (in weeks) • Number of sessions • Number of follow-up sessions
	Structure	• Frequency of sessions • Inclusion of an orientation or initial assessment • Inclusion of a retreat, practicum, or other intensive group practice
	Home practice	• Provision of audio recordings for home practice • Total home practice hours

gram is administered (e.g., in-person groups, individualized, or mixed format); and the program's philosophy and how these perspectives are highlighted in each program (e.g., cognitive restructuring) (Pilla et al., 2020). We considered including program trainer qualifications, but we were not able to thoroughly document the available trainings for included mindfulness programs; thus, we excluded this characteristic from our framework. We discuss the importance of the trainer in the section on implementing mindfulness programs in military settings later in this chapter.

Characteristics of Four Mindfulness Programs

Mindfulness programs can vary widely and can often be characterized by a variety of program design elements, such as duration, setting, and mode of delivery. Implementation of these programs can be informed by how the developers first implemented and evaluated these programs and what types of adaptations and variations have subsequently been tested. In this section, our goal is to summarize the characteristics of four named mindfulness programs (MBSR, MBCT, MMFT, and MBAT), as outlined by the developers of these programs, and to understand the variability in how the programs were implemented in studies included in our systematic review. We used our implementation framework to describe the characteristics of four named mindfulness programs (MBSR, MBCT, MMFT and MBAT). We summarize the characteristics of each program, based on materials from the developers of these interventions. We also include a brief description of the characteristics of programs evaluated in the studies included in our systematic review.

In Table 6.2, we provide an overview of program characteristics for each of the four selected mindfulness programs. Data for these summary descriptions were drawn from multiple proprietary sources from program developers, including the MBSR curriculum; MBCT text; MMFT text, articles, and personal correspondence; and MBAT articles and personal correspondence, as referenced in this chapter. Next, we provide a more detailed overview of each program.

Mindfulness-Based Stress Reduction

MBSR was developed by Jon Kabat-Zinn at the University of Massachusetts Medical Center in 1979 to complement medical care for patients with stress-related conditions (Santorelli et al., 2017). Designed to relieve suffering and increase the well-being of people with medical, psychological, and stress-related conditions, MBSR combines mindfulness meditation and mindful hatha yoga in an intensive curriculum. The program is founded on the premise that mindfulness—or nonjudgmental awareness of the present moment—is developed through practice. MBSR is delivered in person as an eight-week, ten-session group training, totaling 31 hours of classroom instruction. Each sequence starts with an orientation and features a full-day silent retreat between the sixth and seventh sessions. MBSR instructors maintain that both formal (an intentional, set block of time) and informal (throughout the day) practice are critical, and daily mindfulness practice of 40–60 minutes is required for the duration of the program (Santorelli et al., 2017). Students are provided with audio recordings for this purpose, including instructions for common exercises, such as body scan (i.e., mindfully scanning from head to toe to observe bodily sensations) or sitting meditation (i.e., guided meditation focused on awareness of breathing) (Santorelli et al., 2017; Kabat-Zinn and Hanh, 2009). At the end of the eight-week program, MBSR participants are invited to maintain their regular daily meditation practice and to attend free all-day silent retreat sessions with other graduates of the program (Santorelli et al., 2017).

MBSR is the most established of the mindfulness programs we describe in this chapter and has been tested extensively (Chiesa and Serretti, 2009; Khoury et al., 2015; Sharma and Rush, 2014; Fjorback et al., 2011; Parsons et al., 2017). Research suggests that MBSR is beneficial in reducing stress and anxiety in clinical and nonclinical populations, and it has shown promise in improving numerous other psychological and

TABLE 6.2

Overview of Original Characteristics of Mindfulness Programs

Category	Program Characteristic	MBSR	MBCT	MMFT	MBAT
Program goal	Target outcome	Stress reduction	Depressive relapse prevention	Resilience	Cognitive resilience
Target audience	Target population	Individuals with stress-related conditions	Individuals with recurrent depression	Military service members; civilians in high-stress occupations	Military service members; civilians in high-stress occupations
	Tested in military populations	No	No	Yes	Yes
Program structure and design	Format	Group	Mixed individual and group	Mixed individual and group	Group
	Delivery mode	In-person	In-person	In-person	In-person
	Length				
	Total program hours[a]	31	16	20	8
	Program duration (in weeks)	8	8	8	4
	Number of sessions[b]	10	9	9	4
	Number of follow-up sessions	0	4[c]	0	0
	Structure				
	Format of retreat or practicum	8-hour group silent retreat	None	4-hour group skills practicum	None
	Core exercises	• Body scan • Loving-kindness meditation • Sitting meditation • Yoga	• Body scan • Cognitive coping strategies • Sitting meditation • Yoga	• Contact-points guided meditation exercise • Ground-and-release exercise	• Body scan • Guided concentration • Connection exercise • Open monitoring exercise
	Home practice				
	Provision of audio recordings for home practice	Yes	Yes	Yes	Yes
	Total home practice hours[d]	42	36	28	5

NOTE: Programs are represented according to the features described in seminal articles written by the creators of each intervention. Characteristics may vary by population, implementation setting, and other factors.

[a] *Total program hours* provides an estimate of hours spent in instructor-led training and practice, excluding any required or optional time spent in independent home practice or in training follow-up sessions. MBCT was the only program that included follow-up sessions after the conclusion of the eight-week, 16-hour program.

[b] *Number of sessions* refers to the total number of program sessions considered standard for the program, including any initial assessment interview, orientation, or in-depth retreat or practicum session. MBSR included an initial group orientation, MBCT included an initial individual assessment interview, MMFT included an individual practice interview between the second and third weeks, and MBAT did not include any individual session or skills practicum.

[c] MBCT included four follow-up sessions spaced throughout the year following the end of the program.

[d] *Home practice hours* includes an estimate of recommended or required time spent completing practice or homework assignments outside of instructor-led training time.

somatic outcomes in both clinical and nonclinical populations (Chiesa and Serretti, 2009; Khoury et al., 2015; Sharma and Rush, 2014; Fjorback et al., 2011). The mechanisms of action remain unclear, and more research is needed (MacCoon et al., 2012).

We examined the characteristics of MBSR programs evaluated in the studies included in our systematic review. Of the 121 mindfulness interventions in our systematic review, 18 interventions (15 percent) were referred to by the study authors as MBSR programs. These 18 MBSR programs were described across 17 different studies, meaning that one study evaluated two different MBSR programs. Of the 18 MBSR programs, all were standardized or manualized, and none was evaluated in military populations. Consistent with the MBSR curriculum, the majority of MBSR programs were delivered in person ($n = 14$) without a web-based or smartphone application ($n = 16$). Although the MBSR curriculum is based on a group format, four studies evaluated mixed intervention modes delivered in person or virtually (e.g., smartphone or web-based applications). Of note, MBSR programs in our included studies varied widely in their duration: Four studies lasted seven or fewer total program hours, one study lasted 11 hours, three studies lasted 16 hours, and eight studies lasted between 20 and 40 hours. Consistent with the MBSR curriculum, most MBSR programs were completed in eight weeks. Home practice hours also varied by study, from two to 56 hours (versus 42 hours in the standard curriculum). Sixteen MBSR programs were reported by studies that had data to calculate effect sizes. Although we could not conduct pooled analyses to assess the differential effects of named mindfulness meditation programs, we examined variability in effects sizes. Because studies may report effect sizes for multiple outcomes, we looked at the largest effect size in each of the 16 MBSR studies. The 16 effect sizes ranged from −0.08 (a small effect favoring the comparator) to 1.04 (a large effect in favor of MBSR).

Mindfulness-Based Cognitive Therapy

MBCT was developed by Zindel Segal, John Teasdale, and Mark Williams in 2002 as a maintenance treatment to prevent depressive relapse. Rooted in cognitive therapy and MBSR, MBCT was designed to help patients change their relationship with thoughts, feelings, and bodily sensations that contribute to the risk of depressive relapse (Segal, Teasdale, and Williams, 2002, p. 65). The program is delivered in person as an eight-week, nine-session group training totaling 16 hours of classroom instruction (Teasdale et al., 2000; Segal, Teasdale, and Williams, 2002). Each course begins with an hour-long individual assessment interview, which is designed to orient the patient to the program and confirm the appropriateness of MBCT (e.g., screening for suicidality and active substance use) (Segal, Teasdale, and Williams, 2002, p. 83). Early iterations of MBCT did not include a retreat or day-long practice session. Similar to cognitive therapy, a defining feature of MBCT is its assignment of homework, which includes formal mindfulness practice and the documentation of that practice in a written diary (Segal, Teasdale, and Williams, 2002, p. 118). MBCT trainees were originally provided with 45-minute audio recordings developed by Jon Kabat-Zinn for the MBSR program, which included a body scan, guided meditation, and guided hatha yoga. The original implementation of MBCT included four optional follow-up meetings in the year following the end of the program (Segal, Teasdale, and Williams, 2002, p. 85).

MBCT was developed more recently than MBSR, and most research on its efficacy has been limited to the study of MBCT in clinical populations. Systematic reviews of MBCT have suggested that it is more effective than usual care at reducing the risk of depressive relapse (Fjorback et al., 2011; McCartney et al., 2021). More research is needed to determine the mechanism of action of MBCT (van der Velden et al., 2015). Resources to support MBCT training and implementation are publicly available (Oxford Mindfulness Centre, undated).

Of the 121 interventions described in studies in our systematic review, six (5 percent) evaluated MBCT programs. These six MBCT programs were described across five different studies, meaning that one study evaluated two different MBCT programs. Of the six MBCT programs, all were standardized or manualized, and none was evaluated in military populations. Consistent with the MBCT developers' text, MBCT programs evaluated in studies in our systematic review also reported mixed delivery modes; three studies delivered the programs in person, and the remaining three reported a mix of in-person and virtual formats (one study conducted MBCT via self-help). No studies reported MBCT programs administered using a smartphone or web-based application. In contrast to the original MBCT program, which is delivered in a mixture of individual and group sessions, four of the six programs delivered MBCT in group format and one delivered in individual format. Similar to how MBSR programs were adapted (as described earlier), MBCT programs in our data set used mixed delivery modes with wide variations in program duration (12 to 20 total program hours versus 24 program hours in the developers' text). Five MBCT studies in our systematic review had data to calculate effect sizes. The maximum effect size ranged from 0.09 (a small effect bordering on a null effect) to 1.0 (a large effect in favor of MBCT).

Mindfulness-Based Mind Fitness Training

MMFT was developed by Elizabeth Stanley in 2011 by modifying MBSR for individuals in military settings and other high-stress professions (Stanley, 2014). In early studies of MMFT, Stanley partnered with neuroscience collaborator Amishi Jha, who subsequently developed MBAT (Stanley, 2021; Stanley and Jha, 2009; Jha et al., 2010; Jha, Stanley, and Baime, 2010). MMFT was designed specifically for individuals with a history of exposure to trauma or significant stress; therefore, it includes trauma-informed self-regulation skills and concepts derived from trauma-informed psychotherapy interventions (e.g., sensorimotor psychotherapy, somatic experiencing, and the Trauma Resilience Model) (Larsen and Stanley, 2019; Stanley and Jha, 2009). In addition to its course content and mindfulness training, MMFT includes psychoeducation content about the neurobiology of the bodily response to stress (Larsen and Stanley, 2019). The goal of MMFT is to improve decisionmaking and use of self-regulation skills in military and other high-stress occupational environments. MMFT is delivered in person as an eight-week, nine-session group training, with an additional individual practice interview between the second and third weekly sessions. The curriculum includes 20 hours of instruction (Stanley, 2021). Participants are asked to complete 30 minutes of practice per day, divided into exercises ranging from five to 30 minutes (Larsen and Stanley, 2019; Stanley, 2019, p. 255). Participants initially use audio recordings to guide their home practice exercises and are later encouraged to complete home practice without audio support (Stanley, 2014; Stanley, 2019). Core exercises include a contact-points guided meditation exercise and a ground-and-release exercise designed to "release stress activation slowly" (Stanley, 2019, p. 284). Individuals who are new to learning MMFT are discouraged from practicing more-advanced body-based self-regulation exercises until they are more practiced in tolerating their reactions to stress activation (Stanley, 2019, pp. 256–257).

Because MMFT is a newer intervention, the evidence base supporting its efficacy is smaller than that of MBSR or MBCT. Most of the research demonstrating the efficacy of MMFT has been conducted by MMFT program developers (Johnson et al., 2014; Jha et al., 2015; Jha, Witkin, et al., 2017; Jha, Morrison, et al., 2017). Early research suggests that MMFT may be an efficacious tool for reducing activation and encouraging recovery from exposure to stress in military populations (Johnson et al., 2014). MMFT may also protect against working memory degradation and functional impairment in military populations exposed to stress (Jha et al., 2010; Jha, Witkin, et al., 2017). We are not aware of any systematic reviews of MMFT studies. Additional research is needed to determine effectiveness with larger samples and longer follow-ups.

Of the 121 mindfulness interventions described in studies in our systematic review, five (4 percent) evaluated MMFT programs. These five MMFT programs were described across four different studies, meaning that one study evaluated two different MMFT programs. All of the MMFT programs in the dataset were evaluated in military populations. Four of the five MMFT programs were reported in studies conducted and reported by the same investigative team (Jha et al., 2015; Jha, Zanesco, Denkova, Rooks, et al., 2020; Jha, Morrison, et al., 2017). The MMFT programs were relatively homogenous, lasting eight weeks; were delivered in person; and included 28 home practice hours. In contrast to the materials from MMFT program developers, which indicate that the program should be delivered in mixed individual and group formats, three MMFT programs were delivered in a group format, and two were delivered in mixed individual and group format. Similar to other programs highlighted in this chapter, the effect sizes observed in studies in our systematic review varied widely. Of the four studies with data available to calculate effect sizes, the maximum effect sizes ranged from 0.06 (a small effect bordering on a null effect) to 1.56 (a large effect in favor of MMFT).

Mindfulness-Based Attention Training

MBAT was developed by Amishi Jha and colleagues at the University of Miami beginning in 2012 as a short-form mindfulness training program for individuals in highly demanding military and civilian occupations (Denkova et al., 2020; Jha, undated). Like MMFT, MBAT was modeled after MBSR and modified for the military context and implementation considerations, in collaboration with military leaders and mindfulness experts (Zanesco et al., 2019). The goal of MBAT is to support cognitive resilience and enhance psychological health (Zanesco et al., 2019). MBAT is delivered in person as a four-week, four-session group training totaling eight hours of classroom instruction (Jha, 2021). Content revolves around four basic themes, including concentration, body awareness, open monitoring, and connection (Jha, 2021; Zanesco et al., 2019). Participants are required to practice for 15 minutes per day for at least five days per week and are provided with a personal listening device and guided mindfulness practice recordings for this purpose (Jha, 2021). Core exercises include guided body scan and concentration, a connection exercise in which participants engage in acts of kindness toward the self and others, and an open-monitoring exercise (Jha, 2021).

Similar to MMFT, MBAT is a newer intervention and thus has a smaller evidence base supporting its efficacy compared with the evidence bases for MBSR and MBCT. Most of the research to date demonstrating the efficacy of MBAT has been conducted by program developers (Zanesco et al., 2019; Denkova et al., 2020; Jha, Zanesco, Denkova, Morrison, et al., 2020). Early research suggests that MBAT may be effective for cognitive training to improve attention and memory in military populations. MMFT has also been studied as a possible tool for promoting resilience in military populations and other highly demanding professions (e.g., firefighters) (Denkova et al., 2020; Jha, Zanesco, Denkova, Morrison, et al., 2020). Additional research is needed to replicate these findings in larger studies. We are not aware of any systematic reviews of MBAT studies.

Of the 121 mindfulness interventions described in studies in our systematic review, five (4 percent) were MBAT programs. These five MBAT programs were described across three different studies, meaning that two studies each evaluated two different MBAT programs. All programs were reported in studies developed and authored by the same investigative team, and four of the five MBAT programs were evaluated in military populations. Similar to the MMFT programs, the MBAT programs were homogenous and similar to the materials that we received from the developer. Most of these programs were delivered in person and lasted four sessions across four weeks (one study also evaluated a two-week version). Four MBAT programs were delivered in a group format, which aligns with the developer's materials, and one MBAT program was delivered in a mixed individual and group format. Three studies with MBAT had data available to calculate effect sizes, and observed effects varied widely. The maximum within study effect sizes ranged from −0.04 (a virtually null effect) to 0.79 (a large effect favoring MBAT).

Summary Characteristics of Four Mindfulness Programs

In Table 6.3, we provide an overview of selected program characteristics for each of the four mindfulness programs, as described in the studies from our systematic review. In most ways, program characteristics as reported in those studies were similar to the characteristics described by program developers (see Table 6.2). The mean number of program sessions for MBSR, MBCT, and MMFT ranged from seven to nine, delivered

TABLE 6.3

Selected Characteristics of Mindfulness Programs Evaluated in Systematic Review Studies

Characteristic	MBSR Mean (SD)	MBCT Mean (SD)	MMFT Mean (SD)	MBAT Mean (SD)
Number of sessions	9 (5)	7 (2)	7 (2)	4 (0)
Total program hours	19 (10)	14 (5)	14 (8)	8 (0)
Total program weeks	7 (3)	6 (3)	8 (0)	4 (1)
Home practice hours	22 (15)	18 (14)	28 (0)	5 (2)

over six to eight weeks. These programs were all about the same total length (ranging from 14 to 19 hours), although MBSR had the longest mean length of 19 hours. MBSR, MBCT, and MMFT were also roughly similar in mean home practice hours (ranging from 18 to 28 hours). In contrast, MBAT averaged four sessions delivered over four weeks, eight total hours, and five hours of home practice.

Considerations for Implementing Mindfulness Programs in the Military

There are numerous aspects of military settings that should be considered in implementing a mindfulness program. For instance, the military has a unique culture, which could affect service members' acceptance and the subsequent effectiveness of the program (Coll, Akerman, and Cicchetti, 2000). Army life is often characterized by austere settings and competing demands for soldiers' time, which could make it difficult for soldiers to allocate time for new programs. Variation in soldier characteristics (e.g., by component or military occupational specialty) can also make it more challenging to conduct RCTs and other rigorous study methodologies to evaluate the effectiveness of programs delivered in military settings (Jha et al., 2015). In reviewing published literature, we were unable to identify any systematic reviews of mindfulness programs implemented with military populations, However, the literature does contain suggested considerations and possible strategies for adapting mindfulness programs for military populations.

First, to account for the schedules and time demands of service members, it may be important to consider mindfulness programs that have been tested in briefer formats (Zanesco et al., 2019). Service members have limited time available for training and often work long hours completing stressful and physically demanding tasks, particularly in garrison settings (Campbell and Nobel, 2009). More research is needed to determine the minimum effective program duration and length necessary for program efficacy, and modifications should be made with caution until more data are available. One possible strategy to address time and scheduling demands is to devote time during the duty day to mindfulness practice, either for guided or independent mindfulness exercises (Piatt, Teyhen, and Adler, 2021). Alternatively, it might be useful to offer prerecorded or asynchronous training options to accommodate deployments and other unpredictable scheduling conflicts (Jha, 2020; Brintz et al., 2020).

Second, mindfulness programs delivered in military settings should be designed with an understanding of the hierarchical structure of the military and the importance of support from senior military leaders (Adler and Castro, 2013; Meredith et al., 2011). One way of upholding the importance of this hierarchy and supporting the chain of command is to assume a more directive approach to delivering course content (Brintz et al., 2020). Although involving senior military leaders may be important to establish buy-in and support for an intervention, it may also be important to consider the group composition of mindfulness training programs (e.g., by holding separate programs for officers and enlisted soldiers) (Brintz et al., 2020). Furthermore, there is a possibility that some individuals may experience discomfort during mindfulness practice (Lindahl et al.,

2017). Given this, as well as the hierarchical nature of military environments, implementation should allow for soldiers to opt out of participation.

Third, mindfulness programs may benefit from crafting an implementation plan that recognizes the importance of the trainer. Kabat-Zinn, the founder of MBSR, noted that "the quality of MBSR as an intervention is only as good as the MBSR instructor" (Kabat-Zinn, 2011, p. 281). As mindfulness programs have gained popularity, researchers have acknowledged the need to establish a shared standard for mindfulness trainer competencies in research settings (Crane et al., 2012). Accordingly, more research is needed to determine how the quality of the trainer might affect the outcomes of mindfulness training for program participants (Ruijgrok-Lupton, Crane, and Dorjee, 2018; Khoury et al., 2013). In the military, lessons learned from implementing resilience training programs suggest that such programs might be better received if delivered by a fellow service member (Roski et al., 2019). The use of service members as trainers could also make implementation more scalable and cost-effective (Roski et al., 2019). The Master Resilience Training Program is an example of an existing military program with broad reach and an established infrastructure. Master Resilience Trainers are taught using a train-the-trainer model, which has proved to be an efficient strategy for training service members at a scale appropriate for widespread implementation in the military (Reivich, Seligman, and McBride, 2011). In one study that compared MBAT training delivered by civilian mindfulness experts with MBAT training delivered by mindfulness-naïve Army Master Resilience Trainers (i.e., soldiers with expertise in resilience training who received mindfulness training for the study through a train-the-trainer model), soldiers rated the Army Master Resilience Trainers as being significantly more effective at delivering the course content than the civilian mindfulness experts (Jha, Zanesco, Denkova, Morrison, et al., 2020). However, more research is needed to determine whether train-the-trainer models can adequately prepare service members to implement mindfulness programs with fidelity.

Summary

In this chapter, we presented a preliminary framework to characterize the goals, target audience, and program structure and design of four prevalent mindfulness meditation programs. Although they differ in their characteristics, MBSR, MBCT, MMFT, and MBAT have a great deal in common. MBCT, MMFT, and MBAT were each derived from MBSR, and all four programs seek to reduce suffering and increase well-being among participants. MBSR was developed for individuals with chronic pain, illness, and stress-related conditions, and MBCT was developed for individuals with recurrent depression. MMFT and MBAT were designed for nonclinical individuals in high-stress military and other occupations. All four programs use a group format, although MBCT and MMFT each include an individual session in the first few weeks of the program. All were initially developed to be administered in person. MBSR, MBCT, and MMFT are somewhat similar in length, duration, and structure, and MBAT is significantly shorter and less intensive. For example, MBSR, MBCT, and MMFT are similar in total program hours (ranging from 20 to 31) and duration (eight weeks), and MBAT is less than half the length (eight hours) and half the duration (four weeks) of the other three programs, according to the original materials from program developers (see Table 6.2). MBAT also features fewer total sessions (four) than MBSR, MBCT, and MMFT (nine or ten), and it requires significantly less home practice (five hours versus 28–42 hours). Despite these differences, the core exercises of the four programs are relatively similar.

When we examined these four programs in studies included in our systematic review, several patterns emerged. MBSR was the most frequently evaluated program, and many studies evaluated program adaptations, including delivery via virtual, briefer, and mixed group and individual formats. Similarly, studies evaluated adaptations of MBCT in briefer and mixed modalities compared with the characteristics in the developers' source material. This heterogeneity is in contrast to the newer MMFT and MBAT programs, which have been only piloted, mostly by the same investigative teams. Nonetheless, these studies offer important insights because they involved military populations. Finally, when we examined pooled effect sizes for each of these programs, effect sizes ranged from null effects to large effects in favor of the mindfulness program, suggesting varying degrees of evidence.

As Army leaders consider implementing mindfulness meditation programs, they should focus on three key aspects as potential best practices. First, the Army should consider the program's goal and which target behavior the mindfulness meditation is intended to influence. Second, identifying the target audience and whether adaptations are needed will increase the likelihood that the program can be successfully delivered and accepted by participants. Finally, it is important to determine the program structure and design. More research is needed to determine how best to implement mindfulness programs with military populations. Possible adaptations include shortening program length, offering flexible training options to accommodate deployments and workload demands, delivering programs in a manner that upholds the hierarchical structure of the military chain of command, and crafting an implementation plan that recognizes the importance of the program trainer.

CHAPTER SEVEN

Summary and Recommendations

This report describes a systematic review and meta-analyses of published literature on mindfulness programs, with a focus on outcomes relevant to nonclinical soldiers. We supplemented our systematic review by examining how mindfulness meditation could support stress management and exploring the characteristics of selected mindfulness programs. The goal of this effort was to develop recommendations for best practices for mindfulness programs for soldiers, should the Army consider implementing such programs in the future. In this chapter, we discuss the strengths and limitations of our analysis, summarize our key findings, and present our recommendations.

Strengths and Limitations

Our systematic review and meta-analyses had significant strengths. We conducted a comprehensive, highly rigorous systematic review focused on 13 outcomes relevant to soldier performance. The scope of the literature that we examined was broad: We identified and screened 5,900 unique publications and ultimately included 104 articles, representing 106 studies, that met the inclusion and exclusion criteria for our review. We followed established guidelines for conducting high-quality systematic reviews (Higgins et al., 2021; AHRQ, 2014; U.S. Preventive Services Task Force, 2017), and these standards guided the development and implementation of our systematic review protocol. Our rigorous, transparent methods help to ensure the replicability of our findings and minimize potential bias in interpreting the available literature. We strengthened our report by supplementing our systematic review with an overview of literature on stress and parenting stress—two outcomes that are highly relevant to both soldiers and their families.

Our systematic review also had limitations, largely because of the literature available to address our key question. Chiefly, the quality of the existing literature for most outcomes limited our ability to draw strong conclusions about the effect of mindfulness programs on our target outcomes. There were more analogue studies than we expected, and those studies have significant limitations and may have limited relevance for understanding effects of sustained mindfulness practice. Most studies included in the systematic review were of lower overall quality, and the average number of included participants was relatively small. The majority of RCTs did not report intent-to-treat analyses, and most non-randomized trials were selected from a relatively narrow population of participants. Furthermore, most studies assessed outcomes immediately after the completion of the intervention, and few studies included longer-term follow-up assessments. Thus, our analyses of effects were restricted to effects immediately post-intervention, which limited our ability to make conclusions about potential sustained impacts of mindfulness.

The articles included in the review examined a wide variety of mindfulness programs and outcomes, but most outcomes were reported by only a small number of studies. We excluded outcomes that were assessed via brain imaging because we determined that it would be difficult to generate actionable recommendations from those assessments. Nevertheless, we acknowledge that there is a growing literature on the effects of mindfulness practice on the brain and that those studies may provide unique insights into the mechanisms of mindfulness. Additionally, there was a wide variety of suboutcomes for attention, which was the outcome assessed in the most studies in our systematic review. We could have categorized these suboutcomes into fewer or more than the three domains of alerting, orienting, and executive attention that we used. However, given the relatively small number of studies that showed significant effects of mindfulness on attention, we believe it is unlikely that our main conclusions would have changed if we had grouped the attention suboutcomes differently.

For some outcomes—specifically, work-related absenteeism, accidents, interpersonal conflict, and turnover—we identified no studies. As a result of limited available literature, we were unable to directly compare the effectiveness of different mindfulness programs, so we could not identify characteristics that were associated with effective programs (Key Question 1b). Relatedly, few studies included military populations. Thus, effects of mindfulness were largely based on effects estimated in civilian populations. Because so few studies examined military populations, we were unable to address whether the effects of mindfulness programs differed for military and civilian populations (Key Question 1a). To better align results with military populations, our review excluded studies of mindfulness in clinical populations and populations that were much older or younger than military populations. Still, the estimated effects may not be representative of effects that would be observed in military populations. Our coding of the populations for included studies suggests that participants were more likely to be female and university students. There may be further differences on variables that we did not capture in our extraction (e.g., race/ethnicity, trauma history, sociodemographic background). Limitations in the literature also limited our ability to clearly identify best practices when implementing mindfulness meditation programs with soldiers.

Finally, we supplemented our systematic review by examining recent systematic reviews on stress and describing characteristics of four mindfulness programs. These efforts were separate from our systematic review, and we did not incorporate the same rigorous methodological approach for these components as we did for our systematic review. Our description of four selected mindfulness programs and implementation considerations for the Army had some limitations. For instance, in describing the characteristics of the four programs that were documented in studies included in our systematic review, we relied on the authors' characterization of the intervention (i.e., interventions referred to as MBSR were considered MBSR). We were also unable to thoroughly document available leader trainings for the selected mindfulness programs, so we excluded the quality of the mindfulness trainer from our framework.

Key Findings

Considering the results of our analyses, we identified four key findings. Table 7.1 summarizes the findings from our systematic review.

Mindfulness May Improve Some Aspects of Attention and Emotion Regulation, Impulsivity, and Work-Related Morale and Social Support

Guided by existing models of how the processes of attention and emotion regulation work, we performed meta-analyses on five types of attention outcomes (examined across 43 studies) and five types of emotion regulation outcomes (examined across 15 studies). We found that mindfulness may improve accuracy on attention tests that require resolving conflicts or solving problems (executive attention) but not reaction time or self-perception of attention. Regarding emotion regulation, we found that mindfulness may increase the use of a specific adaptive emotion regulation strategy (reappraisal), decrease the use of a specific maladaptive emotion regulation strategy (suppression), and reduce the extent to which negative emotions slow down reac-

TABLE 7.1

Overview of Findings from the Systematic Review

Outcome	Effect of Mindfulness Programs	Strength of the Evidence	Number of Studies
Attention			
Executive attention accuracy (resolving conflicts or solving problems)	Potential small beneficial effect	Moderate	23 studies
Self-perception of attention, reaction time	No effect	Very low to moderate[a]	4–25 studies (per suboutcome)
Decisionmaking	Unknown	Very low	Too few studies to conduct pooled analyses
Emotion regulation			
Reappraisal, suppression, and emotional interference	Potential small to medium beneficial effect	Low	Fewer than 5 studies (per suboutcome)
General emotion regulation and change in negative mood	No effect	Very low to low[a]	Fewer than 5 studies (per suboutcome)
Impulsivity	Potential small beneficial effect	Moderate	Fewer than 5 studies
Work-related outcomes			
Absenteeism, accidents, interpersonal conflict, and turnover	Unknown	Very low	No studies
Communication skills and teamwork	Unknown	Very low	Too few studies to conduct pooled analyses
Morale	Potential small beneficial effect	Moderate	Fewer than 5 studies
Productivity	No effect	Low	Fewer than 5 studies
Social support	Potential medium beneficial effect	Low	Fewer than 5 studies

NOTE: Shaded rows indicate outcomes for which there was evidence of a potential effect of mindfulness programs, although, in many cases, the strength of evidence was low.

[a] These ranges reflect grades for different suboutcomes. Each individual suboutcome had a grade of very low, low, or moderate.

tion time on attention tests (emotional interference). Our analyses did not suggest that mindfulness improves general emotion regulation ability or that it decreases negative mood intensity.

We identified a small number of studies examining the impulsivity, work-related morale, and work-related social support outcomes, so analysis of these outcomes was more limited. Our analyses suggested that mindfulness may have a small beneficial effect on impulsivity, but limitations in the available studies mean that the strength of evidence for this finding was moderate. Furthermore, our analyses showed a small beneficial effect of mindfulness on morale, and the four studies that could not be included in the pooled analysis indicated the same. Likewise, our analyses showed a medium beneficial effect on social support. Our confidence in the conclusions regarding impulsivity was moderate and our confidence in the conclusion for social support was low because the studies were mostly small and relied on different, self-reported measures. Our confidence in the conclusion regarding a beneficial effect on morale was higher—moderate—because of the larger number of studies with similar findings.

The available evidence included studies that examined a variety of mindfulness programs across many populations, often with very small samples. This variation across studies makes it difficult to draw definitive conclusions about the impact of mindfulness on these outcomes, but available evidence suggests some potential benefits that warrant further research.

The Available Evidence Does Not Suggest That Mindfulness Improves Other Outcomes of Interest to the Army

Across the 13 target outcomes in our systematic review, there was inadequate evidence to suggest that mindfulness has an effect on eight of them. Our analysis indicated that mindfulness programs did not have a significant impact on productivity. Our confidence in this conclusion was low because the studies were very small and the measures of productivity were varied. For three outcomes (decisionmaking, communication skills, and teamwork), we identified relevant studies but were not able to conduct pooled analyses. Only one study included an outcome related to communication skills, and that study indicated benefits comparable to communication skills training.

One of the two studies that examined decisionmaking indicated a benefit of mindfulness but only on one of several types of decisionmaking evaluated; the other study did not find an effect of mindfulness. Only one study, which tested an analogue intervention, included a teamwork outcome. This study did not find a significant difference between the intervention and the comparison group. Finally, we did not find any relevant studies for four target outcomes (absenteeism, accidents, interpersonal conflict, and turnover), so the effect of mindfulness on these outcomes is unknown as well. Additional research is necessary to determine whether mindfulness affects these eight outcomes.

Mindfulness Programs Reduce Stress and May Reduce Parental Stress, Which Could Benefit Army Families

Numerous systematic reviews of mindfulness programs for general stress outcomes suggest that MBSR and other mindfulness programs can be effective at reducing stress in nonclinical populations. One 2020 systematic review of self-reported stress outcomes indicated that mindfulness programs were associated with a significant reduction in self-reported stress (Querstret et al., 2020). Through our supplementary analysis of the effect sizes of the subset of RCT studies in that review, we found a medium-sized pooled effect, meaning that mindfulness programs significantly decreased self-reported stress. A 2017 review of physiological outcomes (e.g., cortisol, heart rate, blood pressure) indicated that mindfulness meditation programs were associated with improvements in systolic blood pressure and heart rate in some studies (Pascoe et al., 2017). Similarly, a review of workplace mindfulness found small to medium-sized effects for improvements in physiological measurements of job stress (e.g., cortisol levels, heart rate variability) (Heckenberg et al., 2018). Taken together, this research suggests that the positive impact of mindfulness on general stress reduction is well supported in the literature.

Studies of parenting stress show promising dyadic improvements on both parent and child outcomes. One systematic review of studies on mindful parenting programs indicated small to moderate improvements in parenting stress and symptoms associated with externalizing disorders in children (Townshend et al., 2016). However, the authors did not pool effect sizes for analyses, and the quality of included studies was determined to be weak (Townshend et al., 2016). Another systematic review of MBSR, MBCT, and mindful parenting groups indicated small to moderate effect sizes for decreased parenting stress and moderate effect sizes for improved youth outcomes compared with results from the control condition (Burgdorf, Szabó, and Abbott, 2019). Furthermore, the authors found evidence of dyadic improvements, meaning that improvements in parenting stress also were associated with subsequent improvements in child and youth outcomes, even when only the parents directly participated in the mindfulness programs (Burgdorf, Szabó, and Abbott, 2019). Although none of the studies included in these reviews was conducted in military populations, the literature suggests that mindfulness programs may hold promise in addressing general stress and parenting stress affecting soldiers and their family members.

More Research Is Needed to Identify Best Practices for Implementing Mindfulness Programs in the Military

Although there is evidence to support the efficacy of mindfulness programs to reduce stress and anxiety (Chiesa and Serretti, 2009; Khoury et al., 2015; Sharma and Rush, 2014; Fjorback et al., 2011), the military will need to consider several factors before implementing such programs. However, the research literature on mindfulness-based programs in real-world military settings is scant, and clear guidance about best practices is not yet available. In our brief review of the literature on mindfulness program implementation frameworks, we identified three categories of program characteristics to consider in implementing mindfulness programs: program goal, target audience, and program structure and design. Implementation and evaluation of mindfulness programs—even well-established programs, such as MBSR—can vary widely. In our review of four named mindfulness programs (MBSR, MBCT, MMFT, and MBAT), we used our implementation framework to compare programs and identify commonalities and differences that may be useful in making choices about implementation options. Although the four programs differ, they also have a great deal in common. For instance, all four use a group format, and all were initially developed to be delivered in person. MBSR, MBCT, and MMFT are somewhat similar in length (20–31 hours), duration (eight weeks), structure (weekly), and total home practice hours (28– 42 hours), and MBAT is significantly shorter (four weeks) and less intensive (eight hours long and five home practice hours). Several adaptations of MBSR and MBCT—including shortening the program length, offering various group or individual-based modalities, and implementing programs using web-based applications—have been shown to be effective. Despite these differences, MBCT, MMFT, and MBAT were each derived from MBSR, and the core exercises and overall objective of these four programs are relatively similar.

Through our analysis of these four programs in studies included in our systematic review, we observed several patterns. MBSR was the most frequently evaluated program in our systematic review, and MMFT and MBAT had been piloted only by the developers and their respective investigative teams. Despite being newer and more homogenous in implementation than MBSR and MBCT were in our included studies, MMFT and MBAT were implemented with military populations. In examining the pooled effect sizes for each of the four programs evaluated in studies included in our systematic review, we found effect sizes ranging from null (no effect) to large effects in favor of mindfulness. Our supplementary review of the literature on best practices for implementing mindfulness programs in military populations did not uncover clear guidance on what elements of the programs are most crucial to overall program efficacy. However, we did identify three key considerations for implementing mindfulness programs in military populations. First, particularly in selecting the program structure, duration, and modality, it may be important to consider scheduling constraints and other logistical challenges that service members face. Second, it may be helpful to design programs with the hierarchical structure of the military in mind. Finally, it may be beneficial to consider the importance of the trainer. Lessons learned from resilience training programs suggest that military personnel might find programs delivered by a fellow service member more acceptable and relevant (Roski et al., 2019). However, more research is needed to establish standards for trainer competencies and determine how the quality of the trainer might affect outcomes for mindfulness program participants (Crane et al., 2012; Ruijgrok-Lupton, Crane, and Dorjee, 2018; Khoury et al., 2013).

Recommendations

After considering our findings, we identified two recommendations to inform the Army's decisionmaking process regarding the implementation of mindfulness meditation programs for soldiers.

Recommendation 1. Conduct High-Quality Evaluations of Mindfulness Meditation with Soldiers

Our systematic review suggests that mindfulness meditation could have an impact on a variety of outcomes related to soldier performance, including aspects of attention, emotion regulation, impulsivity, and work-related morale and social support. Estimates of effects ranged from small to medium. But, because of significant limitations in the available literature, the strength of evidence for our conclusions of these potential effects ranged from low to moderate. Thus, the available evidence related to these outcomes alone does not provide strong support for implementing mindfulness meditation programs Army-wide. However, we also highlight the robust evidence that such programs have a medium-sized effect on reducing stress among civilian populations. It remains possible that Army implementation of mindfulness-based programs could support soldiers in managing stress and that there could be additional benefits on other performance-related outcomes, such as morale, social support, and emotion regulation. Although our findings suggest that improvements in performance-related outcomes could be small, if these effects were additive to stress reduction, even small effects could be beneficial, particularly if a program were implemented across a large proportion of the force.

As part of this study, we provided an overview of two mindfulness programs that have been adapted and tested in military populations—MMFT and MBAT. Of the 106 studies included in our systematic review, seven were funded by the U.S. Army or DoD (three studies of MMFT and four of MBAT), indicating the military's interest in assessing the utility of mindfulness in military populations. As with the civilian literature, our systematic review documented significant limitations in the quality of these seven studies, and all showed elements of poor quality, such as

- lack of random assignment of participants to intervention or control groups
- lack of a published protocol for the mindfulness meditation intervention
- small sample size
- lack of power analysis
- lack of assessor blinding
- reliance on only passive controls
- short follow-up assessment times (e.g., assessing outcomes only at the end of the program)
- lack of assessment of program adherence and dropout
- evaluations of a program developed by the authors rather than independent investigators
- failure to implement intent-to-treat analysis (i.e., assessing outcomes only among the participants who completed a program)
- failure to consider important potential confounders (such as age, gender, and prior meditation experience).

As a result of these quality issues, all of which can contribute to significant bias, it is difficult to assess the true effectiveness of MMFT and MBAT or to compare their effectiveness with that of other established mindfulness programs. Although it may be a strength that these programs are adaptations of MBSR for military personnel, it remains important to ensure that any adaptations, such as markedly shortening program length, still yield beneficial effects.

To have evidence-based policies on program implementation, rigorous clinical trials of mindfulness meditation programs must be conducted to establish a program's effectiveness and generalizability. Rigorous trials can help elucidate whether apparent improvements in outcomes are valid and can be attributed to the intervention itself or whether outcomes are a product of bias or weak study methods. In this report, we describe detailed criteria for understanding individual study quality (Appendix J). In short, for RCTs, these criteria include rigorous study design methods (e.g., randomization procedures, concealment of allocation to study condition, blinding of participants and testers, valid and reliable tests, intervention contamination prevention), accurate and detailed reporting (e.g., dropout rates, non-selective reporting of outcome data, intervention description), and analysis (e.g., differences in participant characteristics). Additionally, higher-quality studies include power calculations to determine adequate sample sizes to statistically detect an intervention's effects and include all randomized participants in the analysis (i.e., intent-to-treat analysis) (Schulz et al., 1995; Moher, Dulberg, and Wells, 1994; Moher et al., 2010). Furthermore, high-quality studies include measures of intervention fidelity to assess adherence to the mindfulness program curriculum and the competence or skill of the trainer in delivering the program content. Fidelity measures, such as the Mindfulness-Based Interventions: Teaching Assessment Criteria, may be used to guide fidelity assessment with MBSR, MBCT, and other mindfulness-based interventions. If a modified or adapted form of MBSR or another evidence-based program is studied, researchers should take care to describe any changes made. In addition, the duration of follow-up must be determined at the outset of the study based on the expected clinical effects of the intervention (Spieth et al., 2016), and longer follow-ups represent the robustness of improved outcomes (e.g., six to 12 months after baseline). Publishing findings in journals that are peer-reviewed is also an indication of a study's quality because experts in the same field review the work impartially and scrutinize its merit.

The design of clinical trials can progress along multiple stages; for instance, smaller studies can be succeeded by larger trials after establishing program efficacy (i.e., how well the program works under controlled conditions) and then effectiveness (i.e., how well the program works in the real world) (Rounsaville, Carroll, and Onken, 2001). Stage-one trials, for example, are pilot studies that focus on development of new interventions, manual writing, training, and feasibility testing. If findings are promising, the program could be evaluated in a stage-two trial that uses an RCT to evaluate its efficacy compared with that of a comparator and the mechanisms that underlie that efficacy. An important consideration in stage-two trials is study replicability by independent investigators to ensure objectivity and freedom from bias (Chambles and Hollon, 1998). If the program is found to be efficacious in at least two RCTs, researchers may be justified in evaluating the program in a stage-three trial, which focuses on effectiveness using a larger RCT to evaluate the generalizability of the program, implementation insights, and cost-effectiveness. Understanding which stage of evaluation a program is in may help inform policymakers of the next sequence of studies needed prior to implementing a program population-wide. Furthermore, the Consolidated Standards of Reporting Trials statement provides a checklist of elements to include in clinical trial reporting (Consort, undated; Moher, Schulz, and Altman, 2001; Moher et al., 2010). The Template for Intervention Description and Replication checklist details the information that authors should include about the mindfulness program (Hoffmann et al., 2014).

We recommend that the Army conduct rigorous evaluations of the effects of mindfulness meditation among soldiers, following the three-stage model. Many of the studies included in our systematic review would be considered pilot (i.e., stage-one) evaluations. These types of studies provide important information about feasibility and acceptability, but caution is warranted in interpreting efficacy outcomes. Larger, rigorous RCTs (stage-two trials) with adequate statistical power and longer-term follow-up are needed to assess the efficacy of mindfulness, especially on outcomes that are a high priority in military populations. For example, we found no studies that evaluated the impact of mindfulness meditation on improving the key work-related outcomes of absenteeism, accidents, interpersonal conflict, and teamwork. Understanding the short- and long-term effects of these programs on enhancing readiness and resilience and preventing downstream health consequences could yield significant benefit for the Army.

Recommendation 2. Assess the Effect of Mindfulness Meditation on Military Families

Decreasing stress and improving well-being among military families are high priorities for the Army Resilience Directorate and DoD overall and are goals of ongoing efforts to support military readiness and resilience (U.S. Army, undated-a). Although we did not include stress reduction among the 13 performance-related outcomes in our systematic review, we conducted a supplemental search of recent systematic reviews on mindfulness programs for general stress, parenting, and relationship problems in nonclinical adult populations. The purpose of this supplemental review was to provide a preliminary assessment of available literature on these additional outcomes that are important for military families. Although we found robust evidence that mindfulness meditation reduces general stress and promising evidence that it could reduce parental stress, we did not identify any systematic reviews on relationship problems or other aspects of parenting. Further research is needed to rigorously assess the effect of mindfulness meditation on military families, particularly the effect on outcomes that are important to this population, such as relationship problems, parenting, and child outcomes.

Existing research suggests that mindfulness-based interventions could potentially not only reduce parenting stress but also affect child outcomes. However, the available literature on these interventions is limited. Additional studies or pilot evaluations of these interventions among military families would provide additional guidance on whether these interventions should be made widely available to that population.

Systematic Review Protocol

Methods

The systematic review followed standard documented procedures (Higgins et al., 2021; AHRQ, 2014). The protocol was registered with PROSPERO (2021 CRD42021227957).

Search Strategy

Search strategies were developed in collaboration with a RAND Knowledge Services reference librarian and were informed by a horizon scan of existing systematic reviews on mindfulness interventions on the PROSPERO website. The search strategies for each database are provided in Appendix G, available online.

Sources

We conducted a systematic search of electronic databases for studies published between January 1, 2000, and late August 2020. The databases that we searched are the Allied and Complementary Medicine Database, Business Source Complete, Cochrane Central Register of Controlled Trials, Cochrane Database of Systematic Reviews, Cumulative Index to Nursing and Allied Health Literature, Defense Technical Information Center, PsycINFO, PTSDpubs (formerly the Published International Literature on Traumatic Stress), PubMed, and Web of Science. We searched ClinicalTrials.gov from its inception in February 2000 for controlled trials that enrolled nonclinical adult participants. We also coordinated with the Army to identify Army- and DoD-sponsored mindfulness research and contacted researchers to request publications that we might have missed.

Subsequently, we reference-mined relevant systematic reviews identified during our searches and used Web of Science and Scopus to retrieve references. Reference-mining is an additional search strategy that helps ensure that relevant documents are identified. Specifically, we obtained the reference lists of 42 relevant systematic reviews. We then removed any duplicates and omitted any publications prior to 2000. We also reached out to corresponding authors of relevant studies for additional information as necessary.

Eligibility Criteria

Study inclusion and exclusion criteria are summarized in Table A.1 using the PICOTSS framework.

TABLE A.1

Inclusion and Exclusion Criteria for the Systematic Review

PICOTSS Category	Included	Excluded
Participants	• Studies of adults (18 years or older), with a mean age < 45 years • Studies of nonclinical (healthy) individuals with no clinical diagnoses or in which no more than 20 percent have a clinical diagnosis • Studies of healthy caregivers of individuals with clinical diagnoses • Studies of individuals with concerns not associated with a clinical diagnosis (e.g., bereavement, grief, self-reported cognitive or memory problems, stress)	• Studies with a mean age < 18 years, a mean age ≥ 45 years, or a minimum age ≥ 55 • Studies of individuals recruited for a clinical diagnosis or in which 20 percent or more had a diagnosis of depression or anxiety
Intervention	• Studies that assessed the effects of a mindfulness-based program or intervention, including MBSR, MBCT, mindfulness meditation, Vipassana, Zazen, Zen, Shambala, focused-attention meditation, mindfulness training	• Studies that assessed the effects of yoga, tai chi, qigong, or transcendental meditation without explicit reference to mindfulness • Studies of mind-body interventions without a mindfulness component • Studies that assessed multicomponent interventions for which the effects of the mindfulness component could not be isolated • Studies that assessed interventions with a mindfulness component that was not the central component (e.g., acceptance and commitment therapy, dialectical behavior therapy)
Comparator	• Studies that included active comparators (e.g., fitness training, a didactic program) or passive comparators (e.g., no treatment, treatment as usual, waitlist control)	• Studies that assessed multicomponent interventions that also included mindfulness meditation in such a way that the effect of the meditation component could not be isolated
Outcome	• Studies that assessed attention; decisionmaking; emotion regulation; impulsivity; or work-related absenteeism, accidents, communication skills, interpersonal conflict, morale, productivity, social support, teamwork, or turnover	• Studies that assessed physiological or neurobiological outcomes
Timing	• No limits to the duration of the mindfulness intervention or the timing of follow-up period(s)	
Setting	• No limits on the setting or country	
Study design	• Individual or cluster RCTs or non-randomized trials (non-randomized studies with a control condition)	• Single-arm (uncontrolled) trials, case reports, case series, retrospective observational studies, narrative reviews, and cross-sectional studies
Other limiters	• Full-text, peer reviewed articles or reports in English-language media	• Dissertations, meeting abstracts, commentaries, perspectives, letters, and other opinion pieces

Participants

Studies of individuals aged 18 or older were considered for inclusion. Studies that specifically recruited a population 55 and older and studies in which the average age was 45 or older were excluded to ensure alignment with the average age of military populations. We excluded studies in which individuals were recruited specifically because they had a health or behavioral health diagnosis or were presumed to have a diagnosis based on screening or symptom assessment (e.g., insomnia, chronic pain, eating disorders, diabetes, mild cognitive impairment, cancer recovery, pregnancy, infertility, stillbirth, development disabilities). Relatedly, we excluded studies in which more than 20 percent of the participants were identified as having a diagnosis of depression or anxiety. We included studies in which individuals were recruited specifically based on concerns not typically associated with a clinical diagnosis (e.g., bereavement, grief, self-reported cognitive or memory problems, stress).

Intervention

Studies were considered for inclusion if they assessed the effects of a mindfulness-based program or intervention, including MBSR, MBCT, mindfulness meditation, Vipassana, Zazen, Zen, Shambhala, focused-attention meditation, or mindfulness training. We excluded studies that assessed the effects of yoga (e.g., pranayama, yoga nidra, yoga texts), tai chi, qigong, or transcendental meditation without explicit reference to mindfulness and studies that assessed the effects of mind-body interventions that did not include a mindfulness meditative component (e.g., diaphragmatic breathing, chanting meditation). We also excluded multicomponent studies that assessed the effects of mindfulness meditation in combination with another intervention in such a way that the effect of the meditation component could not be isolated. Studies that assessed the effects of interventions that included mindfulness as a component but not as the central component of the intervention (e.g., acceptance and commitment therapy, dialectical behavior therapy) were also excluded.

Comparator

Studies were considered for inclusion in the systematic review if they included a waitlist control, no treatment control, or other passive or active control conditions. Studies were excluded if the control group received an intervention that would not permit the mindfulness intervention to be assessed in isolation (e.g., a mindfulness program combined with another intervention).

Outcome

Studies were considered for inclusion if they reported one or more of the following outcomes, measured via self-report (i.e., questionnaire or interview), observer rating, or completion of a task: attention; decisionmaking; emotion regulation; impulsivity; or work-related absenteeism, accidents, communication skills, interpersonal conflict, morale, productivity, social support, teamwork, or turnover. Studies that assessed physiological and neurobiological outcomes (e.g., blood pressure) were excluded. Specific outcome measures are listed in Appendix I, which accompanies this report online.

Timing

Studies were considered for inclusion regardless of the duration of the mindfulness intervention or the timing of the follow-up period(s).

Setting

Studies were considered for inclusion regardless of the setting of the intervention (e.g., school, wellness center, clinic, recreation center, research laboratory, virtual). We also considered studies conducted in any country.

Study Design

We considered studies for inclusion if they were multiple-arm RCTs or non-randomized studies (non-randomized trials with a comparison group). The following study designs were excluded: single-arm (uncontrolled) trials, case reports, case series, retrospective observational studies, narrative reviews, and cross-sectional studies. We included crossover trials that met inclusion criteria, but only the first phase of data was included in our analyses.

Other Limiters

Studies published as full-text peer-reviewed articles or reports in English-language publications were considered for inclusion. Meeting abstracts were excluded, however; if they reported on studies of interest, we sought full-text peer-reviewed articles that reported on those studies. Dissertations, commentaries, perspectives, letters, and other opinion pieces were also excluded.

Inclusion Screening

Literature search results were uploaded to the systematic and literature review software platform DistillerSR. Two reviewers independently screened titles and abstracts against the inclusion and exclusion criteria described in the previous section. Those reviewers screened the first approximately 1,700 titles and abstracts, compared results, discussed major decisional differences, and clarified inclusion and exclusion criteria if necessary. They then screened the remaining titles and abstracts independently. Documents selected by either screener went on to full-text screening. Articles selected for full-text screening were obtained and screened independently by two reviewers who used DistillerSR to document their decisions. They reconciled disagreements, and if consensus could not be reached, the principal investigator or another subject-matter expert on the team mediated the decision.

One member of the study team screened citations identified through reference-mining, and a second person performed periodic, random concurrence checks. Any title or abstract that was excluded went through DistillerSR's Continuous AI Reprioritization process for screening against the manually screened references, and the program gave a prediction score ranked by confidence. A second reviewer manually screened references with a score of 0.45 confidence or higher. We excluded titles and abstracts that scored 0.44 confidence or lower. Two independent reviewers conducted full-text screening of articles identified through this process.

We documented screening and final inclusion decisions in a PRISMA flow diagram (see Figure 3.1 in Chapter Three).

Data Extraction

We developed a standardized form in DistillerSR to independently extract study-level data from each eligible study. The process was guided by detailed instructions and rules developed for use during the data-extraction process and documented for reference. Four independent reviewers tested the forms on ten randomly selected eligible studies and then modified the forms for clarity. Next, reviewers abstracted an additional ten publications to ensure consistency and reconciled differences. Two independent reviewers extracted study-level data from each eligible publication, and discrepancies were resolved through discussion. If more than one publication appeared to report on the same study, the reviewers compared the descriptions of participants to ensure that data from the same study population were included in our study only once. Table A.2 lists the types of information extracted from individual studies.

TABLE A.2
Elements Extracted from Included Studies

Domain	Element
Study characteristics	• Study design • Unit of randomization (e.g., participant or study site, if applicable) • Funding source • Financial conflict of interest • Location: country where the study was conducted • Setting: place of intervention (e.g., workplace, community)
Participant characteristics	• Number in each group • Inclusion and exclusion criteria • Population description • Mean age and standard deviation • Gender, percentage who were female • Military service status • Prior experience with mindfulness meditation
Intervention	• Number of intervention arms or groups • Type: MBSR, MBCT, mindfulness meditation training (e.g., Vipassana, Zazen, Zen, Shambhala), or mindfulness analogue intervention or induction • Standardized or manualized • Intervention delivery mode • Integrated smartphone web-based application (yes or no) • Timing of sessions, number of sessions, total program hours, program duration, home practice, intervention format, follow-up support, training or certification of the intervention leader, participant-to-trainer ratio
Comparator	• Number of comparator groups • Number of participants in the control or comparison group • Type: passive (e.g., waitlist control, no treatment) or other active intervention • Active comparator content, format, number of sessions, duration
Outcome	• Related to attention; decisionmaking; emotion regulation; impulsivity; or work-related absenteeism, accidents, communication skills, interpersonal conflict, morale, productivity, social support, teamwork, or turnover • Assessment method • Information provided on reliability and validity • Timepoint of assessments • Analytic approach

Individual Study Quality

Two reviewers independently assessed the individual study quality (also referred to as *risk of bias* or *internal validity*) of each study accepted for inclusion in the systematic review. They used DistillerSR and reconciled differences between their assessments.

We assessed the quality of RCTs using a slightly modified version of the U.S. Preventive Services Task Force assessment tool (Higgins et al., 2011; U.S. Preventive Services Task Force, 2017), which includes the following six domains: selection bias and confounding, performance bias, detection bias, attrition bias, reporting bias, and other sources of bias. Table A.3 lists the individual items for each domain. The items in each of the first five domains were rated as contributing to low, unclear, or high risk of bias; these ratings were operationalized by providing examples of low, unclear, and high risk. For the other potential sources of bias for RCTs (Table A.3), reviewers rated whether the item could be contributing to bias (yes) or whether it was not an issue (no). We assessed the overall quality of each RCT as poor, fair, or good based on the task force's criteria. The ratings are presented in Table J.1 in Appendix J, which accompanies this report online.

Study quality for non-randomized trials (trials that did not use a randomization process to assign participants to experimental or control groups) was assessed using the Newcastle-Ottawa assessment tool for non-randomized studies (Wells et al., 2019). Table A.3 also presents the assessment criteria for these studies. For the Newcastle-Ottawa tool, the quality rating for each item was operationalized by the definitions of *low*, *moderate*, and *high* risk of bias for that item. This tool does not include an overall study quality rating.

TABLE A.3

Domains and Items Used to Assess Individual Study Quality

Domain	Item
RCTs	
Selection bias and confounding	• Random sequence generation • Allocation concealment
Performance bias	• Blinding of participants to their assigned intervention
Detection bias	• Blinding of outcome assessors to the participants' assigned intervention
Attrition bias	• Completeness of reporting of outcome data
Reporting bias	• Selective reporting of outcome data
Other sources of bias	• Differences between intervention groups at the start of a study • Crossover or contamination between groups • Equal, reliable, and valid outcome measurement • Clear definitions of interventions • Intent-to-treat analysis
Non-randomized studies	
Selection	• Representativeness of the exposed cohort • Selection of the non-exposed cohort • Ascertainment of exposure • Demonstration that the outcome of interest was not present at the start of the study
Comparability	• Comparability of cohorts on the basis of the design or analysis (in our case, on gender, age, and meditation experience)
Outcome	• Assessment of the outcome • Follow-up time was long enough for outcomes to occur • Adequacy of follow-up of cohorts (dropout rates within and between cohorts)

Therefore, we did not rate overall study quality for non-randomized trials; these studies were not included in meta-analyses and were not considered in drawing conclusions. The ratings are presented in Table J.2 in Appendix J.

Data Synthesis

We pooled studies for meta-analysis only if there were at least three RCTs with a reported effect size or an effect size that we could calculate from available data *and* all the following criteria were met:

1. The studies implemented the same type of intervention (mindfulness program or analogue; mindfulness programs were not pooled with analogues).
2. The studies had the same type of comparison group (passive or active; passive comparison groups were not pooled with active comparison groups).
3. The studies measured the same type of outcome at the same point in time (e.g., at the end of the intervention or at a longer-term follow-up timepoint; post-intervention outcomes were not pooled with longer-term follow-ups).

When a study had multiple intervention groups, multiple comparison groups, or multiple outcomes of the same type and timepoint, we used a hierarchy of considerations to select which group(s) or outcome to include in the pooled analysis.

When a study had multiple intervention groups, if one of the interventions was a standardized intervention that has been tested in multiple studies, such as MBCT or MBSR, we selected that intervention. If none of the interventions was standardized and the study presented analyses that combined the intervention groups (i.e., the mean across the groups), we used the combined mean. If the interventions were not standardized and could not be combined, we selected the intervention that was most similar to the other interventions in that pooled analysis. Finally, if there was not an obvious choice for the most similar intervention, we selected the intervention was that was most intensive (had the longest duration or the most content).

When a study had multiple comparison groups, we selected the comparison group that was most similar to the other comparison groups in that pooled analysis. If there was not an obvious choice for most similar, then we selected the intervention that was most similar to mindfulness or another established or validated psychological intervention and would therefore provide the strongest comparison. For example, if the two comparison groups were performing relaxation exercises and listening to a recording of someone reading a book with neutral content, we selected the relaxation exercises.

Subject-matter experts reviewed the outcome measures used in each study and provided recommendations on which measures in each of our 13 outcome categories assessed similar concepts and therefore could be pooled. Additional details regarding the process for each outcome assessment are provided in Appendixes C–E. For example, subject-matter experts determined that the emotion regulation outcome measures should be grouped into five subcategories. We conducted separate meta-analyses on each subcategory (Appendix D). When a study had multiple outcome measures from the same subcategory measured at the same point in time, we selected the outcome measure that was most similar to the other outcome measures included in that pooled analysis. If there was not an obvious choice for the most similar measure, we selected the outcome measure that best represented that subcategory according to our subject-matter experts.

For non-randomized studies and other studies that could not be included in pooled analyses, we describe those findings narratively (see Appendixes C–F).

Analyses

The purpose of this systematic review was to summarize results of studies that examined the effectiveness of mindfulness programs for nonclinical populations; estimate the effectiveness of mindfulness programs in nonclinical populations by pooling results across studies; and determine whether effectiveness differs for civilian versus military personnel or by specific characteristics of the program, including the type of mindfulness, duration of the program, and delivery format. We compared effect sizes for the intervention group versus effect sizes for the comparison group (i.e., the control group in RCTs). We calculated SMDs for continuous outcomes and odds ratios for categorical outcomes, along with 95-percent confidence intervals.

We pooled studies according to the requirements described in the previous section. We required at least three RCTs for a pooled analysis so that we could assess between-study variation. We did not include non-randomized studies in any pooled analyses. For each outcome of interest, we estimated pooled effects using the modified Hartung-Knapp-Sidik-Jonkman method for random effects meta-analysis (Hartung, 1999; IntHout, Ioannidis, and Borm, 2014; Jackson et al., 2017; Knapp and Hartung, 2003; Sidik and Jonkman, 2006). Because the type of comparator could affect the size of the effect observed for the mindfulness program, we analyzed studies with active control groups separately from those with passive control groups. We also analyzed studies of mindfulness programs (conducted in realistic settings) separately from analogue studies (conducted in laboratory settings, usually employing a one-time intervention). For studies too heterogeneous to pool, we present a narrative review of study results.

We planned to assess whether the effects of mindfulness programs on each outcome of interest differed for military versus civilian populations and whether the effects of mindfulness programs differed by characteristics of the program, including type of program, length, delivery format, and other variables. Because of the limited number of studies available for each outcome, we could not conduct these comparisons.

When possible, we used sensitivity analyses to assess the robustness of pooled results. Sensitivity analyses could be conducted only when pooling results across at least four studies and were limited to analyses that included outlier studies. We considered a study to be an outlier if the confidence interval of the study's SMD was outside the confidence interval of the pooled result (Viechtbauer and Cheung, 2010). We used sensitivity analyses to estimate the pooled effects with and without outlier studies.

Strength of Evidence

For each outcome for which we were able to draw a conclusion based on a pooled analysis, we assessed the overall strength of the body of evidence underlying each conclusion using the GRADE approach, as modified by AHRQ (Balshem et al., 2011; Guyatt et al., 2011; AHRQ, 2014). As described in Chapter Two, the AHRQ modification of the GRADE approach assesses the strength of evidence across four domains:

1. study quality: based on study design and limitations; assessed as poor, fair, or good[1]
2. directness: the degree to which the assessed outcome represented the true outcome of interest and the findings were based on RCTs; alternatively, in the case of subgroup analyses, whether subgroups were compared within the same study or only indirectly via meta-regression
3. consistency: similarity of effect direction and size across studies
4. precision: degree of certainty around an estimate and, to the extent possible, optimal *information size*—a term for statistical power that considers study size and number.

---

[1] In the U.S. Preventive Services Task Force assessment tool, this first domain is called *study limitations*.

Three experienced team members conducted the assessments.

As described elsewhere, for some of our outcomes of interest, we included studies that reported on a suboutcome (e.g., some studies assessed executive attention reaction time, which is a suboutcome of attention). In some cases, we were able to conduct multiple pooled analyses for each suboutcome; for example, we conducted three meta-analyses for self-perception of attention: mindfulness passive, mindfulness active, and analogue active. In those cases, we assessed the strength of evidence for each pooled analysis separately and report those in Chapter Four (Tables 4.1–4.3). However, we also assessed an aggregate rating across the pooled analyses for each suboutcome and report the single strength-of-evidence grade for those suboutcomes in Table B.1 in Appendix B, because there is no strong agreement among subject-matter experts regarding which study design is superior for assessing the suboutcomes.

Reporting bias is one of the domains examined in the GRADE approach. Reporting bias is present if there is evidence that reported outcomes were not prespecified by the study protocol or that outcomes specified in the protocol were not reported. Reporting bias can also be present if there is evidence that studies that obtained negative or statistically insignificant findings may not have been published (referred to as publication bias). We assessed evidence of failure to prespecify outcomes as part of our assessment of study quality; we assessed and reported publication bias separately (see next section) but did not consider it in determining the quality of evidence (AHRQ, 2014).

As noted in Chapter Two, we report the strength of evidence using the following scale:

- *High* indicates high confidence that the estimated effect reflects the true effect. Further research is unlikely to change the estimate or our confidence in the estimate.
- *Moderate* indicates moderate confidence that the estimated effect reflects the true effect. Further research may change estimates and our confidence in the estimates.
- *Low* indicates low confidence that the estimated effect reflects the true effect. Further research is likely to change estimates and our confidence in the estimates.
- *Very low* indicates that evidence either is unavailable or does not permit a conclusion to be drawn.

Table B.1 presents the strength of evidence and conclusion for each outcome and suboutcome. If data were insufficient to support a conclusion for a particular subquestion of interest, we indicate the reason (e.g., too few studies, inconsistency of findings) in our assessment.

Publication Bias

Publication bias refers to the tendency of studies to be published only if findings are statistically significant. This can cause problems when pooling findings across studies and can bias pooled estimates toward finding a difference between the intervention and control groups. Formal evaluation of publication bias requires a relatively large number of pooled studies.

Funnel plots are created when pooled results include ten or more studies (Sterne et al., 2011). When there are few studies, publication bias can be evaluated informally, by looking at the relationship among sample size, publication year, and the significance of study findings. Evidence of publication bias may exist if older and smaller studies are more likely than newer and larger studies to report statistically significant findings. We did not find any evidence of publication bias for the studies included in our analyses. Detailed description of analyses examining publication bias are provided in Appendix K, available online.

Disclosures

Kimberly A. Hepner is the guarantor of this report's accuracy. The report authors (Hepner, Erika Litvin Bloom, Sydne Newberry, Jessica L. Sousa, Karen Chan Osilla, Marika Booth, Armenda Bialas, Carolyn M. Rutter) drafted the manuscript and were involved in the design of the study. Hepner, Newberry, Sousa, and Bloom developed the search strategy in collaboration with Jody Larkin. Expert consultation on the development of this protocol was provided by Patricia Herman and Sean Robson. The sponsor reviewed and provided feedback on this protocol. Hepner has received compensation from the Beck Institute to deliver provider trainings in cognitive behavioral therapy, which can include how to incorporate mindfulness meditation. She also has a private practice, and mindfulness meditation is one of the interventions used with patients. The other authors do not have any conflicts of interest to declare.

Strength of Evidence and Conclusion for Each Outcome

This appendix provides the results of the GRADE strength-of-evidence assessments and our conclusions, arranged by outcome. Table B.1 builds on the tables in Chapter Four and provides more-detailed results for our four domains (study quality, directness, consistency, and precision) for assessing the strength of evidence for each pooled analysis.

TABLE B.1

Strength of Evidence for Outcomes in Pooled Analyses

Outcome	Intervention, Comparison Type	Pooled Effect Size (95% CI), Number of Pooled Studies, Number of Participants in Sample	Study Quality	Directness	Consistency	Precision	Grade	Strength of Evidence and Conclusion
Attention								
Self-perception of attention	Mindfulness, passive	SMD = 0.17 (95% CI = −0.30, 0.64), 4 studies, $n = 200$	3 poor, 1 good	Direct	Inconsistent	Imprecise	Low	Moderate strength of evidence for **no effect** of mindfulness on self-perception of attention, upgraded for directness and consistency within and across study types
	Mindfulness, active	SMD = −0.05 (95% CI = −0.26, 0.37), 5 studies, $n = 264$	2 poor, 1 fair, 2 good	Direct	Consistent	Imprecise	Low	
	Analogue, active	SMD = 0.15 (95% CI = −0.06, 0.36), 4 studies, $n = 368$	2 poor, 2 fair	Direct	Consistent	Imprecise	Low	
Alerting attention reaction time	Mindfulness, passive	SMD = 0.05 (95% CI = −0.26, 0.37), 4 studies, $n = 177$	4 poor	Indirect	Consistent	Imprecise	Very low	Very low strength of evidence for **no effect** of mindfulness on alerting attention reaction time

Table B.1—Continued

Outcome	Intervention, Comparison Type	Pooled Effect Size (95% CI), Number of Pooled Studies, Number of Participants in Sample	Study Quality	Directness	Consistency	Precision	Grade	Strength of Evidence and Conclusion
Orienting attention reaction time	Mindfulness, passive	SMD = 0.11 (95% CI = −0.22, 0.44), 5 studies, $n = 201$	5 poor	Indirect	Consistent	Imprecise	Low	Moderate strength of evidence for **no effect** of mindfulness on orienting attention reaction time, upgraded for directness and consistency within and across study types
	Mindfulness, active	SMD = 0.13 (95% CI = −0.23, 0.48), 5 studies, $n = 263$	4 poor, 1 fair	Indirect	Consistent	Imprecise	Low	
Executive attention reaction time	Mindfulness, passive	SMD = 0.18 (95% CI = −0.13, 0.48), 11 studies, $n = 503$	10 poor, 1 good	Indirect	Inconsistent	Imprecise	Very low	Very low strength of evidence for **no effect** of mindfulness on executive attention reaction time, downgraded for poor study quality, indirectness, inconsistency, and imprecision
	Mindfulness, active	SMD = 0.36 (95% CI = 0.11, 0.62), 8 studies, $n = 478$[a]	5 poor, 2 fair, 1 good	Indirect	Consistent	Imprecise	Very low	
	Analogue, active	SMD = 0.18 (95% CI = −0.19, 0.54), 6 studies, $n = 338$	6 poor	Indirect	Inconsistent	Imprecise	Very low	
Executive attention accuracy	Mindfulness, passive	SMD = 0.37 (95% CI = 0.16, 0.58), 10 studies, $n = 375$	9 poor, 1 good	Indirect	Consistent	Imprecise	Moderate	Moderate strength of evidence for a **beneficial effect** of mindfulness on executive attention accuracy, upgraded for consistency across study types
	Mindfulness, active	SMD = 0.30 (95% CI = −0.06, 0.54), 9 studies, $n = 582$[a]	7 poor, 1 fair, 1 good	Indirect	Consistent	Imprecise	Low	
	Analogue, active	SMD = 0.00 (95% CI = −0.28, 0.28), 6 studies, $n = 272$	6 poor	Indirect	Consistent	Imprecise	Low	

Table B.1—Continued

Outcome	Intervention, Comparison Type	Pooled Effect Size (95% CI), Number of Pooled Studies, Number of Participants in Sample	Study Quality	Directness	Consistency	Precision	Grade	Strength of Evidence and Conclusion
Emotion regulation								
General emotion regulation ability	Mindfulness, passive	SMD = 0.11 (95% CI = −0.25, 0.47), 4 studies, *n* = 628	3 poor, 1 good	Direct	Inconsistent	Imprecise	Low	Low strength of evidence for **no effect** of mindfulness on general emotion regulation ability, downgraded for inconsistency and imprecision
Reappraisal	Mindfulness, passive	SMD = 0.27 (95% CI = 0.02, 0.52), 4 studies, *n* = 630	2 poor, 1 fair, 1 good	Direct	Inconsistent	Precise	Low	Low strength of evidence for a **beneficial effect** of mindfulness programs on increasing the use of reappraisal as an emotion regulation strategy, downgraded for inconsistency
Suppression	Mindfulness, passive	SMD = 0.17 (95% CI = 0.00, 0.33), 4 studies, *n* = 630	2 poor, 1 fair, 1 good	Direct	Consistent	Precise	Low	Low strength of evidence for a **beneficial effect** of mindfulness on decreasing the use of suppression as an emotion regulation strategy, downgraded for poor study quality
Change in negative mood intensity	Analogue, active	SMD = 0.18 (95% CI = −0.17, 0.53), 3 studies, *n* = 244	3 poor	Indirect	Inconsistent	Imprecise	Very low	Very low strength of evidence for **no effect** of mindfulness on change in negative mood intensity, downgraded for poor study quality, indirectness, inconsistency, and imprecision

Table B.1—Continued

Outcome	Intervention, Comparison Type	Pooled Effect Size (95% CI), Number of Pooled Studies, Number of Participants in Sample	Study Quality	Directness	Consistency	Precision	Grade	Strength of Evidence and Conclusion
Emotional interference	Mindfulness, active	SMD = 0.61 (95% CI = 0.31, 0.92), 4 studies, $n = 174$	4 poor	Indirect	Consistent	Precise	Low	Low strength of evidence for a **beneficial effect** of mindfulness on decreasing emotional interference, downgraded for poor study quality and indirectness
Impulsivity	Mindfulness, passive	SMD = 0.31 (95% CI = 0.10, 0.52), 3 studies, $n = 397$	2 good, 1 fair	Direct	Inconsistent	Precise	Moderate	Low strength of evidence for a **beneficial effect** of mindfulness programs on impulsivity, downgraded for overall study quality
Work-related outcomes								
Morale	Mindfulness, passive	SMD = 0.33 (95% CI = 0.07, 0.58), 4 studies pooled, $n = 244$	3 poor, 1 fair	Direct	Consistent	Precise	Moderate	Moderate strength of evidence for a **beneficial effect** of mindfulness programs on work-related morale, downgraded for overall study quality
Productivity	Mindfulness, passive	SMD = 0.08 (95% CI = −0.20, 0.35), 3 studies pooled, $n = 228$	3 fair	Indirect	Consistent	Precise	Low	Low strength of evidence for **no effect** of mindfulness on work-related productivity, downgraded for overall study quality and indirectness
Social support	Mindfulness, passive	SMD = 0.54 (95% CI = 0.08, 1.00), 3 studies pooled, $n = 343$	2 poor, 1 fair	Direct	Inconsistent	Precise	Low	Low strength of evidence for a **beneficial effect** of mindfulness programs on work-related social support, downgraded for overall study quality

a This SMD value reflects the results with the outlier study removed, as described in Chapter Four.

Effects of Mindfulness Meditation on Attention

In this appendix, we describe the results of our syntheses of findings on two types of attention outcomes: self-report (i.e., an individual's self-perception of their attention or concentration ability or capacity) and performance (reaction time and accuracy) on paper-and-pencil or computerized attention tests. We further categorized the performance outcomes into three types: alerting attention (maintaining an alert state, ready to respond), orienting attention (shifting attention to a specific target), or executive attention (resolving conflicts, solving problems). Box C.1 highlights the key findings discussed in this appendix.

BOX C.1

Key Findings: Effects of Mindfulness Meditation on Attention

- Mindfulness did not have a beneficial effect on self-perception of attentional ability or reaction time.
- Mindfulness had a beneficial effect on accuracy in executive attention tests involving resolving conflicts and solving problems.
- There were not enough studies to evaluate whether mindfulness improved accuracy in alerting or orienting attention tests.

Interpreting Forest Plots

Forest plots are used to display the estimated effect size and 95-percent confidence interval from each of the pooled studies, as well as the overall (pooled) estimate of the effect size. Figure C.1 provides an example of a forest plot. The vertical line at the center of the plot represents a null effect (i.e., no difference between the mindfulness intervention and the comparison group). For pooled analyses of continuous outcomes, the null effect occurs when the SMD equals zero. Each row of the forest plot represents the effect size from one study, and studies are ordered alphabetically by study ID within study type (i.e., RCTs, then non-randomized studies). In this report, the study ID is the first listed author of the study and the year that it was published.[1] The center square on the forest plot shows the effect size for the study, and a horizontal line shows the span of the 95-percent confidence interval around the study's effect size. The size of the center square is proportional to the relative study size (number of participants included in results). When a horizontal line crosses the vertical center line, it means that the confidence interval included the null effect that indicates no effect of mindfulness. The small diamond at the base of the individual study lines represents the pooled effect size and confidence intervals. The calculated study heterogeneity (I^2) appears at the bottom left of the figure.

---

[1] In two cases (Hafenbrack et al., 2020; Norris et al., 2018), two studies were reported in the same publication, and we use 1a and 1b to differentiate the studies. Bibliographic details for all included studies are presented in a separate section of the References list at the end of this report.

FIGURE C.1
Example of a Forest Plot

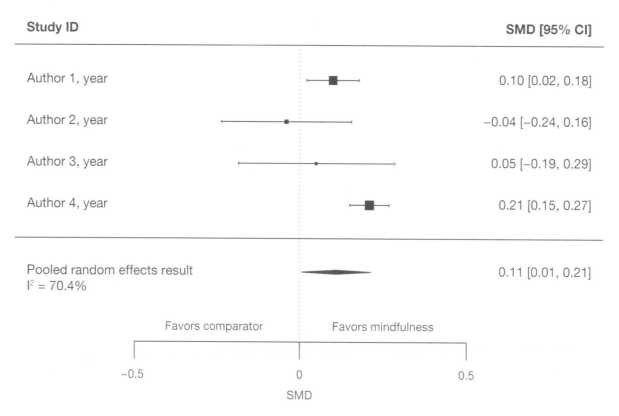

Measuring Attention

For an overview of the attention outcome and suboutcomes, see Chapter Four. In this section, we describe the tests that studies in our systematic review employed to measure attention.

The Attention Network Test

The Attention Network Test (ANT), which was used in 11 studies included in our systematic review, produces reaction time and accuracy outcomes that correspond to each of the three attention networks (alerting, orienting, and executive) in our analysis. In this computerized test of attention, an individual views a series of rows of arrows, one at a time. For each row, they press a key to indicate if the center arrow is pointing to the right or the left. In *congruent* trials, all arrows in the row are pointing the same direction. In *incongruent* trials, the center arrow is pointing in the opposite direction of the other arrows. Reaction time is expected to be slower in incongruent trials. The *executive effect score* is a measure of how quickly the individual is able to resolve conflict among the arrows' directions in incongruent trials and is calculated as the difference in the person's average reaction time between incongruent and congruent trials. A smaller score (i.e., smaller difference) indicates better executive attention. Before some trials, a cue appears on the screen that provides some information about when (known as a *center* or *double* cue) or both when and where (known as a *spatial* cue) the row of arrows is going to appear. The center or double cues tell the individual when to be *alert* and ready to respond. The spatial cues tell the individual where to *orient* their attention. Therefore, reaction time in cued trials is expected to be faster than in no-cue trials, and reaction time in spatial cue trials is expected to be faster than in center or double cue trials. The *alerting effect score* is the difference in average reaction time between center or double cue trials and no-cue trials. The *orienting effect score* is the difference in average reaction time between spatial cue trials and center cue trials (Wang and Fan, 2007). The developer of the ANT has advised that average reaction times for each type of trial (no cue, cue) must be considered when interpreting alerting and orienting scores. For example, a larger alerting score may reflect better attention (i.e., better use of the cue) if the larger score is attributable to a faster average reaction time in the cue conditions but may reflect a deficit in attention if the larger score is attributable to a slower average reaction time in the no-cue condition (Wang and Fan, 2007).

Some of the studies included in our review that used the ANT presented only the network effect scores. Also, interpretation of alerting and orienting effect scores was inconsistent across studies. In our meta-analysis, regardless of the study authors' interpretation, we interpreted all ANT alerting and orienting effect scores in the direction of larger scores indicating better attention, which was the most common interpretation across our studies. We then reviewed the results of each pooled analysis carefully and decided whether to conduct additional sensitivity analyses. In this appendix, we note whether results might change if ANT studies were interpreted the opposite way (i.e., with smaller alerting or orienting scores representing better attention).

Other Common Attention Tests

Three other computerized attention tests were each used in at least five studies included in our review, so we describe them briefly here. All of them require the individual to resolve a conflict before they can respond, so we categorized these tests as measuring executive attention.

The Stroop task was used in 14 studies in our systematic review. In the original Stroop task, which dates to the 1930s, an individual views color words (e.g., red, blue) printed in various colors. The person is instructed to name the color of the ink. When the word and ink color do not match (e.g., the word *red* appears in blue ink), the individual experiences interference between the tendency to respond *red* automatically and the correct response of *blue*; thus, their reaction time is slower than when the word and ink color match. Today, the Stroop task is typically administered via computer, and there are multiple versions available that use various types of words and colors. However, all of these versions measure the *Stroop interference outcome* of the difference in reaction time and accuracy between matching versus nonmatching trials, and they produce other outcome measures, such as overall reaction time and accuracy.

The sustained attention to response task (SART) was used in 12 studies, including all six studies involving U.S. military personnel. In the SART, the individual views a series of single digits (0–9) and is told to press a key when they see any number except a 3 (*non-target* trials) or not to press a key when they do see a 3 (*target* trials). Outcome measures from this task include average reaction time on each type of trial; variability in reaction time; errors of commission (how many times the person pressed the key when a 3 appeared); and *A'*, a composite accuracy score that takes into account the number of errors and correct responses (Jha et al., 2015).

Finally, continuous performance tests, which are similar to the SART and involve viewing a series of letters that appear in rapid succession and pressing a key only when certain letters or a certain series of letters appears, were used in five studies. As with the Stroop task, there are multiple versions of continuous performance tests (Riccio et al., 2002).

Organization of the Results

In the remainder of this appendix, we describe the results of our syntheses, including pooled analyses whenever possible, for each of the seven categories of attention outcomes (self-perception of attention, plus reaction time and accuracy for each of the alerting, orienting, and executive attention outcomes). For each type of outcome, mindfulness RCTs were pooled separately from analogue studies, and within each of those two groups, RCTs with passive comparison groups were pooled separately from those with active comparison groups. The outcomes are described in that order, wherever possible.

In all pooled analyses, the attention outcome was measured at the end of the intervention. Too few studies with longer-term follow-up data were available for pooling. We also summarize the strength of evidence for the effect of mindfulness on each category of attention.

Self-Perception of Attention

Mindfulness Studies

Passive Comparison Groups

We conducted a meta-analysis of four RCTs that assessed the effect of mindfulness programs on self-perception of attention and used passive comparison groups. Additionally, there were three non-randomized studies. We summarize study-level details in Table C.1. The RCTs included two studies of MBSR with civilian adults and two studies involving military personnel (one MMFT, one MBAT). Durations ranged from two to eight weeks. Our pooled analysis did not show a beneficial effect of mindfulness on self-perception of attention (SMD = 0.17; 95% CI = −0.30, 0.64; I^2 = 63.8%) (Figure C.2).

TABLE C.1

Study-Level Details for Studies That Assessed Self-Perception of Attention: Mindfulness Studies with Passive Comparison Groups

Study ID	Participants	Intervention	Comparator	Outcome	Study Quality
RCTs (included in meta-analysis)					
Giannandrea, 2019	60 Italian adults, mean age = 35.7 (SD = 12.1)	In-person, group MBSR	Waitlist	SART probes	Poor
Kral, 2019	140 U.S. adults, 59.3% female, mean age = 44.3 (SD = 12.8)	8-week, in-person, group MBSR	Waitlist	Emotional Style Questionnaire, attention subscale	Poor
Jha, 2015	164 active-duty U.S. Army service members, 1.8% female, mean age = 24.2 (SD = 4.9)	8-week, in-person, mixed individual and group MMFT	No intervention[a]	SART probes	Poor
Zanesco, 2019	120 U.S. special operations forces personnel, 0% female, mean age = 33.1 (SD = 5.6)	2-week, in-person, group MBAT; 4-week, in-person, group MBAT	No intervention	SART probes	Good
Non-randomized studies (not included in meta-analysis)					
Jha, 2017	55 U.S. Marine Corp reservists, 0% female, mean age = 27.8 (SD = 6.4)	8-week, in-person, group MMFT	No intervention	SART probes	Not applicable
Jha, 2019	180 U.S. Army active-duty personnel, 0% female, mean age = 23.3 (SD = 3/0)	4-week, in-person, group MBAT	No intervention	SART probes	Not applicable
Morrison, 2014	58 U.S. psychology and neuroscience university majors, 51.7% female, mean age = 18.2 (SD = 1.3)	7-week, mixed in-person and virtual, mixed individual and group MBSR	Waitlist	SART probes	Not applicable

[a] In this report, *no intervention* and *no treatment* are synonymous, but we present the phrase as used in each study.

FIGURE C.2

Estimates of the Effect on Attention: Self-Perception of Attention in Mindfulness Studies with Passive Comparison Groups

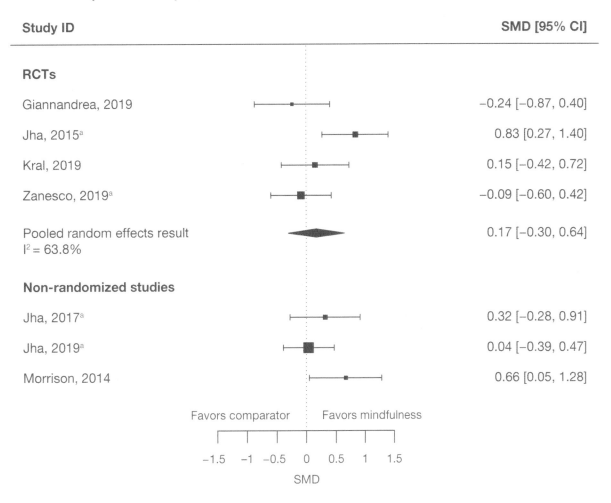

Study ID	SMD [95% CI]
RCTs	
Giannandrea, 2019	−0.24 [−0.87, 0.40]
Jha, 2015[a]	0.83 [0.27, 1.40]
Kral, 2019	0.15 [−0.42, 0.72]
Zanesco, 2019[a]	−0.09 [−0.60, 0.42]
Pooled random effects result $I^2 = 63.8\%$	0.17 [−0.30, 0.64]
Non-randomized studies	
Jha, 2017[a]	0.32 [−0.28, 0.91]
Jha, 2019[a]	0.04 [−0.39, 0.47]
Morrison, 2014	0.66 [0.05, 1.28]

[a] Indicates a study that involved a military population.

Among the non-randomized studies, there was one study of civilians who received MBSR and two that involved military personnel (one MMFT, one MBAT). Neither of the military studies indicated an effect of mindfulness on self-perception of attention, but the third study did find a beneficial effect of MBSR on self-perception of attention.

Active Comparison Groups

We conducted a meta-analysis of five RCTs that assessed the effect of mindfulness programs on self-perception of attention and used active comparison groups. Additionally, there was one non-randomized study. We summarize study-level details in Table C.2. The mindfulness interventions included MBSR (three studies), an in-person group-based program, and a virtual mindfulness program. Durations ranged from two to 12 weeks. Our pooled analysis did not show an effect of mindfulness on self-perception of attention compared with an active comparison group (SMD = 0.05; 95% CI = −0.26, 0.37; I² = 40.3%) (Figure C.3). The cohort study, which involved military personnel who received MMFT, also did not show an effect of mindfulness that was more beneficial than that of the active control group (Figure C.3).

TABLE C.2

Study-Level Details for Studies That Assessed Self-Perception of Attention: Mindfulness Studies with Active Comparison Groups

Study ID	Participants	Intervention	Comparator	Outcome	Study Quality
RCTs (included in meta-analysis)					
Baltar, 2018	40 Brazilian professional football players, 0% female, mean age = 23.6 (SD = 1.4)	12-week, virtual mindfulness meditation training program	Audio recording listening task	Attentional Control Scale	Fair
de Bruin, 2016	126 Dutch adults with elevated stress levels, 73.5% female, mean age = 26.2 (SD = 5.3)	5-week, in-person, group mindfulness meditation training program	Physical activity program	Attentional Control Scale	Poor
Kral, 2019	140 U.S. adults, 59.3% female, mean age = 44.3 (SD = 12.8)	8-week, in-person, group MBSR	Health Enhancement Program	Emotional Styles Questionnaire, attention subscale	Poor
Mrazek, 2013	48 U.S. undergraduate students, 70.8% female, mean age = 20.8 (SD = 2.1)	2-week, in-person group MBSR	Nutrition classes	Mind wandering (mean of three measures)	Good
Rooks, 2017	100 U.S. university athletes, mean age = 19.8 (SD = 1.5)	4-week, mixed in-person and virtual, mixed individual and group MBSR	Relaxation training	SART probes	Good
Non-randomized studies (not included in meta-analysis)					
Jha, 2020	80 U.S. active-duty Army service members, 0% female, mean age = 24.6 (SD = 4.2)	8-week, in-person, group MMFT	Positive emotion resilience training	SART probes	Not applicable

FIGURE C.3

Estimates of the Effect on Self-Perception of Attention in Mindfulness Studies with Active Comparison Groups

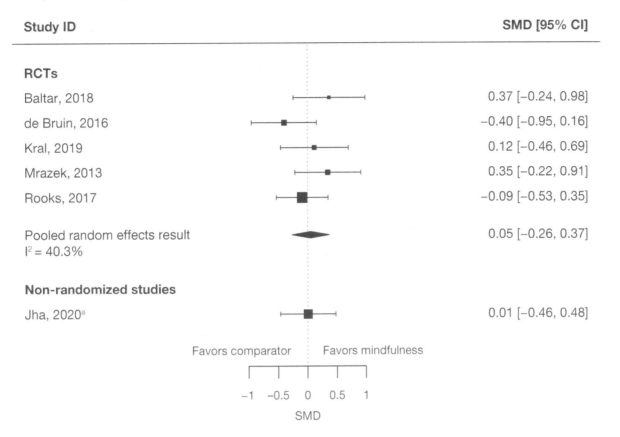

Study ID	SMD [95% CI]
RCTs	
Baltar, 2018	0.37 [−0.24, 0.98]
de Bruin, 2016	−0.40 [−0.95, 0.16]
Kral, 2019	0.12 [−0.46, 0.69]
Mrazek, 2013	0.35 [−0.22, 0.91]
Rooks, 2017	−0.09 [−0.53, 0.35]
Pooled random effects result $I^2 = 40.3\%$	0.05 [−0.26, 0.37]
Non-randomized studies	
Jha, 2020[a]	0.01 [−0.46, 0.48]

Favors comparator   Favors mindfulness

SMD

[a] Indicates a study that involved a military population.

Analogue Studies

We performed a meta-analysis of three RCTs that assessed the effect of mindfulness analogues on self-perception of attention and used active comparison groups, and these studies contributed four effect sizes (Table C.3). One study tested two different mindfulness analogues, each of which had its own corresponding active comparison group. Therefore, we could include two effect sizes from this study (analogue 1 versus control 1 and analogue 2 versus control 2). All four analogues were delivered in virtual format and lasted between 15 and 20 minutes. Our pooled analysis did not show an effect of the analogue interventions on self-perception of attention (SMD = 0.15; 95% CI = −0.06, 0.36; I^2 = 6.9%) (Figure C.4).

TABLE C.3

Study-Level Details for Studies That Assessed Self-Perception of Attention: Analogue Studies with Active Comparison Groups

Study ID	Participants	Intervention	Comparator	Outcome	Study Quality
RCTs (included in meta-analysis)					
Banks, 2019	102 U.S. undergraduate students, 71.8% female, mean age = 19.1 (SD = 2.3)	15-minute virtual mindfulness analogue	15-minute virtual relaxation induction	SART probes	Poor
Diaz, 2013 (aesthetic response group)	132 U.S. university music students, percent female not reported, mean age and SD not reported	15-minute virtual mindfulness analogue paired with music listening and aesthetic response	15-minute music listening and aesthetic response	Self-reported perceived magnitude of attention	Fair
Diaz, 2013 (flow response group)	132 U.S. university music students, percent female not reported, mean age and SD not reported	15-minute virtual mindfulness analogue paired with music listening and flow response	15-minute music listening and flow response	Self-reported perceived magnitude of attention	Fair
Green, 2017	305 U.S. university students in a psychology course, 48.6% female, mean age = 19.3 (SD = 2.8)	20-minute virtual mindfulness analogue	20-minute progressive muscle relaxation video segment	Self-reported concentration during anagram trials	Poor

FIGURE C.4

Estimates of the Effect on Attention: Self-Perception of Attention in Analogue Studies with Active Comparison Groups

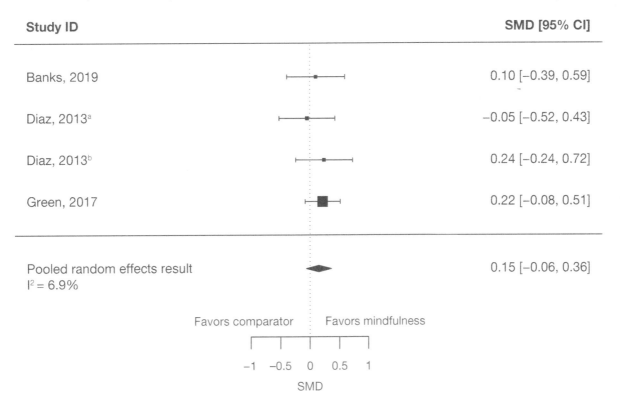

Study ID	SMD [95% CI]
Banks, 2019	0.10 [−0.39, 0.59]
Diaz, 2013[a]	−0.05 [−0.52, 0.43]
Diaz, 2013[b]	0.24 [−0.24, 0.72]
Green, 2017	0.22 [−0.08, 0.51]
Pooled random effects result $I^2 = 6.9\%$	0.15 [−0.06, 0.36]

Favors comparator   Favors mindfulness

−1   −0.5   0   0.5   1
SMD

[a] Indicates the study that used an aesthetic response group.
[b] Indicates the study that used a flow response group.

Additional Studies

One analogue RCT included in the meta-analysis with active comparison groups also had a passive comparison group (Banks et al., 2019). Consistent with the result for the active comparison group, there was no significant difference between the mindfulness intervention and the passive control group on self-perception of attention.

Strength of Evidence for the Effect of Mindfulness on Self-Perception of Attention

Our pooled analyses indicated that mindfulness did not have an effect on self-perception of attention. The strength of the evidence supporting this conclusion was moderate. Most of the studies were of poor quality, and outcomes tended to be imprecise. However, outcomes were consistent across all three pooled analyses. Only one RCT, which involved military personnel who received MMFT, showed a beneficial effect of mindfulness.

Alerting Attention

Reaction Time

Mindfulness Studies

We performed a meta-analysis of four RCTs that assessed the effect of mindfulness programs on alerting attention reaction time and used passive comparison groups. We summarize study-level details in Table C.4. Three programs were delivered in person, and one was virtual; durations ranged from one to eight weeks. Our pooled analysis did not show an effect of the mindfulness interventions on alerting attention reaction time (SMD = 0.05; 95% CI = –0.26, 0.37; I^2 = 14.2%) (Figure C.5).

Additional Studies

Three additional studies—two mindfulness RCTs (Tang et al., 2007; Kwak et al., 2020) and an analogue RCT (Lai, MacNeil, and Frewen, 2015), all with active comparison groups—reported alerting effect scores from the ANT but could not be included in pooled analyses. In one mindfulness study (Tang et al., 2007), undergraduate students received a mindfulness program called integrative body-mind training or a relaxation training program. Both programs lasted 50 days and involved 20 minutes of training per day. In the other mindfulness study (Kwak et al., 2020), participants received a four-day intensive mindfulness meditation program or a relaxation program. In the analogue RCT (Lai, MacNeil, and Frewen, 2015), participants were assigned to a virtual mindfulness analogue or one of two active comparison groups, one of which was to silently count backward from 500. The mindfulness program had no effect on alerting attention reaction time in any of these three studies.

TABLE C.4

Study-Level Details for Studies That Assessed Alerting Attention (Reaction Time): Mindfulness Studies with Passive Comparison Groups

Study ID	Participants	Intervention	Comparator	Outcome	Study Quality
RCTs (included in meta-analysis)					
Ainsworth, 2013	76 UK adults, 86.8% female, mean age = 20.3 (SD = 4.1)	8-day, in-person, group focused-attention meditation; 1.1-week, in-person, group open-monitoring meditation	No intervention	ANT—alerting effect	Poor
Becerra, 2017	62 Australian undergraduate students, 77.4% female, mean age = 33.9 (SD = 12.1)	8-week, in-person, group mindfulness meditation training	Waitlist	ANT—alerting effect	Poor
Burger, 2017	60 U.S. first-semester students pursuing an associate's degree in nursing, 82.7% female, age range = 18–40 (SD not reported)	4-week, virtual, individual mindfulness meditation training	Waitlist	ANT—alerting effect	Poor
Esch, 2016	31 German adults, 77.4% female, mean age = 26.7 (SD = 7.6)	10-day, in-person, group mindfulness meditation training	No intervention	ANT—alerting effect	Poor

NOTE: UK = United Kingdom.

FIGURE C.5

Estimates of the Effect on Alerting Attention (Reaction Time) in Mindfulness Studies with Passive Comparison Groups

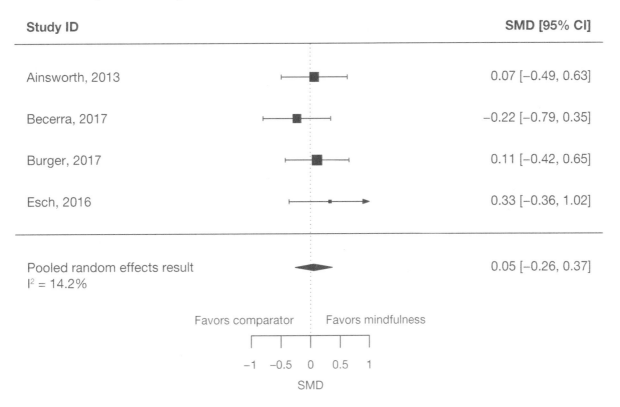

Strength of Evidence for the Effect of Mindfulness on Alerting Attention Reaction Time

Our pooled analysis indicated that mindfulness did not have a beneficial effect on alerting attention reaction time. The strength of the evidence supporting this conclusion was very low. Only four studies—all of which were of poor quality—were included in the pooled analysis, and outcomes were imprecise, although they were consistent across studies.

Accuracy

Only one study, an analogue RCT with an active comparison group, reported a measure of alerting attention accuracy (Schofield, Creswell, and Denson, 2015). In this study, participants completed an "inattentional blindness" task on a computer. In this task, participants viewed black and white letters moving around the screen and counted the number of times that letters touched the edge of the screen. During the task, a red symbol also appeared on the screen. After the task was over, participants were asked if they saw anything "unusual or unexpected" (i.e., the red symbol) during the task (*distractor awareness*, a measure of how alert they were). They were also shown an array of letters and symbols that included the red symbol and asked if they had seen any of those characters during the task (*distractor encoding*, another measure of alerting attention). More participants in the mindfulness group were aware of the red symbol than in the comparison group, but there was no effect of mindfulness on distractor encoding.

Orienting Attention

Reaction Time
Mindfulness Studies
Passive Comparison Groups

We conducted a meta-analysis of five RCTs that assessed the effect of mindfulness programs on orienting attention reaction time and used passive comparison groups. We summarize study-level details in Table C.5. The interventions included MBSR, three in-person programs, and a virtual program. Program durations ranged from one to eight weeks. Our pooled analysis did not show an effect of mindfulness on orienting attention reaction time (SMD = 0.11; 95% CI = –0.22, 0.44; I^2 = 29.8%) (Figure C.6).

TABLE C.5

Study-Level Details for Studies That Assessed Orienting Attention (Reaction Time): Mindfulness Studies with Passive Comparison Groups

Study ID	Participants	Intervention	Comparator	Outcome	Study Quality
RCTs (included in meta-analysis)					
Ainsworth, 2013	76 UK adults, 86.8% female, mean age = 20.3 (SD = 4.1)	8-day, in-person, group focused-attention meditation; 1.1-week, in-person, group open-monitoring meditation	No intervention	ANT—orienting effect	Poor
Becerra, 2017	62 Australian undergraduate students, 77.4% female, mean age = 33.9 (SD = 12.1)	8-week, in-person, group mindfulness meditation training	Waitlist	ANT—orienting effect	Poor
Burger, 2017	60 U.S. first-semester students pursuing an associate's degree in nursing, 82.7% female, age range = 18–40 (SD not reported)	4-week, virtual, individual mindfulness meditation training	Waitlist	ANT—orienting effect	Poor
Esch, 2016	31 German adults, 77.4% female, mean age = 26.7 (SD = 7.6)	10-day, in-person, group mindfulness meditation training	No intervention	ANT—orienting effect	Poor
Jensen, 2012	48 Danish young adults, 62.5% female, age range = 20–36 (SD not reported)	8-week, in-person, group MBSR	No intervention	Spatial and temporal attention network task—reaction time on invalid temporal cues	Poor

FIGURE C.6

Estimates of the Effect on Orienting Attention (Reaction Time) in Mindfulness Studies with Passive Comparison Groups

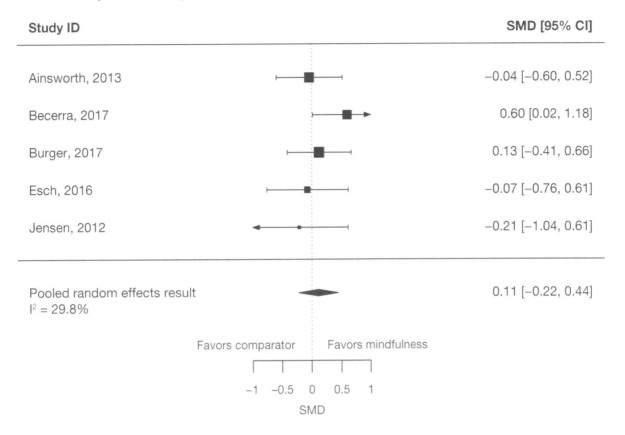

Study ID		SMD [95% CI]
Ainsworth, 2013		−0.04 [−0.60, 0.52]
Becerra, 2017		0.60 [0.02, 1.18]
Burger, 2017		0.13 [−0.41, 0.66]
Esch, 2016		−0.07 [−0.76, 0.61]
Jensen, 2012		−0.21 [−1.04, 0.61]
Pooled random effects result $I^2 = 29.8\%$		0.11 [−0.22, 0.44]

Favors comparator | Favors mindfulness

−1 −0.5 0 0.5 1

SMD

Active Comparison Groups

We conducted a meta-analysis of five RCTs that assessed the effect of mindfulness programs on orienting attention reaction time and used active comparison groups. Additionally, there was one non-randomized study. We summarize study-level details in Table C.6. The RCTs included MBSR, MBCT, three in-person programs, and one program with both in-person and virtual elements. All programs were brief (one week or less), except for the MBSR program, which was eight weeks. Our pooled analysis did not show an effect of mindfulness on orienting attention reaction time (SMD = 0.13; 95% CI = −0.23, 0.48; I^2 = 51.3%) (Figure C.7). The non-randomized study, which tested an 18-week in-person mindfulness program, also did not show a beneficial effect of mindfulness.

TABLE C.6

Study-Level Details for Studies That Assessed Orienting Attention (Reaction Time): Mindfulness Studies with Active Comparison Groups

Study ID	Participants	Intervention	Comparator	Outcome	Study Quality
RCTs (included in meta-analysis)					
Adhikari, 2018	90 Indian university students, 54.1% female, mean age = 21.5 (SD = 2.2)	6-day, in-person, group mindfulness meditation training	Music listening or reading task	Cogstate identification task— reaction time for correct response	Poor
Jensen, 2012	48 Danish young adults, 62.5% female, age range = 20–36 (SD not reported)	8-week, in-person, group MBSR	Non-mindfulness stress reduction	Dual attention to response task—gray digit reaction time	Poor
Kwak, 2020	67 South Korean adults with full-time employment, 75.7% female, mean age = 30.6 (SD = 4.9)	4-day, in-person, group mindfulness meditation training	Relaxation retreat	ANT—orienting effect	Poor
Quan, 2018	48 Chinese undergraduate students, 50.0% female, mean age = 19.2 (SD = 1.3)	1-week, in-person, group MBCT	Relaxation training	ANT—orienting effect	Poor
Tang, 2007	80 Chinese undergraduate students, 45.0% female, mean age = 21.8 (SD not reported)	5-day, mixed in-person and virtual, group integrative body-mind training	Relaxation training	ANT—orienting effect	Fair
Non-randomized studies (not included in meta-analysis)					
Ching, 2015	359 Taiwanese university students, 61.0% female, age range = 18–19 (SD not reported)	18-week, in-person, group mindfulness meditation training	Physical exercise course	Choice reaction times	Not applicable

FIGURE C.7

FIGURE C.7

Estimates of the Effect on Orienting Attention (Reaction Time) in Mindfulness Studies with Active Comparison Groups

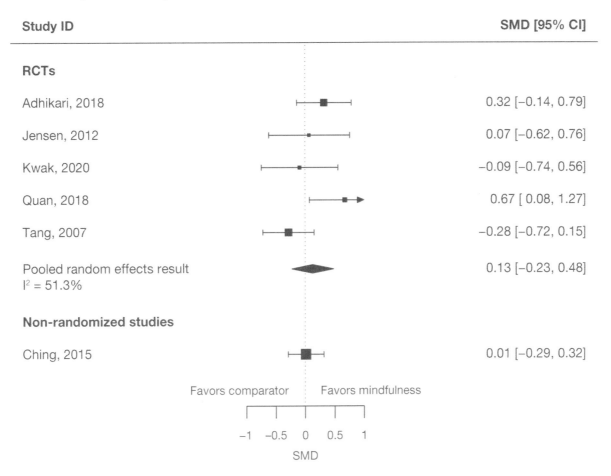

Additional Studies

One analogue RCT (Lai, MacNeil, and Frewen, 2015) that had an active comparison group (a task to count backward) did not find a beneficial effect of mindfulness on orienting attention reaction time over that of the comparison.

Strength of Evidence for the Effect of Mindfulness on Orienting Attention Reaction Time

Our pooled analyses indicated that mindfulness did not have a beneficial effect on orienting attention reaction time. The strength of the evidence supporting this conclusion was moderate. Although most studies included in the analyses were of poor quality and outcomes were imprecise, outcomes were consistent across both pooled analyses. Only two RCTs showed a beneficial effect of mindfulness.

Accuracy

Only one study, an RCT of a mindfulness program with active and passive comparison groups (Jensen et al., 2012), reported an orienting attention accuracy outcome, but it did not show a beneficial effect of mindfulness.

Executive Attention

Reaction Time
Mindfulness Studies
Passive Comparison Groups

We conducted a meta-analysis of 11 RCTs that assessed the effect of mindfulness programs on executive attention reaction time and used passive comparison groups. Additionally, there were four non-randomized studies. We summarize study-level details in Table C.7. All the mindfulness programs were delivered in person and had group-based sessions. Two involved military personnel. Durations ranged from one to 12 weeks. Our pooled analysis did not show an effect of mindfulness on executive attention reaction time (SMD = 0.18; 95% CI = −0.13, 0.48; I^2 = 65.6%) (Figure C.8). Consistent with the results of the pooled analysis, none of the four non-randomized studies (three testing MBSR and one testing MMFT with military personnel) showed an effect of mindfulness on executive attention reaction time.

TABLE C.7

Study-Level Details for Studies That Assessed Executive Attention (Reaction Time): Mindfulness Studies with Passive Comparison Groups

Study ID	Participants	Intervention	Comparator	Outcome	Study Quality
RCTs (included in meta-analysis)					
Ainsworth, 2013	76 UK adults, 86.8% female, mean age = 20.3 (SD = 4.1)	8-day, in-person, group focused-attention meditation; 1.1-week, in-person, group open-monitoring meditation	No intervention	ANT—executive effect	Poor
Anderson, 2007	86 Canadian adults, percent female not reported, mean age = 39.2 (SD not reported)	8-week, in-person, group MBSR	Waitlist	Attention-switching task	Poor
Becerra, 2017	62 Australian undergraduate students, 77.4% female, mean age = 33.9 (SD = 12.1)	8-week, in-person, group mindfulness meditation training	Waitlist	ANT—executive effect	Poor
Burger, 2017	60 U.S. first-semester students pursuing an associate's degree in nursing, 82.7% female, age range = 18–40 (SD not reported)	4-week, virtual, individual mindfulness meditation training	Waitlist	ANT—executive network reaction time difference score	Poor
Esch, 2016	31 German adults, 77.4% female, mean age = 26.7 (SD = 7.6)	10-day, in-person, group mindfulness meditation training	No intervention	ANT—executive network reaction time difference score	
Jensen, 2012	48 Danish young adults, 62.5% female, age range = 20–36 (SD not reported)	8-week, in-person, group MBSR	No intervention	Stroop—color and word task: incongruent block time	Poor
Jha, 2015	164 U.S. active-duty Army service members, 1.8% female, mean age = 24.2 (SD = 4.9)	8-week, in-person, mixed individual and group MMFT	No intervention	SART—reaction time variability (intraindividual coefficient of variation)	Poor

Table C.7—Continued

Study ID	Participants	Intervention	Comparator	Outcome	Study Quality
Li, 2018	34 Chinese adults, 66.7% female, mean age = 29.4 (SD = 9.3)	8-week, in-person, group MBCT	Waitlist	Continuous performance test	Poor
Zanesco, 2019	120 U.S. special operations forces personnel, 0% female, mean age = 33.1 (SD = 5.6)	2-week, in-person, group MBAT	No intervention	SART—reaction time variability	Good
Zhang, 2019	40 Chinese adults, 70.0% female, mean age = 22.5 (SD not reported)	8-week, mixed in-person and virtual, mixed individual and group MBCT	Waitlist	Stroop—incongruent reaction time	Poor
Zhu, 2019	54 Chinese university students, 70.9% female, mean age = 24.2 (SD= 5.2)	12-week, in-person, group MBSR	No intervention	Stroop—mean reaction time	Poor
Non-randomized studies (not included in meta-analysis)					
Jha, 2017	55 U.S. Marine Corps reservists, 0% female, mean age = 27.8 (SD = 6.4)	8-week, in-person, group MBAT	No intervention	SART—mean reaction time	Not applicable
Morrison, 2014	58 U.S. psychology and neuroscience university majors, 51.7% female, mean age = 18.2 (SD = 1.3)	7-week, mixed in-person and virtual, mixed individual and group MBSR	Waitlist	SART—mean reaction time on correct non-target responses	Not applicable
Rodriguez Vega, 2014	103 Spanish resident intern psychiatrists and clinical psychologists, 70.0% female, mean age = 29.6 (SD = 5.6)	8-week, in-person, group MBSR	Waitlist	Stroop—mean reaction time	Not applicable
Wimmer, 2019	222 German university students in a psychology course, 63.9% female, mean age = 24.9 (SD = 3.5)	12-week, in-person, mixed individual and group MBSR	No intervention	Flanker task—reaction time	Not applicable

FIGURE C.8

Estimates of the Effect on Executive Attention (Reaction Time) in Mindfulness Studies with Passive Comparison Groups

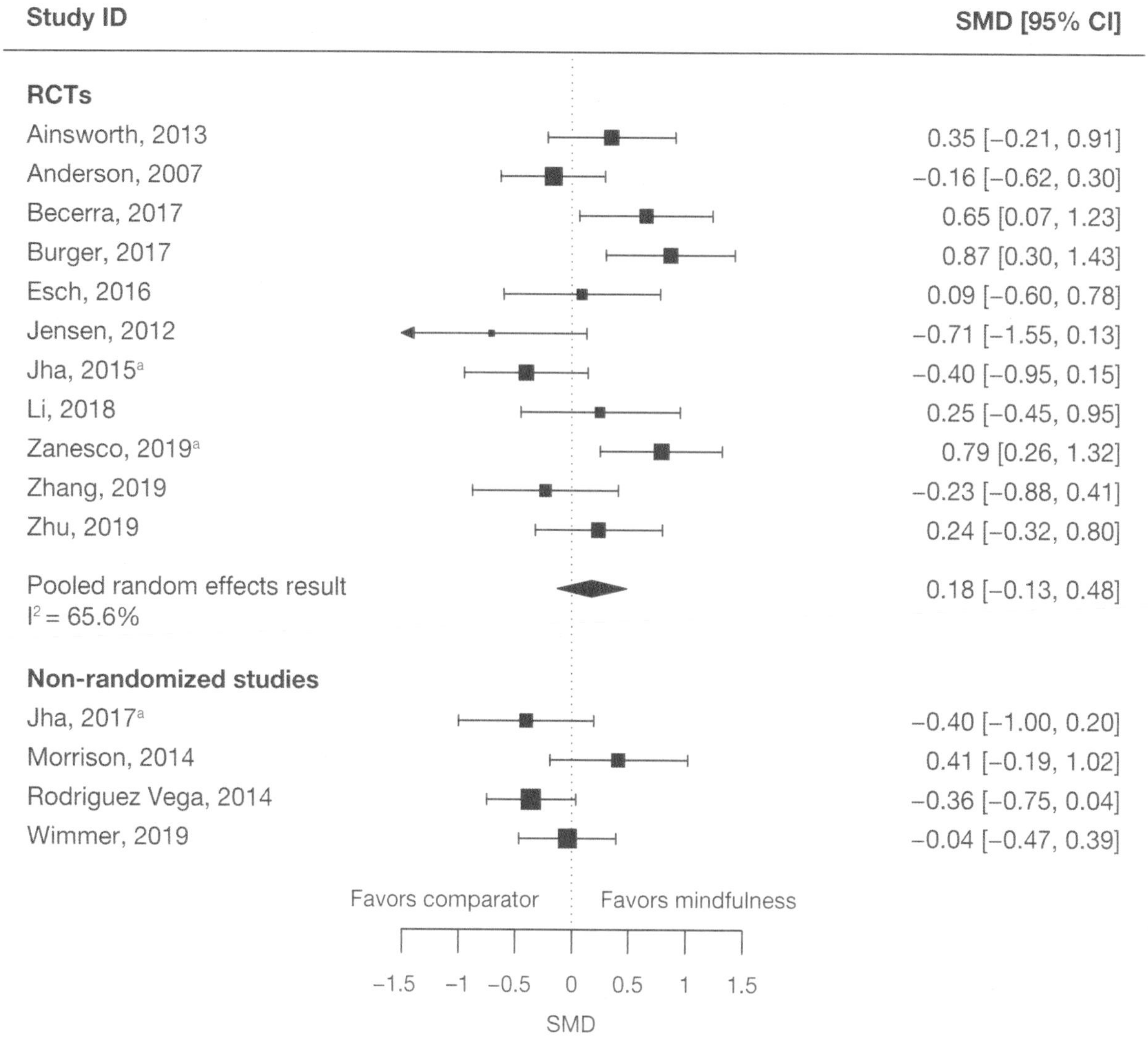

Study ID	SMD [95% CI]

RCTs

Study ID	SMD [95% CI]
Ainsworth, 2013	0.35 [−0.21, 0.91]
Anderson, 2007	−0.16 [−0.62, 0.30]
Becerra, 2017	0.65 [0.07, 1.23]
Burger, 2017	0.87 [0.30, 1.43]
Esch, 2016	0.09 [−0.60, 0.78]
Jensen, 2012	−0.71 [−1.55, 0.13]
Jha, 2015[a]	−0.40 [−0.95, 0.15]
Li, 2018	0.25 [−0.45, 0.95]
Zanesco, 2019[a]	0.79 [0.26, 1.32]
Zhang, 2019	−0.23 [−0.88, 0.41]
Zhu, 2019	0.24 [−0.32, 0.80]

Pooled random effects result
$I^2 = 65.6\%$ — 0.18 [−0.13, 0.48]

Non-randomized studies

Study ID	SMD [95% CI]
Jha, 2017[a]	−0.40 [−1.00, 0.20]
Morrison, 2014	0.41 [−0.19, 1.02]
Rodriguez Vega, 2014	−0.36 [−0.75, 0.04]
Wimmer, 2019	−0.04 [−0.47, 0.39]

Favors comparator   Favors mindfulness

−1.5   −1   −0.5   0   0.5   1   1.5

SMD

[a] Indicates a study that involved a military population.

Active Comparison Groups

We conducted a meta-analysis of nine RCTs that assessed the effect of mindfulness programs on executive attention reaction time and used active comparison groups. We summarize study-level details in Table C.8. Mindfulness interventions included two virtual programs delivered via smartphone applications, MBSR (two studies), and other in-person or mixed in-person and virtual programs. Program durations ranged from five days to eight weeks. Our initial pooled analysis did not show an effect of mindfulness on executive attention reaction time (SMD = 0.25; 95% CI = −0.07, 0.57; I^2 = 66.3%) (Figure C.9). One of the included studies (Quan et al., 2018), which used the ANT, interpreted the executive effect score in the opposite way from other studies (with higher scores—rather than lower scores–indicating better executive attention). To be consistent, in our pooled analysis, we coded all studies that reported this outcome (ANT executive effect score) as lower scores indicating better attention. Furthermore, the effect size in this study was an outlier compared with the effect sizes in the other studies. Therefore, we decided to do a second analysis with this study removed. The second analysis indicated a beneficial effect of mindfulness on executive attention reaction time (SMD = 0.36; 95% CI = 0.11, 0.62; I^2 = 41.7%) (Figure C.10).

TABLE C.8

Study-Level Details for Studies That Assessed Executive Attention (Reaction Time): Mindfulness Studies with Active Comparison Groups

Study ID	Participants	Intervention	Comparator	Outcome	Study Quality
RCTs (included in meta-analysis)					
Balconi, 2019	50 Italian adults with a valid drivers' license, 76.0% female, mean age = 24.2 (SD = 7.0)	3-week, in-person, individual, mindfulness meditation training	Breathing awareness practice	Stroop—time interference	Poor
Bhayee, 2016	43 Canadian community-dwelling adults	6-week, virtual, Calm smartphone application with Muse neurofeedback	Math training program	Stroop—mean reaction time	Poor
Fan, 2014	43 Chinese undergraduate students, 51.2% female, mean age = 21.0 (SD not reported)	5-day, in-person, group integrative body-mind training	Relaxation training	Stroop—interference reaction time	Fair
Jensen, 2012	48 Danish young adults, 62.5% female, age range = 20–36 (SD not reported)	8-week, in-person, group MBSR	Non-mindfulness stress reduction	Stroop—color and word task: incongruent block time	Poor
Kwak, 2020	67 South Korean adults with full-time employment, 75.7% female, mean age = 30.6 (SD = 4.9)	5-day, in-person, group mindfulness meditation training	Relaxation retreat	ANT—executive effect	Poor
Quan, 2018	48 Chinese undergraduate students, 50.0% female, mean age = 19.2 (SD = 1.3)	1-week, in-person, group MBCT	Relaxation training	ANT—executive effect	Poor
Rooks, 2017	100 U.S. university athletes, mean age = 19.8 (SD = 1.5)	4-week, mixed in-person and virtual, mixed individual and group MBSR	Relaxation training	SART—reaction time variability	Good

Table C.8—Continued

Study ID	Participants	Intervention	Comparator	Outcome	Study Quality
Tang, 2007	80 Chinese undergraduate students, 45.0% female, mean age = 21.8 (SD not reported)	5-day, mixed in-person and virtual, group integrative body-mind training	Relaxation training	ANT—executive effect	Fair
Walsh, 2019	108 Canadian undergraduate students, 83.8% female, mean age = 20.0 (SD = 2.5)	3-week, virtual, Wildflowers smartphone application	2048 smartphone application	ANT—executive effect	Poor
Non-randomized studies (not included in meta-analysis)					
Ching, 2015	359 Taiwanese university students, 61.0% female, age range = 18–19 (SD not reported)	18-week, in-person, group mindfulness meditation training	Physical exercise course	Digit vigilance task reaction time	Not applicable
Jha, 2020	80 U.S. active-duty Army service members, 0% female, mean age = 24.6 (SD = 4.2)	8-week, in-person, group MMFT	Positive emotion resilience training	SART—reaction time variability (intraindividual coefficient of variation)	Not applicable
Wimmer, 2019	222 German university students in a psychology course, 63.9% female, mean age = 24.9 (SD = 3.5)	12-week, in-person, mixed individual and group MBSR	Awareness activities	Flanker task—reaction time	Not applicable

FIGURE C.9

Estimates of the Effect on Executive Attention (Reaction Time) in Mindfulness Studies with Active Comparison Groups

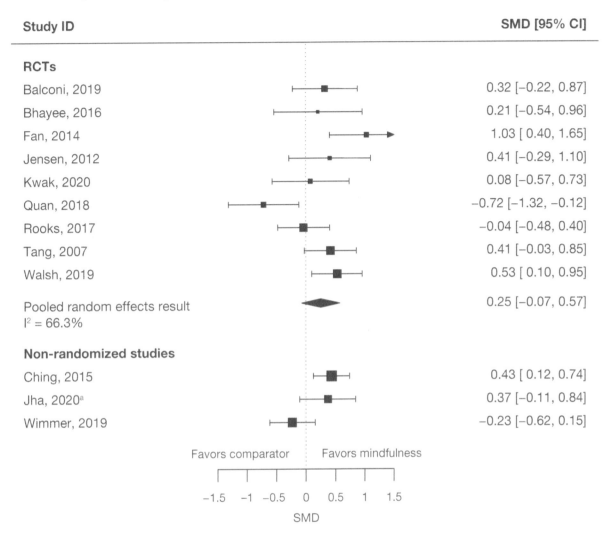

Study ID	SMD [95% CI]
RCTs	
Balconi, 2019	0.32 [−0.22, 0.87]
Bhayee, 2016	0.21 [−0.54, 0.96]
Fan, 2014	1.03 [0.40, 1.65]
Jensen, 2012	0.41 [−0.29, 1.10]
Kwak, 2020	0.08 [−0.57, 0.73]
Quan, 2018	−0.72 [−1.32, −0.12]
Rooks, 2017	−0.04 [−0.48, 0.40]
Tang, 2007	0.41 [−0.03, 0.85]
Walsh, 2019	0.53 [0.10, 0.95]
Pooled random effects result $I^2 = 66.3\%$	0.25 [−0.07, 0.57]
Non-randomized studies	
Ching, 2015	0.43 [0.12, 0.74]
Jha, 2020[a]	0.37 [−0.11, 0.84]
Wimmer, 2019	−0.23 [−0.62, 0.15]

Favors comparator : Favors mindfulness

−1.5 −1 −0.5 0 0.5 1 1.5

SMD

[a] Indicates a study that involved a military population.

FIGURE C.10

Estimates of the Effect on Executive Attention (Reaction Time) in Mindfulness Studies with Active Comparison Groups

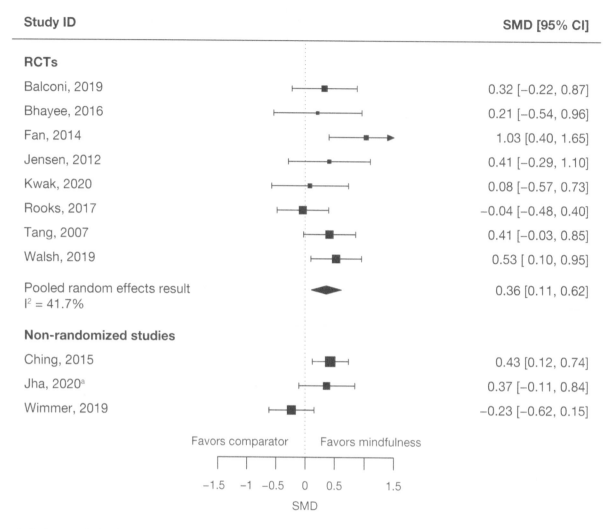

Study ID	SMD [95% CI]
RCTs	
Balconi, 2019	0.32 [−0.22, 0.87]
Bhayee, 2016	0.21 [−0.54, 0.96]
Fan, 2014	1.03 [0.40, 1.65]
Jensen, 2012	0.41 [−0.29, 1.10]
Kwak, 2020	0.08 [−0.57, 0.73]
Rooks, 2017	−0.04 [−0.48, 0.40]
Tang, 2007	0.41 [−0.03, 0.85]
Walsh, 2019	0.53 [0.10, 0.95]
Pooled random effects result $I^2 = 41.7\%$	0.36 [0.11, 0.62]
Non-randomized studies	
Ching, 2015	0.43 [0.12, 0.74]
Jha, 2020[a]	0.37 [−0.11, 0.84]
Wimmer, 2019	−0.23 [−0.62, 0.15]

Favors comparator   Favors mindfulness

−1.5   −1   −0.5   0   0.5   1.5

SMD

[a] Indicates a study that involved a military population.

Analogue Studies

We conducted a meta-analysis of six RCTs that assessed the effect of mindfulness analogues on executive attention reaction time and used active comparison groups. We summarize study-level details in Table C.9. All interventions were delivered in virtual formats except for one, which was delivered in person. Durations ranged from ten to 25 minutes. Our pooled analysis did not show an effect of mindfulness on executive attention reaction time (SMD = 0.18; 95% CI = −0.19, 0.54; I^2 = 65.3%) (Figure C.11).

TABLE C.9

Study-Level Details for Studies That Assessed Executive Attention (Reaction Time): Analogue Studies with Active Comparison Groups

Study ID	Participants	Intervention	Comparator	Outcome	Study Quality
RCTs (included in meta-analysis)					
Banks, 2019	102 U.S. undergraduate students, 71.8% female, mean age = 19.1 (SD = 2.3)	15-minute virtual mindfulness analogue	15-minute virtual relaxation induction	SART reaction time variability	Poor
Jankowski, 2020	81 Polish young adults, 65.4% female, mean age = 22.3 (SD = 2.4)	10-minute virtual mindfulness analogue	10-minute negative affect induction	Attention-switching task—overall reaction time	Poor
Johnson, 2015	92 U.S. university students, 65.0% female, mean age = 23.4 (SD = 8.2)	25-minute virtual mindfulness analogue	25-minute sham meditation	Trail Making Test—parts A and B averaged together	Poor
Lai, 2015	70 Canadian undergraduate psychology students, 65.7% female, mean age = 18.9 (SD = 2.7)	15-minute, in-person, individual mindfulness analogue	15-minute counting-backward task	ANT—executive effect	Poor
Larson, 2013	62 U.S. undergraduate students in a psychology course, 47.3% female, mean age = 19.9 (SD = 2.0)	14-minute, virtual mindfulness analogue	14-minute audio recording listening task	Modified Eriksen flanker task—incongruent trial reaction time	Poor
Norris, 2018 (1a)	40 U.S. undergraduate students, 32.4% female, mean age = 19.5 (SD = 1.2)	10-minute, virtual mindfulness analogue	10-minute audio recording listening task	ANT—executive network reaction time difference score	Poor

FIGURE C.11

Estimates of the Effect on Executive Attention (Reaction Time) in Analogue Studies with Active Comparison Groups

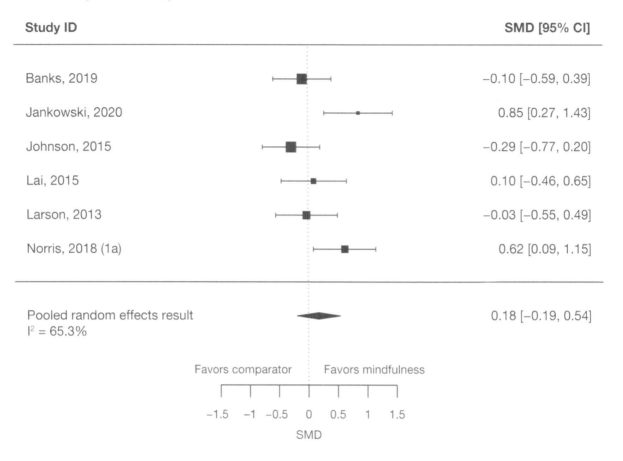

Additional Studies

Two analogue RCTs with passive comparison groups reported an executive attention reaction time outcome. Therefore, results could not be pooled. One study (Banks et al., 2019), which used the SART, did not find an effect of the mindfulness analogue on executive attention reaction time. The other study (Jankowski and Holas, 2020) used an attention-switching task in which participants saw a series of words displayed in various colors. In some trials, they had to indicate whether the word was a plant; in others, they reported whether the word appeared in the color red. Results indicated that the mindfulness group was faster overall than the comparison group, but there was no difference between groups in *switch cost* (the increase in reaction time that occurred when switching from one trial type to the other).

Strength of Evidence for the Effect of Mindfulness on Executive Attention Reaction Time

Across four pooled analyses, results were inconsistent. In two pooled analyses involving mindfulness studies with passive comparison groups and analogue studies with active comparison groups, mindfulness did not have an effect on executive attention reaction time. In two pooled analyses involving mindfulness studies with active comparison groups (the second analysis included the same studies as the first analysis, except we removed an outlier study), only the analysis without the outlier study showed a beneficial effect of mindfulness. In summary, we conclude that mindfulness did not have a beneficial effect on executive attention reaction time, but the strength of the evidence supporting this conclusion was very low. Most studies included in the pooled analyses were of poor quality, and outcomes were imprecise, although they were generally consistent across all pooled analyses.

Accuracy

Mindfulness Studies

Passive Comparison Groups

We conducted a meta-analysis of ten RCTs that assessed the effect of mindfulness programs on executive attention accuracy and used passive comparison groups. Additionally, there were six non-randomized studies. We summarize study-level details in Table C.10. All interventions included in-person and group-based sessions; some additionally included individual sessions or virtual elements. Interventions included MBSR (two studies), MBCT (two studies), MMFT, MBAT, and others. Durations ranged from one to 12 weeks. Our pooled analysis indicated a beneficial effect of mindfulness on executive attention accuracy (SMD = 0.37; 95% CI = 0.16, 0.58; I^2 = 5.4%) (Figure C.12). Of the six non-randomized studies—two of which involved military personnel—three showed a beneficial effect.

TABLE C.10

Study-Level Details for Studies That Assessed Executive Attention (Accuracy): Mindfulness Studies with Passive Comparison Groups

Study ID	Participants	Intervention	Comparator	Outcome	Study Quality
RCTs (included in meta-analysis)					
Esch, 2016	31 German adults, 77.4% female, mean age = 26.7 (SD = 7.6)	1.4-week, in-person, group mindfulness meditation training	No intervention	ANT—overall errors	Poor
Flook, 2013	18 U.S. public elementary school teachers, 88.9% female, mean age = 43.1 (SD = 9.9)	8-week, in-person, group MBSR	Waitlist	Rapid visual information-processing task	Poor
Giannandrea, 2019	60 Italian adults, percent female not reported, mean age = 35.7 (SD = 12.1)	Duration not reported, in-person, group MBSR	Waitlist	SART—errors of commission	Poor
Jensen, 2012	48 Danish young adults, 62.5% female, age range = 20–36 (SD not reported)	8-week, in-person, group MBSR	No treatment	d2 (a test of concentration)—error percentage	Poor
Lacerda, 2018	77 Brazilian adults with stress complaints, 54.5% female, mean age = 36.7 (SD = 2.1)	8-week, in-person, group PROGRESS (a stress reduction program)	Waitlist	Digit symbol substitution test	Poor
Li, 2018	34 Chinese adults, 66.7% female, mean age = 29.4 (SD = 9.3)	8-week, in-person, group MBCT	Waitlist	Continuous performance test error rate	Poor
Menezes, 2013	100 Brazilian university students, 57.0% female, mean age = is 25.0 (SD = 4.4)	6-week, in-person, group focused meditation	Waitlist	Concentrated-attention test total score	Poor
Menezes, 2015	46 Brazilian university students, 57.7% female, mean age = 24.8 (SD = 4.8)	1-week, in-person, group focused meditation	Waitlist	Concentrated-attention test total score	Poor
Zanesco, 2019	120 U.S. special operations forces personnel, 0% female, mean age = 33.1 (SD = 5.6)	2-week, in-person, group MBAT	No intervention	SART A'	Good
Zhu, 2019	54 Chinese university students, 70.9% female, mean age = 24.2 (SD= 5.2)	12-week, in-person, group MBSR	No intervention	Stroop—accuracy percentage	Poor

Table C.10—Continued

Study ID	Participants	Intervention	Comparator	Outcome	Study Quality
Non-randomized studies (not included in meta-analysis)					
Denkova, 2020	121 U.S. firefighters, 19.0% female, mean age = 43.9 (SD = 7.9)	4-week, in-person, mixed individual and group MBAT	No intervention	SART A'	Not applicable
Jha, 2017	55 U.S. Marine Corps reservists, 0% female, mean age = 27.8 (SD = 6.4)	8-week, in-person, group MMFT	No intervention	SART—mean accuracy on target trials	Not applicable
Jha, 2019	180 active-duty U.S. Army personnel, 0% female, mean age = 23.3 (SD = 3.0)	4-week, in-person, group MBAT	No intervention	SART A'	Not applicable
Morrison, 2014	58 U.S. psychology and neuroscience university majors, 51.7% female, mean age = 18.2 (SD = 1.3)	7-week, mixed in-person and virtual, mixed individual and group MBSR	Waitlist	SART—mean overall accuracy	Not applicable
Rodriguez Vega, 2014	103 Spanish resident intern psychiatrists and clinical psychologists, 70.0% female, mean age = 29.6 (SD = 5.6)	8-week, in-person, group MBSR	Waitlist	Stroop—number of errors	Not applicable
Wimmer. 2019	222 German university students in a psychology course, 63.9% female, mean age = 24.9 (SD = 3.5)	12-week, in-person, mixed individual and group MBSR	No intervention	Flanker task—accuracy	Not applicable

FIGURE C.12

Estimates of the Effect on Executive Attention (Accuracy): Mindfulness Studies with Passive Control Groups

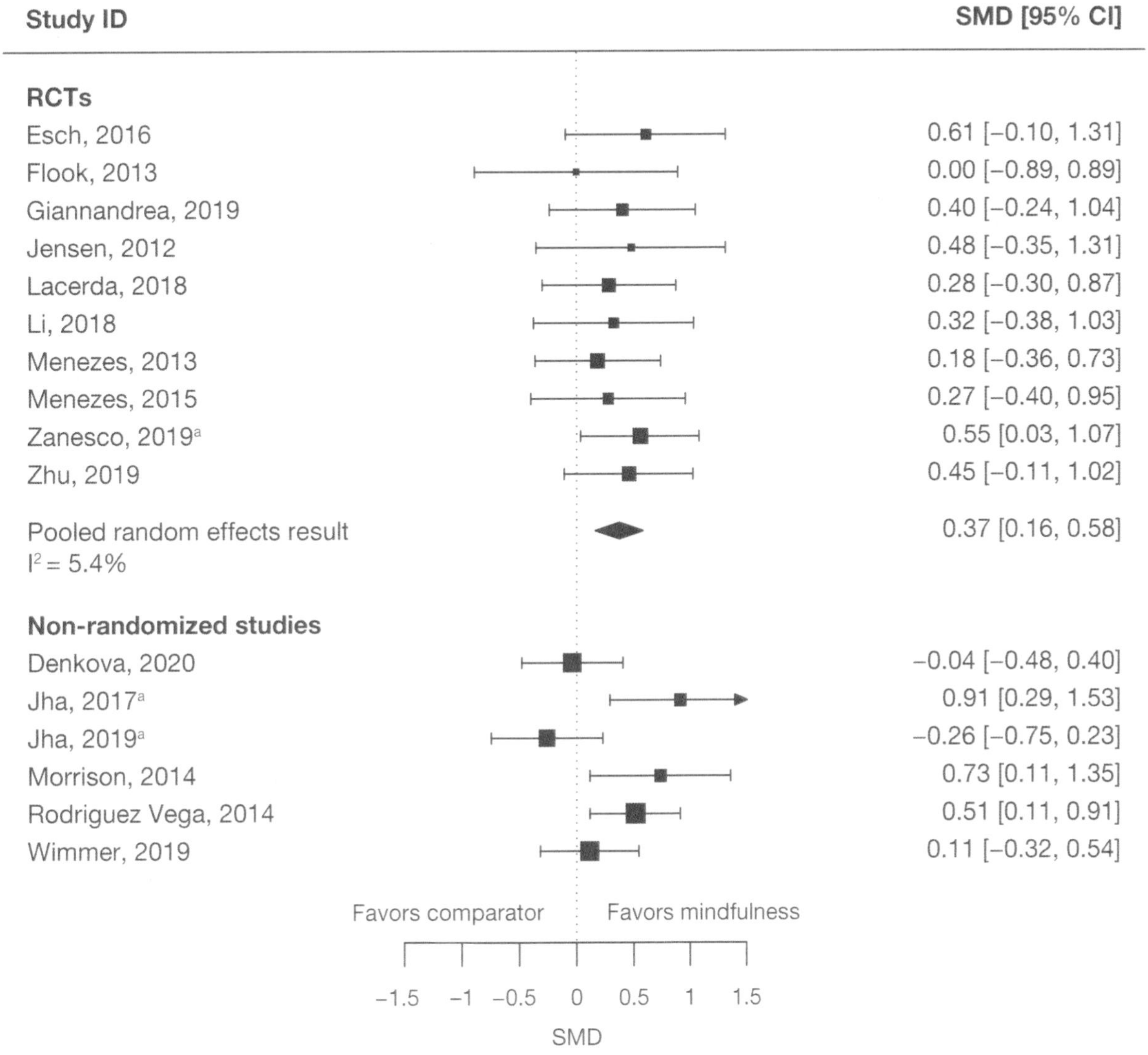

Study ID	SMD [95% CI]
RCTs	
Esch, 2016	0.61 [−0.10, 1.31]
Flook, 2013	0.00 [−0.89, 0.89]
Giannandrea, 2019	0.40 [−0.24, 1.04]
Jensen, 2012	0.48 [−0.35, 1.31]
Lacerda, 2018	0.28 [−0.30, 0.87]
Li, 2018	0.32 [−0.38, 1.03]
Menezes, 2013	0.18 [−0.36, 0.73]
Menezes, 2015	0.27 [−0.40, 0.95]
Zanesco, 2019[a]	0.55 [0.03, 1.07]
Zhu, 2019	0.45 [−0.11, 1.02]
Pooled random effects result $I^2 = 5.4\%$	0.37 [0.16, 0.58]
Non-randomized studies	
Denkova, 2020	−0.04 [−0.48, 0.40]
Jha, 2017[a]	0.91 [0.29, 1.53]
Jha, 2019[a]	−0.26 [−0.75, 0.23]
Morrison, 2014	0.73 [0.11, 1.35]
Rodriguez Vega, 2014	0.51 [0.11, 0.91]
Wimmer, 2019	0.11 [−0.32, 0.54]

Favors comparator · Favors mindfulness

−1.5 −1 −0.5 0 0.5 1 1.5

SMD

[a] Indicates a study that involved a military population.

Active Comparison Groups

We conducted a meta-analysis of ten RCTs that assessed the effect of mindfulness programs on executive attention accuracy and used active comparison groups. Additionally, there were four non-randomized studies. We summarize study-level details in Table C.11. The mindfulness interventions included two virtual programs delivered via smartphone applications, three in-person group-based programs (of which one was MBSR), and other programs with mixed elements. Durations ranged from three days to 24 weeks. Our initial pooled analysis did not show an effect of mindfulness on executive attention accuracy (SMD = 0.83; 95% CI = −0.24, 1.90; I^2 = 97.1%) (Figure C.13). An examination of the forest plot revealed that one study (Rothschild et al., 2017) was an extreme outlier, with a very large effect size in favor of mindfulness that outlier inflated the estimate of the SMD and caused a very wide confidence interval. Therefore, we conducted a second analysis with this study removed, and that analysis indicated a beneficial effect of mindfulness on executive attention accuracy (SMD = 0.30; 95% CI = 0.06, 0.54; I^2 = 39.1%) (Figure C.14). Of the four non-randomized studies, two indicated a beneficial effect.

TABLE C.11

Study-Level Details for Studies That Assessed Executive Attention (Accuracy): Mindfulness Studies with Active Comparison Groups

Study ID	Participants	Intervention	Comparator	Outcome	Study Quality
RCTs (included in meta-analysis)					
Basso, 2019	42 U.S. adults, 64.3% female, mean age and SD not reported	8-week, virtual, individual Journey Meditation	Podcast listening tasks	Stroop—accuracy percentage for congruent trials	Poor
Bhayee, 2016	43 Canadian community-dwelling adults	6-week, virtual, Calm smartphone application with Muse neurofeedback	Math training program	d2—commit error	Poor
Jensen, 2012	48 Danish young adults, 62.5% female, age range = 20–36 (SD not reported)	8-week, in-person, group MBSR	Non-mindfulness stress reduction	Stroop—color and word task: incongruent block error rate	Poor
Kwak, 2020	67 South Korean adults employed full-time, 75.7% female, mean age = 30.6 (SD = 4.9)	4-day, in-person, group mindfulness meditation training	Relaxation retreat	ANT—overall accuracy	Poor
Menezes, 2013	100 Brazilian university students, 57.0% female, mean age = 25.0 (SD = 4.4)	6-week, in-person, group focused meditation	Progressive relaxation	Concentrated-attention test total score	Poor
Rahl, 2017	147 U.S. adults, 49.7% female, mean age = 21.0 (SD = 3.3)	3-day, virtual, individual mindfulness meditation training	Relaxation training; reading tasks	SART discrimination	Poor
Rooks, 2017	100 U.S. university athletes, mean age = 19.8 (SD = 1.5)	4-week, mixed in-person and virtual, mixed individual and group MBSR	Relaxation training	SART A'	Good

Table C.11—Continued

Study ID	Participants	Intervention	Comparator	Outcome	Study Quality
Rothschild, 2017	150 Israel Defense Forces members	24-week, in-person, mixed individual and group mindfulness meditation training	Daily news listening tasks	Digit symbol substitution test	Poor
Zeidan, 2010	49 U.S. university students, 59.4% female, mean age = 22.5 (SD = 8.2)	Duration not reported, in-person, group mindfulness meditation training	Audiobook listening task	Symbol Digit Modalities Test	Fair
Zwilling, 2019	160 U.S. adults, 52.0% female, mean age = 23.8 (SD not reported)	16-week, mixed in-person and virtual, mixed individual and group high-intensity cardio-resistance fitness training and cognitive training with mindfulness meditation	High-intensity cardio-resistance fitness training; active control training	Digit symbol substitution test	Poor
Non-randomized studies (not included in meta-analysis)					
Ching, 2015	359 Taiwanese university students, 61.0% female, age range = 18–19 (SD not reported)	18-week, in-person, group mindfulness meditation training	Physical exercise course	Digit vigilance task—accuracy percentage	Not applicable
Denkova, 2020	121 U.S. firefighters, 19.0% female, mean age = 43.9 (SD = 7.9)	4-week, in-person, mixed individual and group MBAT	Relaxation training	SART A'	Not applicable
Jha, 2020	80 U.S. active-duty Army service members, 0% female, mean age = 24.6 (SD = 4.2)	8-week, in-person, group MMFT	Positive emotion resilience training	SART A'	Not applicable
Wimmer, 2019	222 German university students in a psychology course, 63.9% female, mean age = 24.9 (SD = 3.5)	12-week, in-person, mixed individual and group MBSR	Awareness activities	Flanker task—accuracy	Not applicable

FIGURE C.13

Estimates of the Effect on Executive Attention (Accuracy) in Mindfulness Studies with Active Comparison Groups, with the Outlier Study

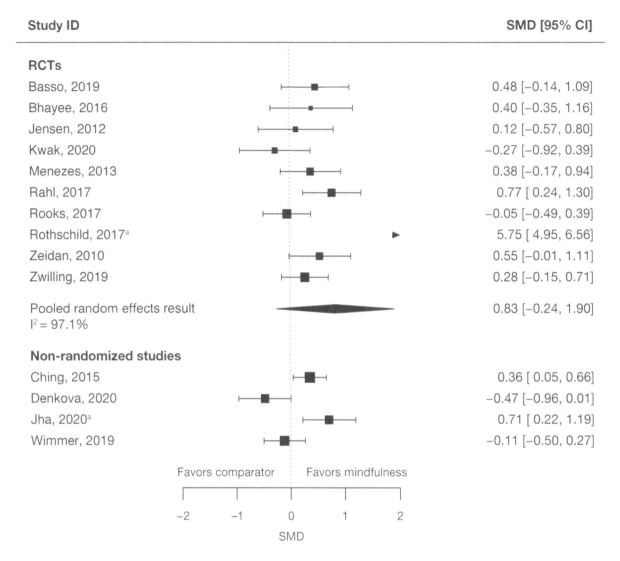

^a Indicates a study that involved a military population.

FIGURE C.14

Estimates of the Effects on Executive Attention (Accuracy) in Mindfulness Studies with Active Comparison Groups, Without the Outlier Study

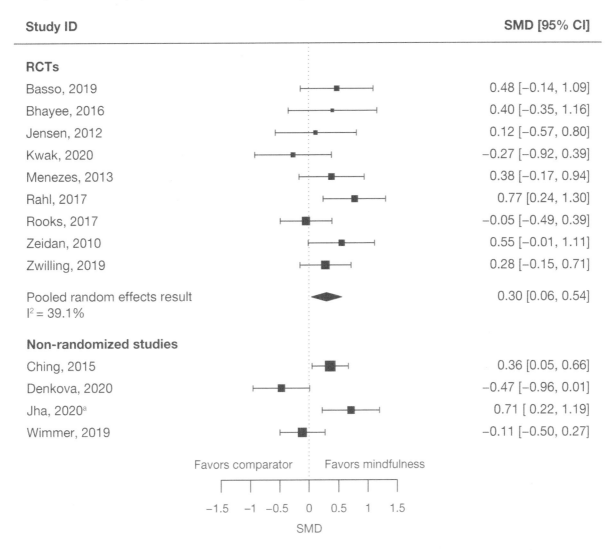

Study ID	SMD [95% CI]
RCTs	
Basso, 2019	0.48 [−0.14, 1.09]
Bhayee, 2016	0.40 [−0.35, 1.16]
Jensen, 2012	0.12 [−0.57, 0.80]
Kwak, 2020	−0.27 [−0.92, 0.39]
Menezes, 2013	0.38 [−0.17, 0.94]
Rahl, 2017	0.77 [0.24, 1.30]
Rooks, 2017	−0.05 [−0.49, 0.39]
Zeidan, 2010	0.55 [−0.01, 1.11]
Zwilling, 2019	0.28 [−0.15, 0.71]
Pooled random effects result $I^2 = 39.1\%$	0.30 [0.06, 0.54]
Non-randomized studies	
Ching, 2015	0.36 [0.05, 0.66]
Denkova, 2020	−0.47 [−0.96, 0.01]
Jha, 2020[a]	0.71 [0.22, 1.19]
Wimmer, 2019	−0.11 [−0.50, 0.27]

Favors comparator   Favors mindfulness

−1.5   −1   −0.5   0   0.5   1   1.5

SMD

[a] Indicates a study that involved a military population.

Analogue Studies

We conducted a meta-analysis of six RCTs that assessed the effect of mindfulness analogues on executive attention accuracy and used active comparison groups. We summarize study-level details in Table C.12. All interventions were delivered virtually except one, which was delivered in person; durations ranged from ten to 25 minutes. Our pooled analysis did not show an effect of mindfulness on executive attention accuracy (SMD = 0.00; 95% CI = −0.28, 0.28; I^2 = 35.9%) (Figure C.15).

TABLE C.12

Study-Level Details for Studies That Assessed Executive Attention (Accuracy): Analogue Studies with Active Control Groups

Study ID	Participants	Intervention	Comparator	Outcome	Study Quality
Banks, 2019	102 U.S. undergraduate students, 71.8% female, mean age = 19.1 (SD = 2.3)	15-minute virtual mindfulness analogue	15-minute virtual relaxation induction	SART—mean accuracy on target trials	Poor
Eisenbeck, 2018	46 Spanish undergraduate psychology students, 58.9% female, mean age = 25.2 (SD = 8.0)	13-minute virtual mindfulness analogue	13-minute audiobook listening task	Concentrated-attention test global index	Poor
Johnson, 2015	92 U.S. university students, 65.0% female, mean age = 23.4 (SD = 8.2)	25-minute virtual mindfulness analogue	25-minute sham meditation	Symbol Digit Modalities Test	Poor
Lai, 2015	70 Canadian undergraduate psychology students, 65.7% female, mean age = 18.9 (SD = 2.7)	15-minute in-person, individual mindfulness analogue	15-minute counting-backward task	ANT—accuracy	Poor
Larson, 2013	62 U.S. undergraduate students in a psychology course, 47.3% female, mean age = 19.9 (SD = 2.0)	14-minute virtual mindfulness analogue	14-minute audio recording listening task	Modified Eriksen flanker task—incongruent-trial error rates	Poor
Norris, 2018 (1a)	40 U.S. undergraduate students, 32.4% female, mean age = 19.5 (SD = 1.2)	10-minute virtual mindfulness analogue	10-minute audio recording listening task	ANT—flanker accuracy	Poor

FIGURE C.15

Estimates of the Effect on Executive Attention (Accuracy) in Analogue Studies with Active Control Groups

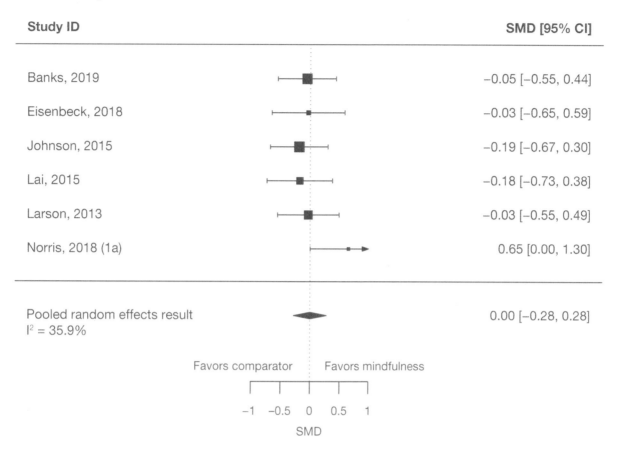

Study ID	SMD [95% CI]
Banks, 2019	−0.05 [−0.55, 0.44]
Eisenbeck, 2018	−0.03 [−0.65, 0.59]
Johnson, 2015	−0.19 [−0.67, 0.30]
Lai, 2015	−0.18 [−0.73, 0.38]
Larson, 2013	−0.03 [−0.55, 0.49]
Norris, 2018 (1a)	0.65 [0.00, 1.30]
Pooled random effects result $I^2 = 35.9\%$	0.00 [−0.28, 0.28]

Favors comparator : Favors mindfulness

−1   −0.5   0   0.5   1

SMD

Additional Studies

One analogue study included in the pooled analysis for active comparison groups also had a passive comparison group (Banks et al., 2019). Consistent with the study's result for the active comparison group, the study did not show a beneficial effect of mindfulness versus the passive comparison group on executive attention accuracy.

Strength of Evidence for the Effect of Mindfulness on Executive Attention Accuracy

In pooled analyses involving mindfulness studies with passive comparison groups and mindfulness studies with active comparison groups (with an extreme outlier removed), mindfulness had a beneficial effect on executive attention accuracy. In a pooled analysis involving analogue studies with active comparison groups, mindfulness did not have a beneficial effect on executive attention accuracy. Given that mindfulness programs are much longer in duration and include more content than analogue interventions do, and given that the total number of studies included in pooled analyses for mindfulness programs (18) was much larger than for analogue studies (six), we conclude that mindfulness did have a beneficial effect on executive attention accuracy. The strength of the evidence supporting this conclusion was moderate. Almost all studies included in the pooled analyses were of poor quality and outcomes were imprecise, but the outcomes were consistent in all pooled analyses.

Summary

This appendix reported the findings from our meta-analyses on the effect of mindfulness programs on attention. Meta-analyses did not show an effect of mindfulness on self-perception of attention, alerting attention reaction time, orienting attention reaction time, or executive attention reaction time. In contrast, meta-analyses involving 18 mindfulness RCTs did show beneficial effects of mindfulness on executive attention accuracy. A meta-analysis involving six analogue RCTs did not show a beneficial effect on executive attention accuracy, which may indicate that brief analogue interventions are not powerful enough to have an impact on this outcome. Although there were many studies included across the meta-analyses and outcomes were mostly consistent, the strength of the evidence for these conclusions was low to moderate, primarily because most of the studies had small sample sizes and were of poor quality, and outcomes were imprecise. Only a few studies reported alerting or orienting accuracy outcomes, and there were not enough studies available to conduct pooled analyses. Therefore, we cannot draw any conclusions about the effect of mindfulness on those outcomes. Overall, more research is needed, particularly large, high-quality studies, to determine whether mindfulness has a beneficial impact on attention.

Effects of Mindfulness Meditation on Emotion Regulation

Emotion regulation refers broadly to an individual's efforts to regulate or control the frequency and intensity of their emotions (Gross, 1998). In this appendix, we describe the results of our syntheses of findings on five aspects of emotion regulation: general emotion regulation ability, use of *reappraisal* (an adaptive emotional regulation strategy involving reassessment of a situation from a different perspective that changes the emotional consequences of that situation) (Gross and John, 2003; Aldao, Nolen-Hoeksema and Schweizer, 2010), use of *suppression* (a maladaptive emotion regulation strategy aimed at trying to inhibit or stop the expression of an emotion), change in negative mood intensity (lower intensity is assumed to reflect successful emotion regulation), and emotional interference with attention (less interference is assumed to reflect successful emotion regulation). Box D.1 highlights key findings discussed in this appendix. For an overview of the emotion regulation outcome and suboutcomes, see Chapter Four.

BOX D.1
Key Findings: Effects of Mindfulness Meditation on Emotion Regulation

- Mindfulness had beneficial effects on increasing the use of reappraisal, decreasing the use of suppression, and decreasing emotional interference with attention.
- Mindfulness did not have an impact on general emotion regulation ability or change in negative mood intensity.

General Emotion Regulation Ability

Mindfulness Studies

We conducted a meta-analysis of four RCTs that assessed the effect of mindfulness programs on general emotion regulation ability and used passive control groups. We summarize study-level details in Table D.1. One program was virtual and self-paced, and another was an online version of MBCT delivered synchronously to groups. The other two programs were delivered in workplace settings with employee participants, including a mostly audio-based program for call center employees and a group-based program for health care workers in a hospital. The programs ranged in duration from two to eight weeks. Our pooled analysis did not show an effect of mindfulness on general emotion regulation ability (SMD = 0.11; 95% CI = -0.25, 0.47; I^2 = 57.8%) (Figure D.1).

TABLE D.1

Study-Level Details for Studies That Assessed General Emotion Regulation Ability

Study ID	Participants	Intervention	Comparator	Outcome	Study Quality
RCTs (included in meta-analysis)					
Barattucci, 2019	594 Italian health care providers, 57.0% female, mean age = 40.4 (SD = 11.0)	Four 8-hour, in-person, group IARA Model Training program meetings	No intervention	Difficulties in Emotion Regulation Scale	Poor
Glück, 2011	40 Swiss community-dwelling adults, 73.5% female, mean age = 35.2 (SD = 13.4)	2-week, virtual mindfulness meditation training	Waitlist	Emotional Competence Self-Assessment (Selbsteinschätzung emotionaler Kompetenzen)	Good
Grégoire, 2015	71 Canadian call center employees, 58.5% female, mean age = 36.1 (SD not reported)	5-week, mixed virtual and in-person mindfulness-based intervention	Waitlist	Two subscales from the Difficulties in Emotion Regulation Scale	Poor
Ma, 2018	192 Chinese adults, 57.9% female, mean age = 27.8 (SD = 7.9)	8-week virtual MBCT program	No intervention	Difficulties in Emotion Regulation Scale	Poor

NOTE: IARA is an Italian abbreviation that translates to "meeting, compliance, responsibility, autonomy" (Barattucci et al., 2019).

FIGURE D.1

Estimates of the Effect on General Emotion Regulation Ability

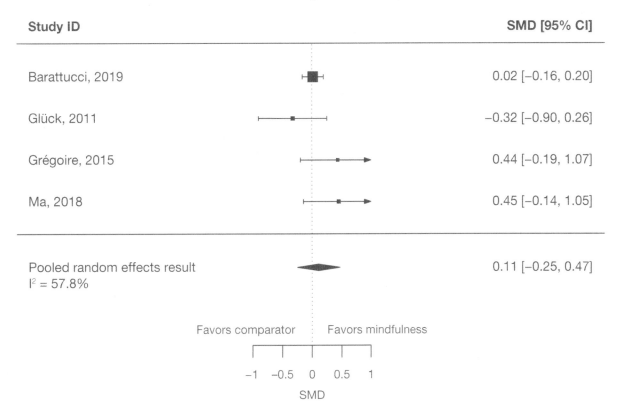

Analogue Studies

One RCT that assessed the effect of a mindfulness analogue and used an active control group could not be included in the meta-analysis. Participants were randomized to listen to a 15-minute audio recording about mindfulness or gardening (control group, "neutral" recording), followed by a mood induction (Watford and Stafford, 2015). This study did not show a significant effect of the mindfulness analogue on "state" (i.e., in that moment) general emotion regulation ability.

Strength of Evidence for the Effect of Mindfulness on General Emotion Regulation Ability

According to our pooled analysis, mindfulness did not have an effect on general emotional regulation ability. However, the strength of the evidence supporting this conclusion was low. The analysis included only four studies, of which study quality was poor in three studies, and the outcomes were inconsistent.

Use of Reappraisal and Suppression

Mindfulness Studies

We conducted meta-analyses of four RCTs that assessed the effect of mindfulness programs on both the use of reappraisal and the use of suppression and used passive control groups. Additionally, there were two non-randomized studies, one of which assessed only the use of reappraisal (see the next section). We summarize study-level details in Table D.2. Three programs were group-based, were delivered in-person, and ranged from four to 16 weeks. Participants in these studies included schoolteachers (two studies) and adult volunteers (one study). In the fourth study, the participants were undergraduate students who received a six-week mindfulness program with mixed in-person and virtual components delivered in a laboratory and at home. Our pooled analysis indicated evidence of beneficial effects of mindfulness on increasing the use of reappraisal (SMD = 0.27; 95% CI = 0.02, 0.52; I^2 = 75.9%) (Figure D.2) and on decreasing the use of suppression (SMD = 0.17; 95% CI = 0.00, 0.33; I^2 = 49.6%) (Figure D.3).

TABLE D.2

Study-Level Details for Studies That Assessed Emotion Regulation: Reappraisal and Suppression

Study ID	Participants	Intervention	Comparator	Outcome	Study Quality
RCTs (included in meta-analysis)					
Cerna, 2020	103 Chilean adults, 74.8% female, age ranges = 18–30 (63.1%), 31–45 (26.2%), 46–60 (7.8%), > 60 (2.9%)	4-week in-person group MBSR program	Waitlist	Emotion Regulation Questionnaire	Poor
Hwang, 2019	185 Australian kindergarten through grade 12 teachers, 83.5% female, mean age = 42.3 (SD = 12.6)	8-week, in-person, group Reconnected program	No Intervention	Emotion Regulation Questionnaire	Poor
Jennings, 2019	224 Malaysian elementary school teachers, 93.0% female, age range = 22–73 (SD not reported)	16-week, mixed in-person and virtual, group CARE program	Waitlist	Emotion Regulation Questionnaire	Good
Wenzel, 2020	125 German undergraduate students, 77.6% female, mean age = 22.9 (SD = 5.1)	5-week, virtual guided breathing meditation program administered in a laboratory	Waitlist	Single-item rating scales for reappraisal and suppression	Fair
Non-randomized studies (not included in meta-analysis)					
Hildebrandt, 2019[a]	332 German adults, 59.3% female, mean age = 40.7 (SD = 9.2)	39-week, in-person, group Resource program	No intervention	Brief COPE inventory and Cognitive Emotion Regulation Questionnaire	N/A
Wimmer, 2019	222 German university students, 63.9% female, mean age = 24.9 (SD = 3.5)	12-week, in-person, mixed individual and group MBSR program	No intervention	Emotion Regulation Questionnaire	N/A

NOTE: CARE = Cultivating Awareness and Resilience in Education; COPE = Coping Orientation to Problems Experienced.

[a] This study included a reappraisal outcome only.

FIGURE D.2

Estimates of the Effect on Emotion Regulation Reappraisal

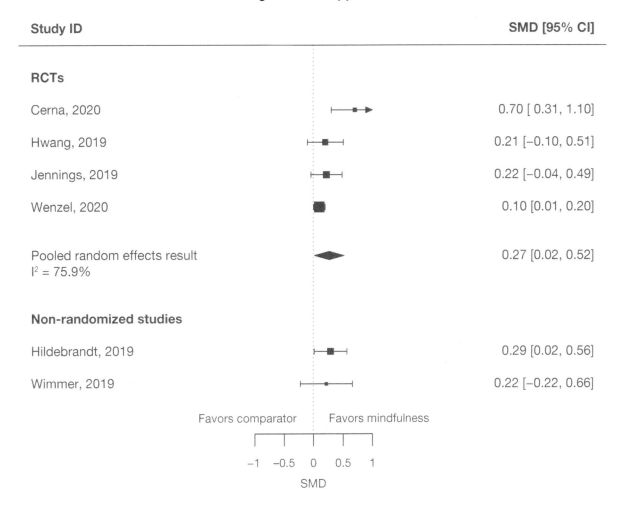

Study ID	SMD [95% CI]
RCTs	
Cerna, 2020	0.70 [0.31, 1.10]
Hwang, 2019	0.21 [−0.10, 0.51]
Jennings, 2019	0.22 [−0.04, 0.49]
Wenzel, 2020	0.10 [0.01, 0.20]
Pooled random effects result $I^2 = 75.9\%$	0.27 [0.02, 0.52]
Non-randomized studies	
Hildebrandt, 2019	0.29 [0.02, 0.56]
Wimmer, 2019	0.22 [−0.22, 0.66]

FIGURE D.3

Estimates of the Effect on Emotion Regulation Suppression

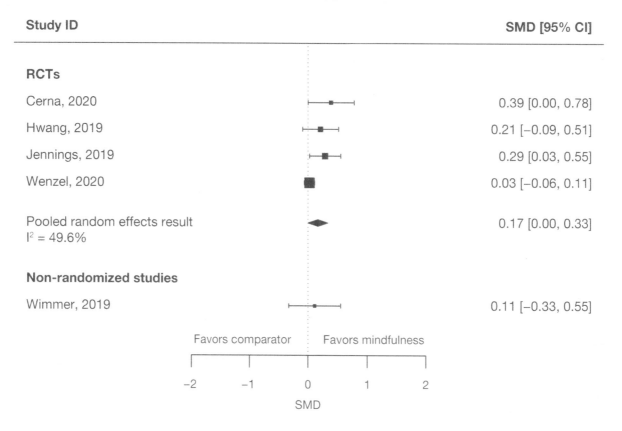

Study ID	SMD [95% CI]
RCTs	
Cerna, 2020	0.39 [0.00, 0.78]
Hwang, 2019	0.21 [−0.09, 0.51]
Jennings, 2019	0.29 [0.03, 0.55]
Wenzel, 2020	0.03 [−0.06, 0.11]
Pooled random effects result $I^2 = 49.6\%$	0.17 [0.00, 0.33]
Non-randomized studies	
Wimmer, 2019	0.11 [−0.33, 0.55]

Additional Studies

We excluded three studies from the pooled analyses. Two non-randomized studies of mindfulness programs with passive comparison groups showed significant effects on the use of reappraisal (Hildebrandt, McCall, and Singer, 2019; Wimmer, von Stockhausen, and Bellingrath, 2019). One of these studies also included a suppression outcome but did not show an effect (Wimmer, von Stockhausen, and Bellingrath, 2019). In contrast to the result of the reappraisal meta-analysis, an RCT that examined the effect of mindfulness analogue and used an active control group did not show a significant effect of mindfulness on the use of reappraisal (Garland et al., 2015). In this study, participants were randomly assigned to listen to a 13-minute audio recording three times over the course of a week. The options were (1) a mindfulness meditation exercise, (2) a recording that encouraged them to suppress unwanted thoughts, or (3) an exercise that encouraged them to let their mind wander freely. Reappraisal was measured at the beginning and end of the week.

Strength of Evidence for the Effect of Mindfulness on the Use of Reappraisal and Suppression

Our pooled analysis indicated that mindfulness had beneficial effects on both increasing the use of reappraisal and decreasing the use of suppression. However, the strength of the evidence supporting these conclusions was low. The same four studies were included in each pooled analysis; study quality was good in one study, poor in two studies, and fair in one study.

Other Adaptive and Maladaptive Emotion Regulation Strategies

We were unable to perform meta-analyses on the effect of mindfulness on the use of other emotion regulation strategies because the number of studies was insufficient to pool. One of the non-randomized studies that showed an effect for mindfulness on increasing the use of reappraisal also reported the use of acceptance and avoidance outcomes (two different measures of each) (Hildebrandt, McCall, and Singer, 2019). The study indicated a beneficial effect on one of the acceptance measures but not on the other and a beneficial effect on both avoidance measures (i.e., reducing avoidance).

Another non-randomized study showed a significant beneficial effect of mindfulness on decreasing rumination (Wimmer, von Stockhausen, and Bellingrath, 2019). However, a study that was included in the pooled analyses for reappraisal and suppression did not show a significant effect on suppression or rumination (Wenzel, Rowland, and Kubiak, 2020). Finally, in one study, the emotion regulation outcome was a specific work-related maladaptive emotion regulation strategy called *surface acting*, which refers to an effort to deliberately alter the emotions shown to other people (e.g., "pretended to have emotions that I did not really have" or "resisted expressing my true feelings") (Hülsheger et al., 2013). Results indicated that participants in the mindfulness group had significant decreases in surface acting.

Change in Negative Mood Intensity

We conducted a meta-analysis of three analogue studies with active comparison groups that reported change in negative mood intensity following a mood induction. All participants were university students. We summarize study level details in Table D.3. This analysis did not indicate evidence to support a difference between the mindfulness and comparison groups in change in negative mood intensity (SMD = 0.18; 95% CI = −0.17, 0.53; I^2 = 45.1%) (Figure D.4).

TABLE D.3

Study-Level Details for Studies That Assessed Emotion Regulation: Change in Negative Mood Intensity

Study ID	Participants	Intervention	Comparator	Outcome	Study Quality
RCTs (included in meta-analysis)					
Arch, 2006	60 U.S. university students, 69.0% female, age range = 18–25	15-minute virtual mindfulness analogue	15-minute virtual instructions (unfocused attention, "let your mind wander")	Positive and Negative Affect Schedule (short version)	Poor
Broderick, 2005	177 U.S. undergraduate students, 78.5% female, mean age = 20.9	30-minute virtual mindfulness analogue	30-minute "distraction" (read booklet with instructions to think of things unrelated to self)	Positive and Negative Affect Schedule	Poor
Keng, 2017	171 Singaporean undergraduate students, 73.6% female, mean age = 20.2 (SD = 1.6)	90-minute virtual mindfulness analogue	90-minute virtual instructions to suppress thoughts and emotions	Single-item rating scale for sadness	Poor

FIGURE D.4

Estimates of the Effect on Emotion Regulation Change in Negative Mood Intensity

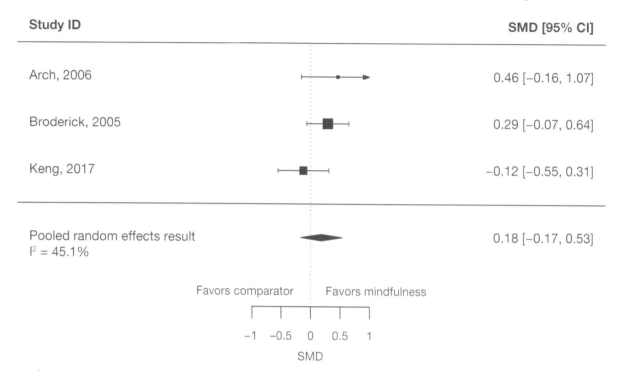

Strength of Evidence for the Effect of Mindfulness on Change in Negative Mood Intensity

According to our pooled analysis, mindfulness did not have an effect on change in negative mood intensity. However, the strength of the evidence supporting this conclusion was very low. The analysis included only three studies, all of which were of poor quality, and findings were inconsistent.

Emotional Interference

Mindfulness Studies

We conducted a meta-analysis of four RCTs of mindfulness programs with active comparison groups in which participants completed a computerized attention test with emotional content. We summarize study-level details in Table D.4. These attention tasks included

- an "affective" number-counting Stroop task in which participants had to count how many numbers they saw on the screen; on *congruent* trials, the numbers matched (e.g., the screen displayed two 2s) and on *incongruent* trials, they did not match (e.g., the screen displayed four 5s) (Allen et al., 2012)
- a visual discrimination task in which the participant had to indicate whether the orientation of two bars was the same or different (Menezes et al., 2013)
- an auditory discrimination task in which the participant had to indicate whether a tone was high or low pitched (Ortner, Kilner and Zelazo, 2007)
- a "dot probe" task in which participants had to indicate the location of a dot on the screen (Wu et al., 2019).

In all four tasks, each trial also included an image on the screen that was intended to be distracting and induce negative emotions. Our pooled analysis indicated evidence of a beneficial effect of mindfulness on decreasing emotional interference (SMD = 0.61; 95% CI = 0.31, 0.92; I^2 = 1.8%) (Figure D.5).

TABLE D.4

Study-Level Details for Studies That Assessed Emotion Regulation: Emotional Interference

Study ID	Participants	Intervention	Comparator	Outcome	Study Quality
RCTs (included in meta-analysis)					
Allen, 2012	61 Danish adults, 55.3% female, mean age = 26.5 (SD not reported)	6-week, in-person, group mindfulness meditation training	Shared reading and listening task	Emotional Stroop task	Poor
Menezes, 2013	100 Brazilian university students, 57.0% female, mean age = 25.0 (SD = 4.4)	6-week, in-person, group focused meditation	Progressive relaxation	Bar orientation discrimination task with unpleasant images	Poor
Ortner, 2007	82 Canadian university students, 76.5% female, mean age = 23.0 (SD not reported)	7-week, in-person, group mindfulness meditation training	Body awareness and relaxation meditation	Tone discrimination task with unpleasant images	Poor
Wu, 2019	43 Chinese university students, 76.2% female, mean age = 21.6 (SD = 2.1)	1-week, virtual synchronous, group mindfulness meditation training	Emotion regulation education	Dot-probe task with images of negative-emotion faces	Poor

Estimates of the Effect on Emotional Interference

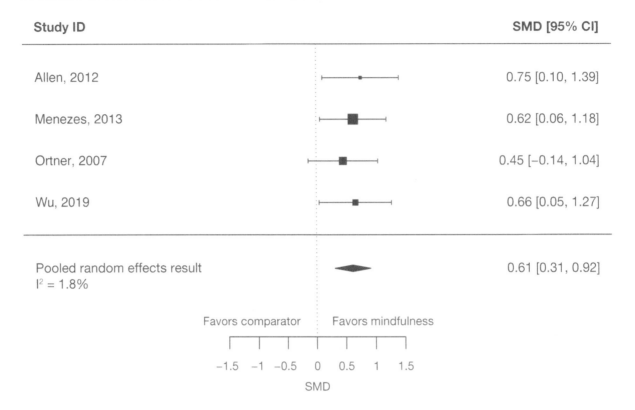

Additional Studies

Three mindfulness studies and three analogue studies could not be pooled because one of the mindfulness studies and two of the analogue studies lacked usable data. However, overall, the results of these studies were consistent with the pooled analysis in that most of the studies showed beneficial effects of mindfulness. These studies used a variety of attention tasks. Two studies—one mindfulness (Flook et al., 2013) and one analogue (Quaglia et al., 2019)—used emotional "go/no-go" tasks in which the participant was presented with a series of emotional words or faces displaying positive or negative emotions on a screen, and they had to press a key to respond to words or faces depicting a target emotion. In both studies, there was a significant effect of mindfulness on improving speed (i.e., reaction time) decreasing errors, or both.

One analogue study administered an emotional Stroop task in which participants had to indicate the font color of emotional and neutral words; the analogue intervention improved performance (decreased reaction time) only among participants in the mindfulness group who reported low levels of mindfulness prior to the intervention (Watier and Dubois, 2016). In another analogue study with active and passive control groups, all participants received a mood induction intended to induce anxiety and then completed an attention-switching task with two different types of trials (deciding whether a word was a plant and deciding whether a word was displayed in red or another color) (Jankowski and Holas, 2020). There was a beneficial effect of mindfulness on overall speed on the attention task but not on *switch cost* (the decrease in speed that occurred when switching from one type of trial to the other type).

A mindfulness study (mindfulness program with passive comparison) (Menezes et al., 2016) used a visual discrimination task with emotional images that was very similar to the task in another study (Menezes et al., 2013); however, the former study did not show an effect of mindfulness on performance. Finally, in one mindfulness study (MBSR with passive comparison) (Alkoby et al., 2019), participants viewed emotional images followed by an instruction to choose and use a specific emotional regulation strategy (reappraisal or distraction). Results indicated that participants in the mindfulness group (MBSR) showed more "flexibility" in their choices; that is, they were more likely to choose reappraisal if the image was low in emotional intensity and more likely to choose distraction if the image was high in emotional intensity.

Strength of Evidence for the Effect of Mindfulness on Emotional Interference

Our pooled analysis indicated that mindfulness had a beneficial effect on decreasing emotional interference. However, the strength of the evidence supporting this conclusion was low. The analysis included only four studies, all of which were of poor quality, and findings were inconsistent.

Summary

This appendix reported the findings of meta-analyses on the effect of mindfulness programs on five types of emotion regulation outcomes. Meta-analyses did not show an effect of mindfulness on general emotion regulation ability or change in negative mood intensity. However, the pooled analyses did show beneficial effects of mindfulness on increasing the use of reappraisal (an adaptive emotion regulation strategy), decreasing the use of suppression (a maladaptive emotion regulation strategy), and decreasing emotional interference with attention. The strength of the evidence for these conclusions was low because of the small numbers of studies, inconsistency in individual study results, and large number of poor-quality studies.

Effects of Mindfulness Meditation on Impulsivity, Morale, Productivity, and Social Support

In this appendix, we describe the results of our syntheses of the findings on the effect of mindfulness meditation on four additional outcomes for which we were able to perform meta-analysis: impulsivity and work-related morale, productivity, and social support. Box E.1 highlights key findings from these analyses. For an overview of each of these outcomes, see Chapter Four.

BOX E.1

Key Findings: Effects of Mindfulness Meditation on Impulsivity, Morale, Productivity, and Social Support

- Few studies assessed the effects of mindfulness meditation programs on impulsivity, morale, productivity, or social support.
- Mindfulness meditation showed beneficial effects on impulsivity, morale, and social support, but the strength of the evidence supporting these conclusions was low (for social support) or moderate at best (for impulsivity and morale).
- Mindfulness meditation appears to have no effect on productivity, but this conclusion was supported by low strength of evidence.

Impulsivity

Mindfulness Studies

We conducted a meta-analysis of three RCTs that assessed the effect of mindfulness meditation on impulsivity. We summarize study-level details in Table E.1. The assessed mindfulness studies enrolled university students and used self-report measures of impulsivity. Our pooled analysis showed a beneficial effect of the programs on self-reported impulsivity (SMD = 0.31; 95% CI = 0.10, 0.52; I^2 = 9.1%) (Figure E.1).

TABLE E.1

Study-Level Details for Studies That Assessed Impulsivity

Study ID	Participants	Intervention	Comparator	Outcome	Study Quality
RCTs (included in meta-analysis)					
Dundas, 2017	138 Norwegian university students, 85% female, mean age = 25.0 (SD = 4.9)	2-week, in-person, group mindfulness meditation training	Waitlist	Self-control scale for healthy impulse control	Good
Throuvala, 2020	252 UK undergraduate students, 82% female, mean age = 20.7 (SD = 3.3)	10-day, virtual, individual Headspace smartphone application	No intervention	Barratt Impulsiveness Scale, self-reported	Fair
Wenzel, 2020	134 German undergraduate students, 78% female, mean age = 22.9 (SD = 5.1)	6-week, in-person, individual mindfulness intervention	Waitlist	State Self-Control Capacity Scale and Self-Control Scale, self-reported measures of healthy impulse control	Good

FIGURE E.1

Estimates of the Effect on Impulsivity

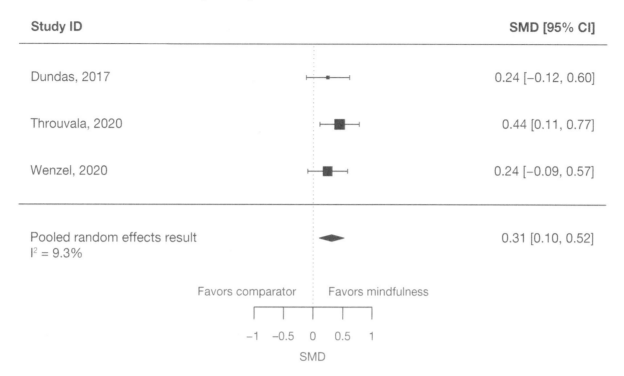

Study ID		SMD [95% CI]
Dundas, 2017		0.24 [−0.12, 0.60]
Throuvala, 2020		0.44 [0.11, 0.77]
Wenzel, 2020		0.24 [−0.09, 0.57]
Pooled random effects result $I^2 = 9.3\%$		0.31 [0.10, 0.52]

Additional Studies

Two analogue studies could not be included in pooled analyses. A 2018 RCT assessed the effects of a brief (ten-minute) mindful body scan practice on performance on a risk-taking behavior task among undergraduate students in a laboratory setting (Upton and Renshaw, 2018). The two groups showed no differences in risk-taking behavior at the end of the intervention period. In addition, a 2019 RCT assessed the effects of a brief (five-minute) mindful breathing exercise on *delay discounting*—a type of behavioral impulsivity that refers to a tendency to select smaller, immediately available rewards over larger but more delayed rewards—among 24 graduate students (Dixon et al., 2019). The mindful breathing group showed no significant difference in delay discounting compared with the comparison group in follow-up test scores.

Strength of the Evidence for the Effect of Mindfulness on Impulsivity

Our pooled analysis indicated that mindfulness programs had a small but beneficial effect on impulsivity. The strength of the evidence supporting this conclusion was moderate. Although outcomes were consistent and study quality was fair to good, the analysis included only three small studies with self-reported outcomes, and the confidence intervals were in the negative range in two of the three studies.

Work-Related Morale

Mindfulness Studies

We conducted a meta-analysis of four RCTs that assessed the impact of mindfulness programs on work-related morale. We also identified two non-randomized studies. We summarize study-level details in Table E.2.

Most of the four RCTs implemented MBSR-type programs, ranging in duration from five to eight weeks. All assessed self-reported measures of morale or job satisfaction. The forest plot in Figure E.2 shows a significant difference for the four studies combined (SMD = 0.33; 95% CI = 0.07, 0.58; I^2 = 1.1%, suggesting low heterogeneity). This finding indicates that mindfulness programs had a significant beneficial effect on work-related morale.

We identified two trials that met our inclusion criteria but assigned participants to a program or a waitlist control without randomization. At the end of the three-week program in one of these trials, the MBCT group showed a significant improvement in work-related morale compared with the control group (SMD = 0.85; 95% CI = 0.16, 1.55). The second non-randomized trial showed a statistically significant benefit of mindfulness meditation in terms of scores on a measure of global job satisfaction compared with the control group at eight weeks (SMD = 1.51; 95% CI = 0.93, 2.09) and at three months (SMD = 1.49; 95% CI = 0.86, 2.11).

TABLE E.2

Study-Level Details for Studies That Assessed Work-Related Morale

Study ID	Participants	Intervention	Comparator	Outcome	Study Quality
RCTs (included in meta-analysis)					
Hülsheger, 2013	64 German workers, 72% female, mean age = 38.6 (SD = 11.1)	2-week, virtual MBSR	Waitlist	Job satisfaction questions	Poor
Klatt, 2017	81 Danish bank employees, 69% female, mean age = 42.9 (SD = 9.3)	8-week, in-person, group Mindfulness in Motion intervention	Waitlist	Utrecht Work Engagement Scale	Poor
Lin, 2019	110 Chinese nurses, 93% female, mean age = 31.5 (SD = 6.8)	8-week, mixed in-person and virtual, group MBSR	Waitlist	McCloskey/Mueller Satisfaction Scale	Poor
Pang, 2019	34 Swiss community-dwelling adults, 69% female, mean age = 44.2 (SD = 10.0)	8-week, in-person, group MBSR	Waitlist	Job satisfaction questionnaire	Fair
Non-randomized studies (not included in meta-analysis)					
Coo, 2018	36 Spanish hospital employees, 80% female, mean age = 37.1 (SD = 6.4)	3-week, in-person, group MBCT	Waitlist	Utrecht Work Engagement Scale	Not applicable
Van Gordon, 2017	73 UK adults, fully employed and suffering from "workaholism," 41% female, mean age = 38.7 (SD = 8.4)	8-week, in-person, mixed individual and group meditation awareness training	Waitlist	Abridged Job in General Scale	Not applicable

FIGURE E.2

Estimates of the Effect on Work-Related Morale

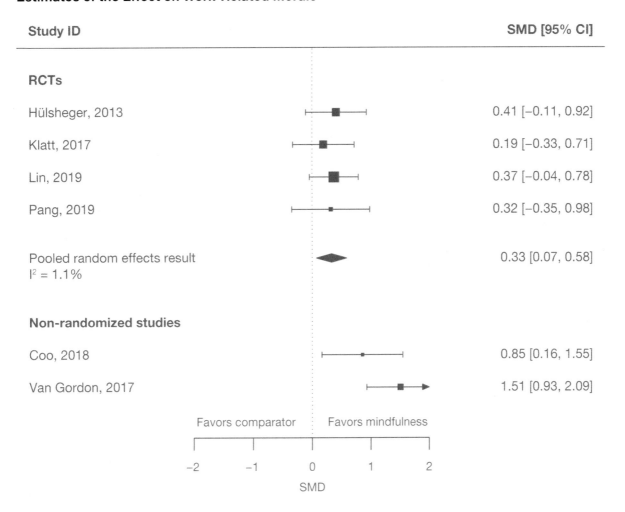

Additional Studies

We identified two additional RCTs that could not be included in pooled analysis. One study could not be included because it did not report a standard deviation (Steinberg, Klatt, and Duchemin, 2016), and another could not be included because it reported its findings as odds ratios (Ghawadra et al., 2020).

The Steinberg, Klatt, and Duchemin (2016) study was a small, eight-week study that compared the effect of the Mindfulness in Motion program with the effect of a waitlist control. Total follow-up scores on the Utrecht Work Engagement Scale were significantly higher than they were prior to program participation in the active intervention group but not in the control group; however, we could not determine the difference between the scores of the intervention group and the control group. The Ghawadra et al. (2020) study was a large trial that compared the effect of a multicomponent mindfulness program with that of a passive comparison on the odds of scoring within the normal range on the Job Satisfaction Scale for Nurses. The study reported a significant beneficial effect of the program on job satisfaction (odds ratio = 8.83; 95% CI = 1.96, 39.82).

Strength of Evidence for the Effect of Mindfulness on Work-Related Morale

Our pooled analysis indicated a beneficial effect of mindfulness training on work-related morale. The strength of the evidence supporting this conclusion was moderate. Four pooled RCTs showed direct, fairly consistent effects in favor of the programs, although the lower limit of the confidence interval was in the negative for all of the studies, and study quality was poor to fair.

Work-Related Productivity

Mindfulness Studies

We conducted a meta-analysis of three RCTs that assessed the effect of mindfulness programs on work-related productivity. We summarize study-level details in Table E.3. All three studies compared an in-person intervention with a passive control in groups of workers. One of the studies used a self-report measure of productivity, the Work Limitations Questionnaire, and two used observer-based measures of productivity—monthly work performance or the supervisor-completed Task Performance Questionnaire.

The forest plot in Figure E.3 shows a nonsignificant pooled effect size (SMD = 0.08; 95% CI = −0.20, 0.35; I^2 = 4.8%, suggesting low heterogeneity). This finding indicates that mindfulness programs had no observable effect on work-related productivity.

TABLE E.3

Study-Level Details for Studies That Assessed Work-Related Productivity

Study ID	Participants	Intervention	Comparator	Outcome	Study Quality
RCTs (included in meta-analysis)					
Allexandre, 2016	45 U.S. corporate call center employees, 83% female, mean age = 40.0 (SD = 12.6)	8-week, virtual, individual Stress Free Now course; 8-week, mixed in-person and virtual, group Stress Free Now course	Waitlist control	Reported monthly work performance	Fair
Pang, 2019	34 Swiss community-dwelling adults, 69% female, mean age = 44.2 (SD = 10.0)	8-week, in-person, group MBSR; 8-week, in-person, group mindfulness-based strengths practice	Waitlist control	Task Performance Questionnaire for supervisory rating of performance	Fair
Wolever, 2012	149 U.S. insurance company employees, 77% female, mean age = 42.9 (SD = 9.7)	12-week, in-person, group Mindfulness at Work; 12-week, virtual synchronous, group Mindfulness at Work	No intervention	Work Limitations Questionnaire	Fair

FIGURE E.3

Estimates of the Effect on Work-Related Productivity

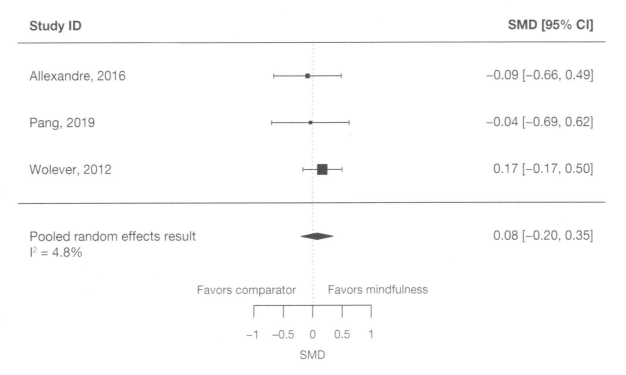

Study ID		SMD [95% CI]
Allexandre, 2016		−0.09 [−0.66, 0.49]
Pang, 2019		−0.04 [−0.69, 0.62]
Wolever, 2012		0.17 [−0.17, 0.50]
Pooled random effects result $I^2 = 4.8\%$		0.08 [−0.20, 0.35]

Additional Studies

One study was not included in the pooled analysis because it had an active comparison group (Deady et al., 2020). In this study, productivity was assessed using a self-report measure, the Health and Work Performance Questionnaire. This RCT indicated no difference in outcomes between the intervention and control group at the end of the study, but when the authors reassessed the participants at three and 12 months of follow-up, the group that received the mindfulness program had significantly higher self-reported productivity than the comparison group did.

Strength of Evidence for the Effect of Mindfulness on Work-Related Productivity

We found no evidence for an effect of mindfulness on work-related productivity. However, the strength of the evidence supporting this conclusion was low, meaning that additional studies could show a net beneficial effect of mindfulness on productivity or could strengthen the evidence for no effect. The findings among pooled studies were consistent and precise, but the number of studies that met the inclusion criteria was small, the studies included small samples, and different outcome measures were used.

Work-Related Social Support

Mindfulness Studies

We conducted a meta-analysis of three RCTs that assessed the effect of mindfulness programs on measures of work-related social support. We summarize study-level details in Table E.4. All three studies used a mindfulness intervention and passive controls. Study duration for the three mindfulness interventions ranged from eight to ten weeks, and intervention content and format varied somewhat. The forest plot in Figure E.4 shows a significant difference in favor of a beneficial effect of mindfulness on work-related social support (SMD = 0.54; 95% CI = 0.08, 1.00; I^2 = 70.0%, suggesting considerable heterogeneity).

Additional Studies

One article reported on two additional studies—denoted in this report as Hafenbrack, 2020 (1a), and Hafenbrack, 2020 (1b). These could not be included in the pooled analysis because one tested an analogue intervention, and both employed active comparison groups. Both studies reported that participants in the intervention groups had higher scores for providing social support than did their respective control groups, based on self-, team member, and supervisor evaluations. These findings also support a beneficial effect of a mindfulness on social support.

Strength of Evidence for the Effect of Mindfulness on Work-Related Social Support

Our pooled analysis indicated a beneficial effect of mindfulness training on work-related social support. The strength of the evidence supporting this conclusion was low. Three pooled RCTs showed direct, relatively consistent effects in favor of the mindfulness programs, but two of the studies were small, the lower limit of the 95-percent confidence interval was slightly in the negative for one of the studies, and study quality was poor to fair. The findings of an analogue study supported the findings of the pooled analysis, but that study had poor quality.

TABLE E.4

Study-Level Details for Studies That Assessed Work-Related Social Support

Study ID	Participants	Intervention	Comparator	Outcome	Study Quality
RCTs (included in meta-analysis)					
Bostock, 2019	238 UK high-tech and pharmaceutical employees, 59% female, mean age = 35.5 (SD = 7.7)	8-week, virtual Headspace smartphone application	Waitlist	Workplace social support 5-item questionnaire	Poor
Molek-Winiarska, 2018	66 Polish mining and other underground workers, 0% female, mean age = 40.4 (SD = 6.8)	10-week, in-person, mixed individual and group MBSR	No intervention	Job Content Questionnaire	Poor
Wingert, 2020	58 U.S. working undergraduate students, 52.6% female, mean age = 18.9 (SD = 1.3)	8-week, in-person, group mindfulness-based strengths practice	No intervention	Workplace PERMA profiler relationships subscale	Fair

NOTE: PERMA = positive emotion, engagement, relationships, meaning, and accomplishment.

FIGURE E.4

Estimates of the Effect on Work-Related Social Support

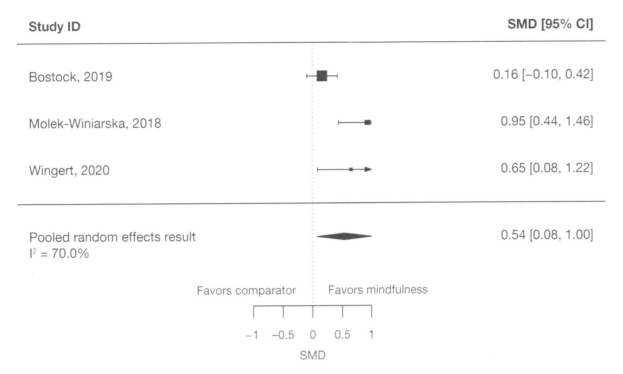

Study ID		SMD [95% CI]
Bostock, 2019		0.16 [−0.10, 0.42]
Molek-Winiarska, 2018		0.95 [0.44, 1.46]
Wingert, 2020		0.65 [0.08, 1.22]
Pooled random effects result $I^2 = 70.0\%$		0.54 [0.08, 1.00]

Summary

This appendix reported the findings of meta-analyses on the effect of mindfulness programs on four outcomes: impulsivity, morale, productivity, and social support. We found beneficial effects of mindfulness meditation programs on impulsivity, morale, and social support. However, because of the small numbers of studies, the strength of evidence was moderate for our conclusions regarding impulsivity and morale and low for the conclusion on social support. Finally, our analysis showed no benefit of mindfulness on productivity, and that conclusion was also supported by only a low strength of evidence.

Effects of Mindfulness Meditation on Decisionmaking, Communication Skills, and Teamwork

In this appendix, we describe the findings for outcomes that could not be included in a meta-analysis because the number of studies was too small, the studies' important characteristics (e.g., the type of intervention or comparison group used) were too dissimilar to be combined in a pooled analysis, or no studies met the inclusion criteria. These outcomes are decisionmaking, communication skills, and teamwork. Box F.1 highlights selected key findings that are presented in this chapter. For an overview of each of the outcomes examined here, see Chapter Four.

BOX F.1

Key Findings: Effects of Mindfulness Meditation on Decisionmaking, Communication Skills, and Teamwork

- Few studies were identified that evaluated the effects of mindfulness meditation on decisionmaking, communication skills, or teamwork.
- The impact of mindfulness on decisionmaking, communication skills, and teamwork is unknown, and more studies are needed before drawing conclusions.

Decisionmaking

Mindfulness Interventions

Although measures of decisionmaking are varied and can be context-specific, many are either self-reported or task-based performance measures (Bruine de Bruin, Parker and Fischhoff, 2007). We identified two studies that met our inclusion criteria and assessed the effect of mindfulness meditation on decisionmaking. Both used performance-based outcomes. We summarize study-level details in Table F.1.

A 2019 RCT that enrolled 61 U.S. law enforcement officers from six local police departments assessed the effects of mindfulness-based resilience training on the Shooter Bias Task, a type of decisionmaking test that requires participants to determine whether individuals shown in computer simulations and varying in apparent racial identity are carrying a weapon (Hunsinger, Christopher, and Schmidt, 2019). The officers were randomized to the mindfulness intervention or a no-intervention control group and were tested before, immediately after, and three months after the intervention. The intervention program design was based on MBSR (Kabat-Zinn, 2012). No differences in task performance were observed between the groups either at baseline or after the intervention. Thus mindfulness-based resilience training had no apparent impact on this type of decisionmaking.

A 2019 RCT that enrolled 160 U.S. community-dwelling adults assessed the effects of including a mindfulness meditation component in a multimodal intervention on decisionmaking (Zwilling et al., 2019). The 16-week intervention combined in-person high-intensity cardio-resistance fitness training and virtual cognitive training with in-person weekly mindfulness meditation sessions. An active comparison group received only the fitness and cognitive components. Decisionmaking was assessed through the Adult Decision-Making Competence test, which uses seven groups of tasks to assess how well individuals make decisions. The tasks are structured around what are thought to be the three key aspects of decisionmaking competency: value assessment (the capacity to assess the value of possible actions and their consequences), belief assessment (the ability to assess the likelihood that or the subjective belief that an event will occur), and information integration (the ability to combine available information to make a reasonable choice). Compared with the comparison group, the group that received the mindfulness intervention showed improved performance after the intervention, but the improvement was only in the value assessment domain. The groups did not differ in their post-intervention performance, but pre-intervention performance was significantly lower in the group that received the mindfulness intervention.

TABLE F.1

Study-Level Details for Studies That Assessed Decisionmaking

Study ID	Participants	Intervention	Comparator	Outcome	Study Quality
Hunsinger, 2019	61 U.S. law enforcement officers, 10% female, mean age = 44.0 (SD = 6.0)	8-week, in-person, mindfulness-based resilience training	No intervention	Shooter Bias Task performance	Poor
Zwilling, 2019	160 U.S. community-dwelling adults, 52% female, mean age = 23.8 (SD not reported)	16-week, mixed in-person and virtual, mixed individual and group high-intensity cardio-resistance fitness training with mindfulness meditation training	Fitness training and cognitive skills training	Adult Decision-Making Competence test: 7 sets of tasks	Poor

Strength of the Evidence for the Effect of Mindfulness on Decisionmaking

With the findings from two studies that were highly heterogeneous with respect to interventions and outcome measures, the evidence for the effect of mindfulness meditation on decisionmaking is insufficient to draw a conclusion about the effect of mindfulness on decisionmaking.

Work-Related Communication Skills

Mindfulness Interventions

We identified one study that met our inclusion criteria and assessed the effect of mindfulness meditation on communication skills. We summarize study-level details in Table F.2. This 2019 study of health care workers in New Zealand compared the effects of a four-week mindfulness training program with the effects of a communication skills training program on the self-reported Interpersonal Communication Competence Scale at three time points: the end of the four weeks, three months later, and six months later. The study showed comparable improvements in workplace communication skills for both groups at the end of the intervention, and the effects were sustained at three and six months.

Strength of the Evidence for the Effect of Mindfulness on Work-Related Communication Skills

The evidence from this one study is insufficient to draw a conclusion about the effect of mindfulness meditation on work-related communication skills.

Work-Related Teamwork

Mindfulness Interventions

We identified two studies that that met our inclusion criteria and assessed the effect of mindfulness program on a measure of work-related teamwork (Table F.3). We summarize study-level details in Table F.3.

A 2014 study (Shonin et al., 2014) randomized 152 middle managers in a UK company to an eight-week mindfulness training program or an educational program on cognitive behavioral therapy theory and principles. At the end of three months, the group that had received mindfulness training had significantly higher scores on a survey of teamwork (SMD = 1.55; 95% CI = 1.17, 1.94).

TABLE F.2

Study-Level Details for Studies That Assessed Work-Related Communication Skills

Study ID	Participants	Intervention	Comparator	Outcome	Study Quality
Baby, 2019	127 New Zealand health care workers, 78% female, age reported in quantiles	4-week, in-person, mindfulness training	Communication skills training	Interpersonal Communication Competence Scale	Fair

TABLE F.3

Study-Level Details for Studies That Assessed Work-Related Teamwork

Study ID	Participants	Intervention	Comparator	Outcome	Study Quality
Shonin, 2014	152 UK office middle managers, 57% female, mean age = 40.1 (SD = 8.1)	8-week meditation awareness training	Education on cognitive behavioral therapy theory and principles	Role-Based Performance Scale team member performance	Good
Hafenbrack, 2020 (1a)	146 U.S. insurance company employees, 83% female, mean age = 41.1 (SD = 10.5)	7-minute virtual mindfulness analogue	Radio show recording	Rating of teamwork by other team members	Poor

Although the Hafenbrack et al., (2020) publication reported on five studies, only one study (Hafenbrack, 2020 (1a)) met inclusion criteria for this analysis. This study randomly assigned employees of an insurance company in the United States to a brief (seven-minute) mindfulness analogue or an active comparison condition. The analogue intervention consisted of listening to an audio recording of a focused breathing mindfulness meditation, while the comparison group listened to a radio news report on a technology topic. At the end of the workday, each participant rated how much they helped coworkers during that day. Teamwork did not differ significantly between groups.

Strength of the Evidence for the Effect of Mindfulness on Work-Related Teamwork

The evidence from the two studies identified is insufficient to draw a conclusion about the effect of mindfulness on work-related teamwork.

Summary

This appendix reviewed the evidence for the effect of mindfulness meditation programs on three outcomes—decisionmaking, work-related communication skills, and work-related teamwork—for which we identified an insufficient number of similar studies to conduct meta-analyses. There was thus insufficient evidence to support conclusions about the effects on these outcomes, and more studies are needed to better assess the potential effect of mindfulness meditation.

Abbreviations

AHRQ	Agency for Healthcare Research and Quality
AMSTAR 2	A MeaSurement Tool to Assess Systematic Reviews, 2nd version
ANT	Attention Network Test
CI	confidence interval
DoD	U.S. Department of Defense
GRADE	Grading of Recommendation, Assessment, Development, and Evaluation
MBAT	mindfulness-based attention training
MBCT	mindfulness-based cognitive therapy
MBSR	mindfulness-based stress reduction
MMFT	mindfulness-based mind fitness training
PICOTSS	participants, intervention, comparator, outcome, timing, setting, and study design
PRISMA	Preferred Reporting Items for Systematic Reviews and Meta-Analyses
PROSPERO	International Prospective Register of Systematic Reviews
RCT	randomized controlled trial
SART	sustained attention to response task
SD	standard deviation
SMD	standardized mean difference
UK	United Kingdom

References

Sources Cited

Adhikari, Kishor, Farida Kothari, and Anjana Khadka, "The Effect of Short-Term Training of Vipassana's Body-Scan on Select Cognitive Functions," *Psychological Studies*, Vol. 63, No. 3, August 2018, pp. 228–235.

Adler, Amy B., and Carl Andrew Castro, "An Occupational Mental Health Model for the Military," *Military Behavioral Health*, Vol. 1, No. 1, January 1, 2013, pp. 41–45.

Adler, Amy B., Jason Williams, Dennis McGurk, Andrew Moss, and Paul D. Bliese, "Resilience Training with Soldiers During Basic Combat Training: Randomisation by Platoon," *Applied Psychology: Health and Well-Being*, Vol. 7, No. 1, March 2015, pp. 85–107.

Agency for Healthcare Research and Quality, *Methods Guide for Effectiveness and Comparative Effectiveness Reviews*, Washington, D.C., AHRQ Publication No. 10(14)-EHC063-EF, January 2014.

AHRQ—*See* Agency for Healthcare Research and Quality.

Alavinia, Seyed M., Duco Molenaar, and Alex Burdorf, "Productivity Loss in the Workforce: Associations with Health, Work Demands, and Individual Characteristics," *American Journal of Industrial Medicine*, Vol. 52, No. 1, January 2009, pp. 49–56.

Aldao, Amelia, Susan Nolen-Hoeksema, and Susanne Schweizer, "Emotion-Regulation Strategies Across Psychopathology: A Meta-Analytic Review," *Clinical Psychology Review*, Vol. 30, No. 2, 2010, pp. 217–237.

Alkoby, Alon, Ruthie Pliskin, Eran Halperin, and Nava Levit-Binnun, "An Eight-Week Mindfulness-Based Stress Reduction (MBSR) Workshop Increases Regulatory Choice Flexibility," *Emotion*, Vol. 19, No. 4, June 1, 2019, pp. 593–604.

Allen, Micah, Martin Dietz, Karina S. Blair, Martijn van Beek, Geraint Rees, Peter Vestergaard-Poulsen, Antoine Lutz, and Andreas Roepstorff, "Cognitive-Affective Neural Plasticity Following Active-Controlled Mindfulness Intervention," *Journal of Neuroscience*, Vol. 32, No. 44, October 31, 2012, pp. 15601–15610.

Alsubaie, Modi, Rebecca Abbott, Barnaby Dunn, Chris Dickens, Tina Frieda Keil, William Henley, and Willem Kuyken, "Mechanisms of Action in Mindfulness-Based Cognitive Therapy (MBCT) and Mindfulness-Based Stress Reduction (MBSR) in People with Physical and/or Psychological Conditions: A Systematic Review," *Clinical Psychology Review*, Vol. 55, July 2017, pp. 74–91.

American Psychological Association, "Stress Effects on the Body," webpage, November 1, 2018. As of July 7, 2021: https://www.apa.org/topics/stress/body

Anheyer, Dennis, Heidemarie Haller, Jurgen Barth, Romy Lauche, Gustav Dobos, and Holger Cramer, "Mindfulness-Based Stress Reduction for Treating Low Back Pain: A Systematic Review and Meta-Analysis," *Annals of Internal Medicine*, Vol. 166, No. 11, June 6, 2017, pp. 799–807.

Balshem, Howard, Mark Helfand, Holger Schunemann, Andrew Oxman, Regina Kunz, Jan Brozek, Gunn Vist, Yngve Falck-Ytter, Joerg Meerpohl, Susan Norris, and Gordon Guyatt, "GRADE Guidelines: 3. Rating the Quality of Evidence," *Journal of Clinical Epidemiology*, Vol. 64, No. 4, April 2011, pp. 401–406.

Bandoli, Gretchen, Laura Campbell-Sills, Ronald C. Kessler, Steven G. Heeringa, Matthew K. Nock, Anthony J. Rosellini, Nancy A. Sampson, Michael Schoenbaum, Robert J. Ursano, and Murray B. Stein, "Childhood Adversity, Adult Stress, and the Risk of Major Depression or Generalized Anxiety Disorder in US Soldiers: A Test of the Stress Sensitization Hypothesis," *Psychological Medicine*, Vol. 47, No. 13, October 1, 2017, pp. 2379–2392.

Banks, Jonathan B., Amishi P. Jha, Audrey V. B. Hood, Haley G. Goller, and Lindsay L. Craig, "Reducing the TUTs that Hurt: The Impact of a Brief Mindfulness Induction on Emotionally Valenced Mind Wandering," *Journal of Cognitive Psychology*, Vol. 31, No. 8, 2019, pp. 785–799.

Barattucci, Massimiliano, Anna M. Padovan, Ermanno Vitale, Venerando Rapisarda, Tiziana Ramaci, and Andrea De Giorgio, "Mindfulness-Based IARA Model® Proves Effective to Reduce Stress and Anxiety in Health Care Professionals. A Six-Month Follow-Up Study," *International Journal of Environmental Research and Public Health*, Vol. 16, No. 22, November 12, 2019.

Bartlett, Larissa, Angela Martin, Amanda L. Neil, Kate Memish, Petr Otahal, Michelle Kilpatrick, and Kristy Sanderson, "A Systematic Review and Meta-Analysis of Workplace Mindfulness Training Randomized Controlled Trials," *Journal of Occupational Health Psychology*, Vol. 24, No. 1, February 2019, pp. 108–126.

Be Mindful, homepage, Wellmind Health Ltd., undated. As of May 24, 2021:
https://www.bemindfulonline.com

Beaton, Dorcas, Claire Bombardier, Reuben Escorpizo, Wei Zhang, Diane Lacaille, Annelies Boonen, Richard H. Osborne, Aslam H. Anis, C. Vibeke Strand, and Peter S. Tugwell, "Measuring Worker Productivity: Frameworks and Measures," *Journal of Rheumatology*, Vol. 36, No. 9, September 2009, pp. 2100–2109.

Black, Sandra A., M. Shayne Gallaway, Michael R. Bell, and Elspeth C. Ritchie, "Prevalence and Risk Factors Associated with Suicides of Army Soldiers 2001–2009," *Military Psychology*, Vol. 23, No. 4, July 1, 2011, pp. 433–451.

Brief, Arthur P., and Howard M. Weiss, "Organizational Behavior: Affect in the Workplace," *Annual Review of Psychology*, Vol. 53, No. 1, 2002, pp. 279–307.

Brintz, Carrie E., Shari Miller, Kristine R. Olmsted, Michael Bartoszek, Joel Cartwright, Paul N. Kizakevich, Michael Butler, Nakisa Asefnia, Alex Buben, and Susan A. Gaylord, "Adapting Mindfulness Training for Military Service Members with Chronic Pain," *Military Medicine*, Vol. 185, No. 3–4, March 2, 2020, pp. 385–393.

Bruine de Bruin, Wändi, Andrew M. Parker, and Baruch Fischhoff, "Individual Differences in Adult Decision-Making Competence," *Journal of Personality and Social Psychology*, Vol. 92, No. 5, 2007, pp. 938–956.

Brunyé, Tad T., Randy Brou, Tracy Jill Doty, Frederick D. Gregory, Erika K. Hussey, Harris R. Lieberman, Kari L. Loverro, Elizabeth S. Mezzacappa, William H. Neumeier, Debra J. Patton, Jason W. Soares, Thaddeus P. Thomas, and Alfred B. Yu, "A Review of US Army Research Contributing to Cognitive Enhancement in Military Contexts," *Journal of Cognitive Enhancement*, Vol. 4, No. 4, December 1, 2020, pp. 453–468.

Burgdorf, Virginia, Marianna Szabó, and Maree J. Abbott, "The Effect of Mindfulness Interventions for Parents on Parenting Stress and Youth Psychological Outcomes: A Systematic Review and Meta-Analysis," *Frontiers in Psychology*, Vol. 10, June 6, 2019, article 1336.

Campbell, Donald J., and Orly Ben-Yoav Nobel, "Occupational Stressors in Military Service: A Review and Framework," *Military Psychology*, Vol. 21, Supp. 2, October 15, 2009, pp. S47–S67.

Campbell-Sills, Laura, Robert J. Ursano, Ronald C. Kessler, Xiaoying Sun, Steven G. Heeringa, Matthew K. Nock, Nancy A. Sampson, Sonia Jain, and Murray B. Stein, "Prospective Risk Factors for Post-Deployment Heavy Drinking and Alcohol or Substance Use Disorder Among US Army Soldiers," *Psychological Medicine*, Vol. 48, No. 10, July 10, 2018, pp. 1624–1633.

Chambles, Dianne L., and Steven D. Hollon, "Defining Empirically Supported Therapies," *Journal of Consulting and Clinical Psychology*, Vol. 66, No. 1, 1998, pp. 7–18.

Chamorro, Jaime, Silvia Bernardi, Marc N. Potenza, Jon E. Grant, Rachel Marsh, Shuai Wang, and Carlos Blanco, "Impulsivity in the General Population: A National Study," *Journal of Psychiatric Research*, Vol. 46, No. 8, August 2012, pp. 994–1001.

Chiesa, Alberto, "Zen Meditation: An Integration of Current Evidence," *Journal of Alternative and Complementary Medicine*, Vol. 15, No. 5, May 2009, pp. 585–592.

Chiesa, Alberto, and Peter Malinowski, "Mindfulness-Based Approaches: Are They All the Same?" *Journal of Clinical Psychology*, Vol. 67, No. 4, April 2011, pp. 404–424.

Chiesa, Alberto, and Alessandro Serretti, "Mindfulness-Based Stress Reduction for Stress Management in Healthy People: A Review and Meta-Analysis," *Journal of Alternative and Complementary Medicine*, Vol. 15, May 15, 2009, pp. 593–600.

———, "A Systematic Review of Neurobiological and Clinical Features of Mindfulness Meditations," *Psychological Medicine*, Vol. 40, No. 8, August 2010, pp. 1239–1252.

Ching, Ho-Hoi, Malcolm Koo, Tsung-Huang Tsai, and Chiu-Yuan Chen, "Effects of a Mindfulness Meditation Course on Learning and Cognitive Performance Among University Students in Taiwan," *Evidence-Based Complementary and Alternative Medicine*, Vol. 2015, 2015, article 254358.

Coll, Cynthia Garcia, Anna Akerman, and Dante Cicchetti, "Cultural Influences on Developmental Processes and Outcomes: Implications for the Study of Development and Psychopathology," *Development and Psychopathology*, Vol. 12, No. 3, Summer, 2000, pp. 333–356.

Consort, homepage, undated. As of January 31, 2022:
http://www.consort-statement.org/

Crane, R. S., J. Brewer, C. Feldman, J. Kabat-Zinn, S. Santorelli, J. M. G. Williams, and W. Kuyken, "What Defines Mindfulness-Based Programs? The Warp and the Weft," *Psychological Medicine*, Vol. 47, No. 6, April 2017, pp. 990–999.

Crane, Rebecca S., and Frederick M. Hecht, "Intervention Integrity in Mindfulness-Based Research," *Mindfulness*, Vol. 9, No. 5, 2018, pp. 1370–1380.

Crane, Rebecca S., Willem Kuyken, J. Mark G. Williams, Richard P. Hastings, Lucinda Cooper, and Melanie J. V. Fennell, "Competence in Teaching Mindfulness-Based Courses: Concepts, Development and Assessment," *Mindfulness*, Vol. 3, No. 1, March 2012, pp. 76–84.

Creswell, J. David, "Mindfulness Interventions," *Annual Review of Psychology*, Vol. 68, No. 1, March 1, 2017, pp. 491–516.

Crowe, Marie, Jennifer Jordan, Beverley Burrell, Virginia Jones, Deborah Gillon, and Shirley Harris, "Mindfulness-Based Stress Reduction for Long-Term Physical Conditions: A Systematic Review," *Australian and New Zealand Journal of Psychiatry*, Vol. 50, No. 1, January 2016, pp. 21–32.

Deady, Mark, Nicholas Glozier, Rafael Calvo, David Johnston, Andrew Mackinnon, David Milne, Isabella Choi, Aimee Gayed, Dorian Peters, Richard Bryant, Helen Christensen, and Samuel B. Harvey, "Preventing Depression Using a Smartphone App: A Randomized Controlled Trial," *Psychological Medicine*, July 6, 2020, pp. 1–10.

Denkova, Ekaterina, Anthony P. Zanesco, Scott L. Rogers, and Amishi P. Jha, "Is Resilience Trainable? An Initial Study Comparing Mindfulness and Relaxation Training in Firefighters," *Psychiatry Research*, Vol. 285, January 16, 2020, article 112794.

Deuster, Patricia A., and Eric Schoomaker, "Mindfulness: A Fundamental Skill for Performance Sustainment and Enhancement," *Journal of Special Operations Medicine*, Vol. 15, No. 1, Spring 2015, pp. 93–99.

Dimidjian, Sona, and Zindel V. Segal, "Prospects for a Clinical Science of Mindfulness-Based Intervention," *American Psychologist*, Vol. 70, No. 7, October 2015, pp. 593–620.

DiRenzo, Marco S., Jennifer Tosti-Kharas, and Edward H. Powley, "Called to Serve: Exploring the Relationship Between Career Calling, Career Plateaus, and Organizational Commitment in the U.S. Military," *Journal of Career Assessment*, Vol. 30, No. 1, 2022, pp. 60–77.

Dixon, Mark R., Dana Paliliunas, Jordan Belisle, Ryan C. Speelman, Karl F. Gunnarsson, and Jordan L. Shaffer, "The Effect of Brief Mindfulness Training on Momentary Impulsivity," *Journal of Contextual Behavioral Science*, Vol. 11, January 2019, pp. 15–20.

DoD—*See* U.S. Department of Defense.

Dreeben, Samuel J., Michelle Mamberg, and Paul Salmon, "The MBSR Body Scan in Clinical Practice," *Mindfulness*, Vol. 4, No. 4, 2013, pp. 394–401.

Eberth, Juliane, and Peter Sedlmeier, "The Effects of Mindfulness Meditation: A Meta-Analysis," *Mindfulness*, Vol. 3, No. 3, May 2, 2012, pp. 174–189.

Emerson, Lisa-Marie, Natalja Nabinger de Diaz, Ashra Sherwood, Allison Waters, and Lara Farrell, "Mindfulness Interventions in Schools: Integrity and Feasibility of Implementation," *International Journal of Behavioral Development*, Vol. 44, No. 1, 2020, pp. 62–75.

Everson, Ronald Blaine, Carol Anderson Darling, and Joseph R. Herzog, "Parenting Stress Among US Army Spouses During Combat-Related Deployments: The Role of Sense of Coherence," *Child & Family Social Work*, Vol. 18, No. 2, 2013, pp. 168–178.

Fan, Jin, Bruce D. McCandliss, Tobias Sommer, Amir Raz, and Michael I. Posner, "Testing the Efficiency and Independence of Attentional Networks," *Journal of Cognitive Neuroscience*, Vol. 14, No. 3, 2002, pp. 340–347.

Faraone, Stephen V., "Interpreting Estimates of Treatment Effects: Implications for Managed Care," *Pharmacy & Therapeutics*, Vol. 33, No. 12, December 2008, pp. 700–711.

Fjorback, L. O., M. Arendt, E. Ornbøl, P. Fink, and H. Walach, "Mindfulness-Based Stress Reduction and Mindfulness-Based Cognitive Therapy: A Systematic Review of Randomized Controlled Trials," *Acta Psychiatrica Scandinavica*, Vol. 124, No. 2, August 2011, pp. 102–119.

Flook, Lisa, Simon B. Goldberg, Laura Pinger, Katherine A. Bonus, and Richard J. Davidson, "Mindfulness for Teachers: A Pilot Study to Assess Effects on Stress, Burnout, and Teaching Efficacy," *Mind, Brain, and Education*, Vol. 7, No. 3, December 7, 2013.

Freeman, Nicholas, and Mark Muraven, "Self-Control Depletion Leads to Increased Risk Taking," *Social Psychological and Personality Science*, Vol. 1, No. 2, 2010, pp. 175–181.

Friborg, Oddgeir, Dag Barlaug, Monica Martinussen, Jan H. Rosenvinge, and Odin Hjemdal, "Resilience in Relation to Personality and Intelligence," *International Journal of Methods in Psychiatric Research*, Vol. 14, No. 1, 2005, pp. 29–42.

Garland, Eric L., Adam Hanley, Norman A. Farb, and Brett E. Froeliger, "State Mindfulness During Meditation Predicts Enhanced Cognitive Reappraisal," *Mindfulness*, Vol. 6, No. 2, April 1, 2015, pp. 234–242.

Gewirtz, Abigail H., David S. DeGarmo, and Osnat Zamir, "Testing a Military Family Stress Model," *Family Process*, Vol. 57, No. 2, June 1, 2018, pp. 415–431.

Ghawadra, Sajed F., Khatijah Lim Abdullah, Wan Yuen Choo, Mahmoud Danaee, and Cheng Kar Phang, "The Effect of Mindfulness-Based Training on Stress, Anxiety, Depression and Job Satisfaction Among Ward Nurses: A Randomized Control Trial," *Journal of Nursing Management*, Vol. 28, No. 5, July 2020, pp. 1088–1097.

Gilmartin, Heather, Anupama Goyal, Mary C. Hamati, Jason Mann, Sanjay Saint, and Vineet Chopra, "Brief Mindfulness Practices for Healthcare Providers—A Systematic Literature Review," *American Journal of Medicine*, Vol. 130, No. 10, October 1, 2017, pp. 1219.e1211–1219.e1217.

Goldberg, Simon B., Raymond P. Tucker, Preston A. Greene, Tracy L. Simpson, David J. Kearney, and Richard J. Davidson, "Is Mindfulness Research Methodology Improving over Time? A Systematic Review," *PLOS ONE*, Vol. 12, No. 10, 2017, article e0187298.

Grant, Sean, Benjamin Colaiaco, Aneesa Motala, Roberta M. Shanman, Marika Booth, Melony E. Sorbero, and Susanne Hempel, "Mindfulness-Based Relapse Prevention for Substance Use Disorders: A Systematic Review and Meta-Analysis," *Journal of Addiction Medicine*, Vol. 11, No. 5, September–October 2017, pp. 386–396.

Gratz, Kim L., and Lizabeth Roemer, "Multidimensional Assessment of Emotion Regulation and Dysregulation: Development, Factor Structure, and Initial Validation of the Difficulties in Emotion Regulation Scale," *Journal of Psychopathology and Behavioral Assessment*, Vol. 26, No. 1, March 2004, pp. 41–54.

Grier, Rebecca A., "Military Cognitive Readiness at the Operational and Strategic Levels: A Theoretical Model for Measurement Development," *Journal of Cognitive Engineering and Decision Making*, Vol. 6, No. 4, 2012, pp. 358–392.

Gross, James J., "The Emerging Field of Emotion Regulation: An Integrative Review," *Review of General Psychology*, Vol. 2, No. 3, September 1, 1998, pp. 271–299.

Gross, James J., and Oliver P. John, "Individual Differences in Two Emotion Regulation Processes: Implications for Affect, Relationships, and Well-Being," *Journal of Personality and Social Psychology*, Vol. 85, No. 2, August 2003, pp. 348–362.

Gutierrez, Ian A., Elizabeth A. Alders, Zainah Abulhawa, and Patricia A. Deuster, "VICTORS: A Conceptual Framework for Implementing and Measuring Military Spiritual Fitness," *Military Behavioral Health*, Vol. 9, No. 4, 2021, pp. 375–389.

Guyatt, Gordon, Andrew Oxman, Elie Aki, Regina Kunz, Gunn Vist, Jan Brozek, Susan Norris, Yngve Falck-Ytter, Paul Glasziou, Hans deBeer, Roman Jaeschke, David Rind, Joerg Meerpohl, Philipp Dahm, and Holger Schunemann, "GRADE Guidelines: 1. Introduction—GRADE Evidence Profiles and Summary of Findings Tables," *Journal of Clinical Epidemiology*, Vol. 64, No. 4, April 2011, pp. 383–394.

Hafenbrack, Andrew. C., Lindsey D. Cameron, Gretchen M. Spreitzer, Chen Zhang, Laura J. Noval, and Samah Shaffakat, "Helping People by Being in the Present: Mindfulness Increases Prosocial Behavior," *Organizational Behavior and Human Decision Processes*, Vol. 159, July 2020, pp. 21–38.

Harms, Peter D., Dina V. Krasikova, Adam J. Vanhove, Mitchel Norman Herian, and Paul B. Lester, "Stress and Emotional Well-Being in Military Organizations," in Pamela L. Perrewe, Christopher C. Rosen, and Jonathon R. B. Halbesleben, eds., *The Role of Emotion and Emotion Regulation in Job Stress and Well Being*, Bingley, United Kingdom: Emerald Group Publishing Limited, 2013, pp. 103–132.

Harris, J. Irene, Ann Marie Winskowski, and Brian E. Engdahl, "Types of Workplace Social Support in the Prediction of Job Satisfaction," *Career Development Quarterly*, Vol. 56, No. 2, 2007, pp. 150–156.

Hartung, Joachim, "An Alternative Method for Meta-Analysis," *Biometric Journal*, Vol. 41, No. 8, 1999, pp. 906–916.

Hausman, C., B. N. Meffert, M. K. Mosich, and A. J. Heinz, "Impulsivity and Cognitive Flexibility as Neuropsychological Markers for Suicidality: A Multi-Modal Investigation Among Military Veterans with Alcohol Use Disorder and PTSD," *Archives of Suicide Research*, Vol. 24, No. 3, July–September 2020, pp. 313–326.

Heckenberg, Rachel A., Pennie Eddy, Stephen Kent, and Bradley J. Wright, "Do Workplace-Based Mindfulness Meditation Programs Improve Physiological Indices of Stress? A Systematic Review and Meta-Analysis," *Journal of Psychosomatic Research*, Vol. 114, November 2018, pp. 62–71.

Hedges, Larry V., "Distribution Theory for Glass's Estimator of Effect Size and Related Estimators," *Journal of Educational Statistics*, Vol. 6, No. 2, Summer 1981, pp. 107–128.

Herman, Aleksandra M., Hugo D. Critchley, and Theodora Duka, "Risk-Taking and Impulsivity: The Role of Mood States and Interoception," *Frontiers in Psychology*, Vol. 9, August 29, 2018, article 1625.

Higgins, Julian, Douglas G. Altman, Peter Gotzsche, Peter Juni, David Moher, Andrew Oxman, Jelena Savovic, Kenneth Schulz, Laura Weeks, and Jonathan Sterne, "The Cochrane Collaboration's Tool for Assessing Risk of Bias in Randomised Trials," *British Medical Journal*, Vol. 343, 2011, article d5928.

Higgins, Julian P. T., James Thomas, Jacqueline Chandler, Miranda Cumpston, Tianjing Li, Matthew J. Page, and Vivian A. Welch, eds., *Cochrane Handbook for Systematic Reviews of Interventions*, online version 6.2, February 2021. As of May 21, 2021:
https://training.cochrane.org/handbook

Hildebrandt, Lea K., Cade McCall, and Tania Singer, "Socioaffective Versus Sociocognitive Mental Trainings Differentially Affect Emotion Regulation Strategies," *Emotion*, Vol. 19, No. 8, December 2019, pp. 1329–1342.

Hilton, Lara, Susanne Hempel, Brett A. Ewing, Eric Apaydin, Lea Xenakis, Sydne Newberry, Ben Colaiaco, Alicia Ruelaz Maher, Roberta M. Shanman, Melony E. Sorbero, and Margaret A. Maglione, "Mindfulness Meditation for Chronic Pain: Systematic Review and Meta-Analysis," *Annals of Behavioral Medicine*, Vol. 51, No. 2, April 2017, pp. 199–213.

Hilton, Lara, Alicia Ruelaz Maher, Benjamin Colaiaco, Eric Apaydin, Melony E. Sorbero, Marika Booth, Roberta M. Shanman, and Susanne Hempel, "Meditation for Posttraumatic Stress: Systematic Review and Meta-Analysis," *Psychological Trauma: Theory, Research, Practice, and Policy*, Vol. 9, No. 4, July 2017, pp. 453–460.

Hoffmann, Tammy C., Paul P. Glasziou, Isabelle Boutron, Ruairidh Milne, Rafael Perera, David Moher, Douglas G. Altman, Virginia Barbour, Helen Macdonald, Marie Johnston, Sarah E. Lamb, Mary Dixon-Woods, Peter McCulloch, Jeremy C. Wyatt, An-Wen Chan, and Susan Michie, "Better Reporting of Interventions: Template for Intervention Description and Replication (TIDieR) Checklist and Guide," *British Medical Journal*, Vol. 348, 2014, article g1687.

Hofmann, Stefan G., Paul Grossman, and Devon E. Hinton, "Loving-Kindness and Compassion Meditation: Potential for Psychological Interventions," *Clinical Psychology Review*, Vol. 31, No. 7, November 2011, pp. 1126–1132.

Hofmann, Stefan G., Nicola Petrocchi, James Steinberg, Muyu Lin, Kohki Arimitsu, Shelley Kind, Adriana Mendes, and Ulrich Stangier, "Loving-Kindness Meditation to Target Affect in Mood Disorders: A Proof-of-Concept Study," *Evidence-Based Complementary and Alternative Medicine*, Vol. 2015, 2015, article 269126.

Hofmann, Stefan G., Alice T. Sawyer, Ashley A. Witt, and Diana Oh, "The Effect of Mindfulness-Based Therapy on Anxiety and Depression: A Meta-Analytic Review," *Journal of Consulting and Clinical Psychology*, Vol. 78, No. 2, April 2010, pp. 169–183.

Hourani, Laurel L., Thomas V. Williams, and Amii M. Kress, "Stress, Mental Health, and Job Performance Among Active Duty Military Personnel: Findings from the 2002 Department of Defense Health-Related Behaviors Survey," *Military Medicine*, Vol. 171, No. 9, September 2006, pp. 849–856.

Hülsheger, Ute R., Hugo J. E. M. Alberts, Alina Feinholdt, and Jonas W. B. Lang, "Benefits of Mindfulness at Work: The Role of Mindfulness in Emotion Regulation, Emotional Exhaustion, and Job Satisfaction," *Journal of Applied Psychology*, Vol. 98, No. 2, March 1, 2013, pp. 310–325.

Hunsinger, Matthew, Michael Christopher, and Andi M. Schmidt, "Mindfulness Training, Implicit Bias, and Force Response Decision-Making," *Mindfulness*, Vol. 10, No. 12, December 1, 2019, pp. 2555–2566.

Huth-Bocks, Alissa C., and Honore M. Hughes, "Parenting Stress, Parenting Behavior, and Children's Adjustment in Families Experiencing Intimate Partner Violence," *Journal of Family Violence*, Vol. 23, No. 4, 2008, pp. 243–251.

IntHout, Joanna, John P. A. Ioannidis, and George Borm, "The Hartung-Knapp-Sidik-Jonkman Method for Random Effects Meta-Analysis Is Straightforward and Considerably Outperforms the Standard DerSimonian-Laird Method," *BMC Medical Research Methodology*, Vol. 14, No. 25, 2014.

Jackson, Dan, Martin Law, Gerta Rücker, and Guido Schwarzer, "The Hartung-Knapp Modification for Random-Effects Meta-Analysis: A Useful Refinement but Are There Any Residual Concerns?" *Statistics in Medicine*, Vol. 36, No. 25, November 10, 2017, pp. 3923–3934.

Jankowski, Tomasz, and Pawel Holas, "Effects of Brief Mindfulness Meditation on Attention Switching," *Mindfulness*, Vol. 11, No. 5, May 1, 2020, pp. 1150–1158.

Jayewardene, Wasantha P., David K. Lohrmann, Ryan G. Erbe, and Mohammad R. Torabi, "Effects of Preventive Online Mindfulness Interventions on Stress and Mindfulness: A Meta-Analysis of Randomized Controlled Trials," *Preventive Medicine Reports*, Vol. 5, 2017, pp. 150–159.

Jensen, Christian G., Signe Vangkilde, Vibe Frokjaer, and Steen G. Hasselbalch, "Mindfulness Training Affects Attention—or Is It Attentional Effort?" *Journal of Experimental Psychology: General*, Vol. 141, No. 1, February 2012, pp. 106–123.

Jha, Amishi P., "Mindfulness-Based Attention Training," webpage, Jha Lab, undated. As of July 7, 2021: http://www.amishi.com/lab/mbat_project/

———, telephone communication with Jessica Sousa, December 12, 2020.

———, telephone communication with Jessica Sousa, May 18, 2021.

Jha, Amishi P., Alexandra B. Morrison, Justin Dainer-Best, Suzanne Parker, Nina Rostrup, and Elizabeth A. Stanley, "Minds 'at Attention': Mindfulness Training Curbs Attentional Lapses in Military Cohorts," *PLOS ONE*, Vol. 10, No. 2, 2015, article e0116889.

Jha, Amishi P., Alexandra B. Morrison, Suzanne C. Parker, and Elizabeth A. Stanley, "Practice Is Protective: Mindfulness Training Promotes Cognitive Resilience in High-Stress Cohorts," *Mindfulness*, Vol. 8, No. 1, 2017, pp. 46–58.

Jha, Amishi P., Elizabeth A. Stanley, and Michael J. Baime, "What Does Mindfulness Training Strengthen? Working Memory Capacity as a Functional Marker of Training Success," in R. A. Baer, ed., *Assessing Mindfulness and Acceptance Processes in Clients: Illuminating the Theory and Practice of Change*, New York: New Harbinger Publications, 2010, pp. 207–221.

Jha, Amishi P., Elizabeth A. Stanley, Anastasia Kiyonaga, Ling Wong, and Lois Gelfand, "Examining the Protective Effects of Mindfulness Training on Working Memory Capacity and Affective Experience," *Emotion*, Vol. 10, No. 1, 2010, pp. 54–64.

Jha, Amishi P., J. E. Witkin, Alexandra B. Morrison, N. Rostrup, and Elizabeth A. Stanley, "Short-Form Mindfulness Training Protects Against Working Memory Degradation over High-Demand Intervals," *Journal of Cognitive Enhancement*, Vol. 1, No. 2, 2017, pp. 154–171.

Jha, Amishi P., Anthony P. Zanesco, Ekaterina Denkova, Alexandra B. Morrison, Nicolas Ramos, Keith Chichester, John W. Gaddy, and Scott L. Rogers, "Bolstering Cognitive Resilience via Train-the-Trainer Delivery of Mindfulness Training in Applied High-Demand Settings," *Mindfulness*, Vol. 11, No. 3, March 1, 2020, pp. 683–697.

Jha, Amishi P., Anthony P. Zanesco, Ekaterina Denkova, Joshua Rooks, Alexandra B. Morrison, and Elizabeth A. Stanley, "Comparing Mindfulness and Positivity Trainings in High-Demand Cohorts," *Cognitive Therapy and Research*, Vol. 44, No. 2, April 1, 2020, pp. 311–326.

Jnitova, Victoria, Sondoss Elsawah, and Michael Ryan, "Review of Simulation Models in Military Workforce Planning and Management Context," *Journal of Defense Modeling and Simulation*, Vol. 14, No. 4, 2017, pp. 447–463.

John, Oliver P., and James J. Gross, "Healthy and Unhealthy Emotion Regulation: Personality Processes, Individual Differences, and Life Span Development," *Journal of Personality*, Vol. 72, No. 6, December 2004, pp. 1301–1333.

Johnson, Douglas C., Nathanial J. Thom, Elizabeth A. Stanley, Lori Haase, Alan N. Simmons, Pei-an A. Shih, Wesley K. Thompson, Eric G. Potterat, Thomas R. Minor, and Martin P. Paulus, "Modifying Resilience Mechanisms in At-Risk Individuals: A Controlled Study of Mindfulness Training in Marines Preparing for Deployment," *American Journal of Psychiatry*, Vol. 171, No. 8, August 2014, pp. 844–853.

Judkins, Jason L., and Devvon L. Bradley, "A Review of the Effectiveness of a Combat and Operational Stress Control Restoration Center in Afghanistan," *Military Medicine*, Vol. 182, No. 7, July 1, 2017, pp. e1755–e1762.

Juster, Robert-Paul, Bruce S. McEwen, and Sonia J. Lupien, "Allostatic Load Biomarkers of Chronic Stress and Impact on Health and Cognition," *Neuroscience & Biobehavioral Reviews*, Vol. 35, No. 1, September 2010, pp. 2–16.

Kabat-Zinn, Jon, "Some Reflections on the Origins of MBSR, Skillful Means, and the Trouble with Maps," *Contemporary Buddhism*, Vol. 12, No. 1, 2011, pp. 281–306.

———, *Mindfulness for Beginners: Reclaiming the Present Moment and Your Life*, Louisville, Colo.: Sounds True, Inc., 2012.

———, *Mindfulness-Based Stress Reduction (MBSR): Authorized Curriculum Guide*, Worcester, Mass.: Center for Mindfulness in Medicine, Health Care and Society, University of Massachusetts Medical School, 2017.

Kabat-Zinn, Jon, and Thich Nhat Hanh, *Full Catastrophe Living: Using the Wisdom of Your Body and Mind to Face Stress, Pain, and Illness*, New York: Random House Publishing Group, 2009.

Khoury, Bassam, Tania Lecomte, Guillaume Fortin, Marjolaine Masse, Phillip Therien, Vanessa Bouchard, Marie-Andreé Chapleau, Karine Paquin, and Stefan G. Hofmann, "Mindfulness-Based Therapy: A Comprehensive Meta-Analysis," *Clinical Psychology Review*, Vol. 33, No. 6, August 2013, pp. 763–771.

Khoury, Bassam, Manoj Sharma, Sarah E. Rush, and Claude Fournier, "Mindfulness-Based Stress Reduction for Healthy Individuals: A Meta-Analysis," *Journal of Psychosomatic Research*, Vol. 78, No. 6, June 2015, pp. 519–528.

Kim, Hye-Geum, Eun-Jin Cheon, Dai-Seg Bai, Young Hwan Lee, and Bon-Hoon Koo, "Stress and Heart Rate Variability: A Meta-Analysis and Review of the Literature," *Psychiatry Investigation*, Vol. 15, No. 3, March 2018, pp. 235–245.

Knapp, Guido, and Joachim Hartung, "Improved Tests for a Random Effects Meta-Regression with a Single Covariate," *Statistics in Medicine*, Vol. 22, No. 17, September 15, 2003, pp. 2693–2710.

Kosni, N. A., M. R. Abdullah, S. N. W. Azman, A. B. H. M. Maliki, R. M. Musa, A. Adnan, S. M. Mat-Rasid, and H. Juahir, "Comparison of Psychological Readiness Factors Among the Collegiate Armed Uniform," *Academic Research in Business & Social Science*, Vol. 8, No. 2, 2018, pp. 97–115.

Kreplin, Ute, Miguel Farias, and Inti A. Brazil, "The Limited Prosocial Effects of Meditation: A Systematic Review and Meta-Analysis," *Scientific Reports*, Vol. 8, February 5, 2018, article 2403.

Kuyken, Willem, Rod S. Taylor, Barbara Barrett, Alison Evans, Sarah Byford, Ed Watkins, Emily Holden, Kat White, Richard Byng, Eugene Mullan, and John Teasdale, "Mindfulness-Based Cognitive Therapy to Prevent Relapse in Recurrent Depression," *Journal of Consulting and Clinical Psychology*, Vol. 76, No. 6, 2008, pp. 966–978.

Kwak, Seoyeon, So-Yeon Kim, Dahye Bae, Wu-Jeong Hwang, Kang Ik Kevin Cho, Kyung-Ok Lim, Hye-Yoon Park, Tae Young Lee, and Jun Soo Kwon, "Enhanced Attentional Network by Short-Term Intensive Meditation," *Frontiers in Psychology*, Vol. 10, February 7, 2020, article 3073.

Lai, Constantine, Benjamin MacNeil, and Paul Frewen, "A Comparison of the Attentional Effects of Single-Session Mindfulness Meditation and Fp-HEG Neurofeedback in Novices," *Mindfulness*, Vol. 6, No. 5, 2015, pp. 1012–1020.

Larsen, Kelsey L., and Elizabeth A. Stanley, "Mindfulness-Based Mind Fitness Training (MMFT): Mindfulness Training for High-Stress and Trauma-Sensitive Contexts," in Itai Ivtzan, ed., *The Handbook of Mindfulness-Based Programmes: Mindfulness Interventions from Education to Health and Therapy*, London: Routledge, 2019, pp. 53–63.

Lavee, Yoav, Shlomo Sharlin, and Ruth Katz, "The Effect of Parenting Stress on Marital Quality: An Integrated Mother–Father Model," *Journal of Family Issues*, Vol. 17, No. 1, 1996, pp. 114–135.

Lench, Heather C., Sarah A. Flores, and Shane W. Bench, "Discrete Emotions Predict Changes in Cognition, Judgment, Experience, Behavior, and Physiology: A Meta-Analysis of Experimental Emotion Elicitations," *Psychological Bulletin*, Vol. 137, No. 5, September 2011, pp. 834–855.

Lester, Patricia, and Eric Flake, "How Wartime Military Service Affects Children and Families," *Future Child*, Vol. 23, No. 2, Fall 2013, pp. 121–141.

Li, Wen, Matthew O. Howard, Eric L. Garland, Patricia McGovern, and Michael Lazar, "Mindfulness Treatment for Substance Misuse: A Systematic Review and Meta-Analysis," *Journal of Substance Abuse Treatment*, Vol. 75, April 2017, pp. 62–96.

Lim, Julian, and David F. Dinges, "A Meta-Analysis of the Impact of Short-Term Sleep Deprivation on Cognitive Variables," *Psychological Bulletin*, Vol. 136, No. 3, 2010, pp. 375–389.

Lindahl, Jared R., Nathan E. Fisher, David J. Cooper, Rochelle K. Rosen, and Willoughby B. Britton, "The Varieties of Contemplative Experience: A Mixed-Methods Study of Meditation-Related Challenges in Western Buddhists," *PLOS ONE*, Vol. 12, No. 5, 2017, article e0176239.

Ludwig, David S., and Jon Kabat-Zinn, "Mindfulness in Medicine," *Journal of the American Medical Association*, Vol. 300, No. 11, September 17, 2008, pp. 1350–1352.

Ma, Ying, Zhaozhuo She, Angela Fung-Ying Siu, Xianlong Zeng, and Xinghua Liu, "Effectiveness of Online Mindfulness-Based Interventions on Psychological Distress and the Mediating Role of Emotion Regulation," *Frontiers in Psychology*, Vol. 9, October 2018, article 2090.

MacCoon, Donal G., Zac E. Imel, Melissa A. Rosenkranz, Jenna G. Sheftel, Helen Y. Weng, Jude C. Sullivan, Katherine A. Bonus, Catherine M. Stoney, Tim V. Salomons, Richard J. Davidson, and Antoine Lutz, "The Validation of an Active Control Intervention for Mindfulness Based Stress Reduction (MBSR)," *Behaviour Research and Therapy*, Vol. 50, No. 1, January 2012, pp. 3–12.

Madrid, Hector P., "Emotion Regulation, Positive Affect, and Promotive Voice Behavior at Work," *Frontiers in Psychology*, Vol. 11, 2020, article 1739.

Mansfield, Alyssa J., Jay S. Kaufman, Charles C. Engel, and Bradley N. Gaynes, "Deployment and Mental Health Diagnoses Among Children of US Army Personnel," *Archives of Pediatrics & Adolescent Medicine*, Vol. 165, No. 11, November 2011, pp. 999–1005.

Mathias, Jane L., and Patricia Wheaton, "Changes in Attention and Information-Processing Speed Following Severe Traumatic Brain Injury: A Meta-Analytic Review," *Neuropsychology*, Vol. 21, No. 2, March 2007, pp. 212–223.

McCartney, Mark, Sarah Nevitt, Annette Lloyd, Ruaraidh Hill, Ross White, and Rui Duarte, "Mindfulness-Based Cognitive Therapy for Prevention and Time to Depressive Relapse: Systematic Review and Network Meta-Analysis," *Acta Psychiatrica Scandinavica*, Vol. 143, No. 1, January 2021, pp. 6–21.

McCroskey, James C., and Linda L. McCroskey, "Self-Report as an Approach to Measuring Communication Competence," *Communication Research Reports*, Vol. 5, No. 2, 1988, pp. 108–113.

McEwen, Bruce S., and Eliot Stellar, "Stress and the Individual: Mechanisms Leading to Disease," *Archives of Internal Medicine*, Vol. 153, No. 18, September 27, 1993, pp. 2093–2101.

Menezes, Carolina Baptista, Maria Clara de Paula Couto, Luciano G. Buratto, Fatima Erthal, Mirtes G. Pereira, and Lisiane Bizarro, "The Improvement of Emotion and Attention Regulation After a 6-Week Training of Focused Meditation: A Randomized Controlled Trial," *Evidence-Based Complementary and Alternative Medicine*, Vol. 2013, 2013, article 984678.

Menezes, Carolina Baptista, Mirtes G. Pereira, Izabela Mocaiber, and Lisiane Bizarro, "Brief Meditation and the Interaction Between Emotional Interference and Anxiety," *Psicologia: Teoria e Pesquisa*, Vol. 32, No. 2, 2016, pp. 1–8.

Meredith, Lisa S., Cathy D. Sherbourne, Sarah J. Gaillot, Lydia Hansell, Hans V. Ritschard, Andrew M. Parker, and Glenda Wrenn, *Promoting Psychological Resilience in the U.S. Military*, Santa Monica, Calif.: RAND Corporation, MG-996-OSD, 2011. As of June 3, 2021:
https://www.rand.org/pubs/monographs/MG996.html

Michie, Susan, Maartje M. van Stralen, and Robert West, "The Behaviour Change Wheel: A New Method for Characterising and Designing Behaviour Change Interventions," *Implementation Science*, Vol. 6, April 23, 2011, article 42.

Moher, David, Corinne S. Dulberg, and George A. Wells, "Statistical Power, Sample Size, and Their Reporting in Randomized Controlled Trials," *Journal of the American Medical Association*, Vol. 272, No. 2, July 13, 1994, pp. 122–124.

Moher, David, Sally Hopewell, Kenneth F. Schulz, Victor Montori, Peter C. Gøtzsche, P. J. Devereaux, Diana Elbourne, Matthias Egger, and Douglas G. Altman, "CONSORT 2010 Explanation and Elaboration: Updated Guidelines for Reporting Parallel Group Randomised Trials," *British Medical Journal*, Vol. 340, March 24, 2010, article c869.

Moher, David, Kenneth F. Schulz, and Douglas G. Altman, "The CONSORT Statement: Revised Recommendations for Improving the Quality of Reports of Parallel-Group Randomised Trials," *The Lancet*, Vol. 357, No. 9263, April 14, 2001, pp. 1191–1194.

Moore, Graham F., Suzanne Audrey, Mary Barker, Lyndal Bond, Chris Bonell, Wendy Hardeman, Laurence Moore, Alicia O'Cathain, Tannaze Tinati, Daniel Wight, and Janis Baird, "Process Evaluation of Complex Interventions: Medical Research Council Guidance," *British Medical Journal*, Vol. 350, 2015, article h1258.

Ngamkham, Srisuda, Janean E. Holden, and Ellen Lavoie Smith, "A Systematic Review: Mindfulness Intervention for Cancer-Related Pain," *Asia-Pacific Journal of Oncology Nursing*, Vol. 6, No. 2, April–June 2019, pp. 161–169.

Nindl, Bradley C., John W. Castellani, Bradley J. Warr, Marilyn A. Sharp, Paul C. Henning, Barry A. Spiering, and Dennis E. Scofield, "Physiological Employment Standards III: Physiological Challenges and Consequences Encountered During International Military Deployments," *European Journal of Applied Physiology*, Vol. 113, No. 11, November 2013, pp. 2655–2672.

Norris, Catherine J., Daniel Creem, Reuben Hendler, and Hedy Kober, "Brief Mindfulness Meditation Improves Attention in Novices: Evidence from ERPs and Moderation by Neuroticism," *Frontiers in Human Neuroscience*, Vol. 12, August 1, 2018, article 315.

Odum, Amy L., "Delay Discounting: I'm a k, You're a k," *Journal of the Experimental Analysis of Behavior*, Vol. 96, No. 3, November 2011, pp. 427–439.

Okoro, Ephraim, Melvin C. Washington, and Otis Thomas, "The Impact of Interpersonal Communication Skills on Organizational Effectiveness and Social Self-Efficacy: A Synthesis," *International Journal of Language and Linguistics*, Vol. 4, No. 3, 2017, pp. 28–32.

Ortner, Catherine N. M., Sachne J. Kilner, and Philip David Zelazo, "Mindfulness Meditation and Reduced Emotional Interference on a Cognitive Task," *Motivation and Emotion*, Vol. 31, No. 4, 2007, pp. 271–283.

Overdale, Sarah, and Dianne Gardner, "Social Support and Coping Adaptability in Initial Military Training," *Military Psychology*, Vol. 24, No. 3, 2012, pp. 312–330.

Oxford Mindfulness Centre, "Implementing MBCT," webpage, undated. As of June 11, 2021:
https://implementing-mindfulness.co.uk/

Page, Matthew J., Joanne E. McKenzie, Patrick M. Bossuyt, Isabelle Boutron, Tammy C. Hoffmann, Cynthia D. Mulrow, Larissa Shamseer, Jennifer M. Tetzlaff, Elie A. Akl, Sue E. Brennan, Roger Chou, Julie Glanville, Jeremy M. Grimshaw, Asbjørn Hróbjartsson, Manoj M. Lalu, Tianjing Li, Elizabeth W. Loder, Evan Mayo-Wilson, Steve McDonald, Luke A. McGuinness, Lesley A. Stewart, James Thomas, Andrea C. Tricco, Vivian A. Welch, Penny Whiting, and David Moher, "The PRISMA 2020 Statement: An Updated Guideline for Reporting Systematic Reviews," *British Medical Journal*, Vol. 372, March 29, 2021, article n71.

Parmentier, Fabrice B. R., Mauro García-Toro, Javier García-Campayo, Aina M. Yañez, Pilar Andrés, and Margalida Gili, "Mindfulness and Symptoms of Depression and Anxiety in the General Population: The Mediating Roles of Worry, Rumination, Reappraisal and Suppression," *Frontiers in Psychology*, Vol. 10, 2019, article 506.

Parsons, Christine E., Catherine Crane, Liam J. Parsons, Lone Overby Fjorback, and Willem Kuyken, "Home Practice in Mindfulness-Based Cognitive Therapy and Mindfulness-Based Stress Reduction: A Systematic Review and Meta-Analysis of Participants' Mindfulness Practice and Its Association with Outcomes," *Behaviour Research and Therapy*, Vol. 95, August 2017, pp. 29–41.

Pascoe, Michaela C., David R. Thompson, Zoe M. Jenkins, and Chantal F. Ski, "Mindfulness Mediates the Physiological Markers of Stress: Systematic Review and Meta-Analysis," *Journal of Psychiatric Research*, Vol. 95, December 1, 2017, pp. 156–178.

Patton, Jim H., Matthew S. Stanford, and Ernest S. Barratt, "Factor Structure of the Barratt Impulsiveness Scale," *Journal of Clinical Psychology*, Vol. 51, No. 6, November 1995, pp. 768–774.

Pflanz, Steven E., and Alan D. Ogle, "Job Stress, Depression, Work Performance, and Perceptions of Supervisors in Military Personnel," *Military Medicine*, Vol. 171, No. 9, September 2006, pp. 861–865.

Piatt, Walter, Deydre Teyhen, and Amy Adler, "Leading with Attention: Mindfulness Takes Hold as Army Embraces the Now," Association of the United States Army, March 19, 2021. As of July 7, 2021: https://www.ausa.org/articles/leading-attention-mindfulness-takes-hold-army-embraces-now

Pilla, David, Joanne Qina'au, Aparna Patel, Brianna Meddaoui, Nicholas Watson, Sanjana Dugad, and Mitchell Saskin, "Toward a Framework for Reporting and Differentiating Key Features of Meditation- and Mindfulness-Based Interventions," *Mindfulness*, Vol. 11, No. 11, 2020, pp. 2613–2628.

Posner, Michael I., and Mary K. Rothbart, "Research on Attention Networks as a Model for the Integration of Psychological Science," *Annual Review of Psychology*, Vol. 58, 2007, pp. 1–23.

Quaglia, Jordan T., Fadel Zeidan, Peter G. Grossenbacher, Sara P. Freeman, Sarah E. Braun, Alexandra Martelli, Robert J. Goodman, and Kirk Warren Brown, "Brief Mindfulness Training Enhances Cognitive Control in Socioemotional Contexts: Behavioral and Neural Evidence," *PLOS ONE*, Vol. 14, No. 7, July 19, 2019, article e0219862.

Quan, Peng, Wenna Wang, Chengjin Chu, and Lingfeng Zhou, "Seven Days of Mindfulness-Based Cognitive Therapy Improves Attention and Coping Style," *Social Behavior and Personality: An International Journal*, Vol. 46, No. 3, 2018, pp. 421–430.

Querstret, Dawn, Linda Morison, Sophie Dickinson, Mark Cropley, and Mary John, "Mindfulness-Based Stress Reduction and Mindfulness-Based Cognitive Therapy for Psychological Health and Well-Being in Nonclinical Samples: A Systematic Review and Meta-Analysis," *International Journal of Stress Management*, Vol. 27, No. 4, 2020, pp. 394–411.

Reivich, Karen J., Martin E. P. Seligman, and Sharon McBride, "Master Resilience Training in the U.S. Army," *American Psychologist*, Vol. 66, No. 1, January 2011, pp. 25–34.

Riccio, Cynthia A., Cecil R. Reynolds, Patricia Lowe, and Jennifer J. Moore, "The Continuous Performance Test: A Window on the Neural Substrates for Attention?" *Archives of Clinical Neuropsychology*, Vol. 17, No. 3, 2002, pp. 235–272.

Rogers, Mary M., Karen Kelley, and Cliff McKinney, "Trait Impulsivity and Health Risk Behaviors: A Latent Profile Analysis," *Personality and Individual Differences*, Vol. 171, 2021, article 110511.

Roski, Joachim, Bruce L. Gillingham, Jeffrey Millegan, Derik R. Zitelman, Sonja V. Batten, and Eileen M. Delaney, "Building Resilience for Greater Health and Performance: Learning from the Military," *Health Affairs Blog*, August 12, 2019. As of June 11, 2021: https://www.healthaffairs.org/do/10.1377/hblog20190807.768196/full/

Rothschild, Sarit, Gilat Kaplan, Tomer Golan, and Yoram Barak, "Mindfulness Meditation in the Israel Defense Forces: Effect on Cognition and Satisfaction with Life—A Randomized Controlled Trial," *European Journal of Integrative Medicine*, Vol. 10, February 1, 2017, pp. 71–74.

Rounsaville, Bruce J., Kathleen M. Carroll, and Lisa S. Onken, "A Stage Model of Behavioral Therapies Research: Getting Started and Moving on from Stage I," *Clinical Psychology: Science and Practice*, Vol. 8, No. 2, 2001, pp. 133–142.

Ruijgrok-Lupton, Pauline Eva, Rebecca S. Crane, and Dusana Dorjee, "Impact of Mindfulness-Based Teacher Training on MBSR Participant Well-Being Outcomes and Course Satisfaction," *Mindfulness*, Vol. 9, No. 1, February 2018, pp. 117–128.

Rung, Jillian M., and Gregory J. Madden, "Experimental Reductions of Delay Discounting and Impulsive Choice: A Systematic Review and Meta-Analysis," *Journal of Experimental Psychology: General*, Vol. 147, No. 9, September 2018, pp. 1349–1381.

Russell, Dale W., David M. Benedek, James A. Naifeh, Carol S. Fullerton, Nikki Benevides, Robert J. Ursano, Cristel A. Russell, Robert D. Forsten, and John T. Cacciopo, "Social Support and Mental Health Outcomes Among U.S. Army Special Operations Personnel," *Military Psychology*, Vol. 28, No. 6, 2016, pp. 361–375.

Russo, Theresa J., and Moira A. Fallon, "Coping with Stress: Supporting the Needs of Military Families and Their Children," *Early Childhood Education Journal*, Vol. 43, No. 5, 2015, pp. 407–416.

Ruths, Florian A., Nicole de Zoysa, Sonya J. Frearson, Jane Hutton, J. Mark G. Williams, and James Walsh, "Mindfulness-Based Cognitive Therapy for Mental Health Professionals—A Pilot Study," *Mindfulness*, Vol. 4, No. 4, 2013, pp. 289–295.

Salzberg, Sharon, "Mindfulness and Loving-Kindness," *Contemporary Buddhism*, Vol. 12, No. 1, May 1, 2011, pp. 177–182.

Santorelli, Saki F., Jon Kabat-Zinn, Melissa Blacker, Florence Meleo-Meyer, and Lynn Koerbel, *Mindfulness-Based Stress Reduction (MBSR) Authorized Curriculum Guide*, Worcester, Mass.: Center for Mindfulness in Medicine, Health Care, and Society, University of Massachusetts Medical School, 2017.

Schofield, Timothy P., J. David Creswell, and Thomas F. Denson, "Brief Mindfulness Induction Reduces Inattentional Blindness," *Consciousness and Cognition*, Vol. 37, December 1, 2015, pp. 63–70.

Schulz, Kenneth F., Iain Chalmers, Richard J. Hayes, and Douglas G. Altman, "Empirical Evidence of Bias: Dimensions of Methodological Quality Associated with Estimates of Treatment Effects in Controlled Trials," *Journal of the American Medical Association*, Vol. 273, No. 5, February 1995, pp. 408–412.

Segal, Zindel V., John Teasdale, and Mark G. Williams, *Mindfulness-Based Cognitive Therapy for Depression: A New Approach to Preventing Relapse*, New York: Guilford Press, 2002.

Sharma, Manoj, and Sarah E. Rush, "Mindfulness-Based Stress Reduction as a Stress Management Intervention for Healthy Individuals: A Systematic Review," *Journal of Evidence-Based Complementary & Alternative Medicine*, Vol. 19, No. 4, October 2014, pp. 271–286.

Shea, Beverley J., Barnaby C. Reeves, George Wells, Micere Thuku, Candyce Hamel, Julian Moran, David Moher, Peter Tugwell, Vivian Welch, Elizabeth Kristjansson, and David A. Henry, "AMSTAR 2: A Critical Appraisal Tool for Systematic Reviews That Include Randomised or Non-Randomised Studies of Healthcare Interventions, or Both," *British Medical Journal*, Vol. 358, September 21, 2017, article j4008.

Shi, Ran, Louise Sharpe, and Maree Abbott, "A Meta-Analysis of the Relationship Between Anxiety and Attentional Control," *Clinical Psychology Review*, Vol. 72, August 2019, article 101754.

Shonin, Edo, William Van Gordon, Thomas J. Dunn, Nirbhay N. Singh, and Mark D. Griffiths, "Meditation Awareness Training (MAT) for Work-Related Wellbeing and Job Performance: A Randomised Controlled Trial," *International Journal of Mental Health and Addiction*, Vol. 12, No. 6, December 2014, pp. 806–823.

Sidik, Kurex, and Jeffrey Jonkman, "Robust Variance Estimation for Random Effects Meta-Analysis," *Computational Statistics & Data Analysis*, Vol. 50, No. 12, 2006, pp. 3681–3701.

Singh, Jitendra Kuma, and Mini Jain, "A Study of Employees' Job Satisfaction and Its Impact on Their Performance," *Journal of Indian Research*, Vol. 1, No. 4, 2013.

Sloan, Elise, Kate Hall, Richard Moulding, Shayden Bryce, Helen Mildred, and Petra K. Staiger, "Emotion Regulation as a Transdiagnostic Treatment Construct Across Anxiety, Depression, Substance, Eating and Borderline Personality Disorders: A Systematic Review," *Clinical Psychology Review*, Vol. 57, November 1, 2017, pp. 141–163.

Smith, Brian N., Rachel A. Vaughn, Dawne Vogt, Daniel W. King, Lynda A. King, and Jillian C. Shipherd, "Main and Interactive Effects of Social Support in Predicting Mental Health Symptoms in Men and Women Following Military Stressor Exposure," *Anxiety, Stress & Coping: An International Journal*, Vol. 26, No. 1, 2013, pp. 52–69.

Solano López, Ana L., "Effectiveness of the Mindfulness-Based Stress Reduction Program on Blood Pressure: A Systematic Review of Literature," *Worldviews on Evidence-Based Nursing*, Vol. 15, No. 5, October 1, 2018, pp. 344–352.

Sookermany, Anders McD, "What Is a Skillful Soldier? An Epistemological Foundation for Understanding Military Skill Acquisition in (Post) Modernized Armed Forces," *Armed Forces & Society*, Vol. 38, No. 4, 2012, pp. 582–603.

Spieth, Peter Markus, Anne Sophie Kubasch, Ana Isabel Penzlin, Ben Min-Woo Illigens, Kristian Barlinn, and Timo Siepmann, "Randomized Controlled Trials—A Matter of Design," *Neuropsychiatric Disease and Treatment*, Vol. 12, June 30, 2016, pp. 1341–1349.

Stanley, Elizabeth A., "Mindfulness-Based Fitness Training (MMFT): An Approach for Enhancing Performance and Building Resilience in High Stress Contexts," in Amanda Ie, Christelle T. Ngnoumen, and Ellen J. Langer, eds., *The Wiley-Blackwell Handbook of Mindfulness*, London: Wiley-Blackwell, 2014, pp. 964–985.

———, *Widen the Window: Training Your Brain and Body to Thrive During Stress and Recover from Trauma*, London: Yellow Kite, Hodder & Soughton Ltd, 2019.

———, telephone communication with Jessica Sousa, May 14, 2021.

Stanley, Elizabeth A., and Amishi P. Jha, "Mind Fitness: Improving Operational Effectiveness and Building Warrior Resilience," *Joint Force Quarterly*, 2009.

Stanley, Elizabeth A., John M. Schaldach, Anastasia Kiyonaga, and Amishi P. Jha, "Mindfulness-Based Mind Fitness Training: A Case Study of a High-Stress Predeployment Military Cohort," *Cognitive and Behavioral Practice*, Vol. 18, No. 4, 2011, pp. 566–576.

Steinberg, Beth A., Maryanna Klatt, and Anne-Marie Duchemin, "Feasibility of a Mindfulness-Based Intervention for Surgical Intensive Care Unit Personnel," *American Journal of Critical Care*, Vol. 26, No. 1, December 1, 2016, pp. 10–18.

Sterne, Jonathan A. C., Alex J. Sutton, John P. A. Ioannidis, Norma Terrin, David R. Jones, Joseph Lau, James Carpenter, Gerta Rücker, Roger M. Harbord, Christopher H. Schmid, Jennifer Tetzlaff, Jonathan J. Deeks, Jaime Peters, Petra Macaskill, Guido Schwarzer, Sue Duval, Douglas G. Altman, David Moher, and Julian P. T. Higgins, "Recommendations for Examining and Interpreting Funnel Plot Asymmetry in Meta-Analyses of Randomised Controlled Trials," *British Medical Journal*, Vol. 343, July 22, 2011, article d4002.

Strough, JoNell, Andrew M. Parker, and Wändi Bruine de Bruin, "Understanding Life-Span Developmental Changes in Decision-Making Competence," in Thomas M. Hess, JoNell Strough, and Corinna E. Löckenhoff, eds., *Aging and Decision Making: Empirical and Applied Perspectives*, San Diego, Calif.: Elsevier Academic Press, 2015, pp. 235–257.

Tang, Yi-Yuan, Britta K. Hölzel, and Michael I. Posner, "The Neuroscience of Mindfulness Meditation," *Nature Reviews Neuroscience*, Vol. 16, No. 4, April 10, 2015, pp. 213–225.

Tang, Yi-Yuan, Yinghua Ma, Junhong Wang, Yaxin Fan, Shigang Feng, Qilin Lu, Qingbao Yu, Danni Sui, Mary K. Rothbart, Ming Fan, and Michael I. Posner, "Short-Term Meditation Training Improves Attention and Self-Regulation," *Proceedings of the National Academy of Sciences of the United States of America*, Vol. 104, No. 43, October 23, 2007, pp. 17152–17156.

Teasdale, John D., Zindel V. Segal, J. Mark Williams, Valerie A. Ridgeway, Judith M. Soulsby, and Mark A. Lau, "Prevention of Relapse/Recurrence in Major Depression by Mindfulness-Based Cognitive Therapy," *Journal of Consulting and Clinical Psychology*, Vol. 68, No. 4, August 2000, pp. 615–623.

Thomas, Maria L., and Michael B. Russo, "Neurocognitive Monitors: Toward the Prevention of Cognitive Performance Decrements and Catastrophic Failures in the Operational Environment," *Aviation, Space, and Environmental Medicine*, Vol. 78, No. 5 Suppl, May 2007, pp. B144–B152.

Townshend, Kishani, Zoe Jordan, Matthew Stephenson, and Komla Tsey, "The Effectiveness of Mindful Parenting Programs in Promoting Parents' and Children's Wellbeing: A Systematic Review," *JBI Database of Systematic Reviews Implementation Reports*, Vol. 14, No. 3, March 2016, pp. 139–180.

Upton, Shelley R., and Tyler L. Renshaw, "Immediate Effects of the Mindful Body Scan Practice on Risk-Taking Behavior," *Mindfulness*, Vol. 10, No. 1, May 16, 2018, pp. 78–88.

U.S. Army, "Army Ready and Resilient," undated-a. As of June 1, 2021:
https://www.armyresilience.army.mil/ard/R2/index.html

———, "Army Ready and Resilient: Practice Mindfulness for Better Quality of Life," webpage, undated-b. As of May 4, 2021:
https://www.armyresilience.army.mil/ard/R2/Mindfulness.html

———, "Army Ready and Resilient: R2 Performance Centers," webpage, undated-c. As of May 4, 2021:
https://www.armyresilience.army.mil/ard/R2/R2-Performance-center.html

———, "Army Personal Readiness and Resilience," webpage, September 13, 2019a. As of May 4, 2021:
https://www.army.mil/standto/archive/2019/09/13/

———, *The Army People Strategy*, Washington, D.C., October 2019b.

U.S. Department of Defense, *Doctrine for the Armed Forces of the United States*, Joint Publication 1, Washington, D.C., incorporating change 1, July 12, 2017.

U.S. Preventive Services Task Force, "Appendix VI. Criteria for Assessing Internal Validity of Individual Studies," in U.S. Preventive Services Task Force, *Procedure Manual*, Rockville, Md., July 2017.

Valentine, Melissa A., Ingrid M. Nembhard, and Amy C. Edmondson, "Measuring Teamwork in Health Care Settings: A Review of Survey Instruments," *Medical Care*, Vol. 53, No. 4, April 2015, pp. e16–e30.

Van Aert, Robbie C. M., and Dan Jackson, "A New Justification of the Hartung-Knapp Method for Random-Effects Meta-Analysis Based on Weighted Least Squares Regression," *Research Synthesis Methods*, Vol. 10, No. 4, December 2019, pp. 515–527.

van der Velden, Anne M., Willem Kuyken, Ulla Wattar, Catherine Crane, Karen Johanne Pallesen, Jesper Dahlgaard, Lone Overby Fjorback, and Jacob Piet, "A Systematic Review of Mechanisms of Change in Mindfulness-Based Cognitive Therapy in the Treatment of Recurrent Major Depressive Disorder," *Clinical Psychology Review*, Vol. 37, April 2015, pp. 26–39.

Victorson, David E., Christina M. Sauer, Lauren Wolters, Carly Maletich, Kai Lukoff, and Nat Sufrin, "Meta-Analysis of Technology-Enabled Mindfulness-Based Programs for Negative Affect and Mindful Awareness," *Mindfulness*, Vol. 11, No. 8, August 1, 2020, pp. 1884–1899.

Viechtbauer, Wolfgang, and Mike W.-L. Cheung, "Outlier and Influence Diagnostics for Meta-Analysis," *Research Synthesis Methods*, Vol. 1, No. 2, April 2010, pp. 112–125.

Waldeck, Jennifer, Cathryn Durante, Briana Helmuth, and Brandon Marcia, "Communication in a Changing World: Contemporary Perspectives on Business Communication Competence," *Journal of Education for Business*, Vol. 87, No. 4, 2012, pp. 230–240.

Walsh, Roger, and Shauna L. Shapiro, "The Meeting of Meditative Disciplines and Western Psychology: A Mutually Enriching Dialogue," *American Psychologist*, Vol. 61, No. 3, 2006, pp. 227–239.

Wang, Hongbin, and Jin Fan, "Human Attentional Networks: A Connectionist Model," *Journal of Cognitive Neuroscience*, Vol. 19, No. 10, October 2007, pp. 1678–1689.

Wang, Xiang, Peihuan Li, Chen Pan, Lisha Dai, Yan Wu, and Yunlong Deng, "The Effect of Mind-Body Therapies on Insomnia: A Systematic Review and Meta-Analysis," *Evidence-Based Complementary and Alternative Medicine*, Vol. 13, February 2019, article 9359807.

Wang, Xiang, Huan Zhou, and Xiongzhao Zhu, "Attention Deficits in Adults with Major Depressive Disorder: A Systematic Review and Meta-Analysis," *Asian Journal of Psychiatry*, Vol. 53, October 2020, article 102359.

Watford, Tanya S., and Jane Stafford, "The Impact of Mindfulness on Emotion Dysregulation and Psychophysiological Reactivity Under Emotional Provocation," *Psychology of Consciousness: Theory, Research, and Practice*, Vol. 2, No. 1, 2015, pp. 90–109.

Watier, Nicholas, and Michael Dubois, "The Effects of a Brief Mindfulness Exercise on Executive Attention and Recognition Memory," *Mindfulness*, Vol. 7, No. 3, 2016, pp. 745–753.

Weller, Joshua, Andrea Ceschi, Lauren Hirsch, Riccardo Sartori, and Arianna Costantini, "Accounting for Individual Differences in Decision-Making Competence: Personality and Gender Differences," *Frontiers in Psychology*, Vol. 9, November 2018, article 2258.

Wells, G., B. Shea, D. O'Connell, J. Peterson, V. Welch, M. Losos, and P. Tugwell, "The Newcastle-Ottawa Scale (NOS) for Assessing the Quality of Nonrandomised Studies in Meta-Analyses," Ottowa Hospital, 2019. As of August 14, 2020:
http://www.ohri.ca/programs/clinical_epidemiology/oxford.asp

Wenzel, Mario, Zarah Rowland, and Thomas Kubiak, "How Mindfulness Shapes the Situational Use of Emotion Regulation Strategies in Daily Life," *Cognition and Emotion*, Vol. 34, No. 7, May 6, 2020, pp. 1408–1422.

Wimmer, Lena, Lisa von Stockhausen, and Silja Bellingrath, "Improving Emotion Regulation and Mood in Teacher Trainees: Effectiveness of Two Mindfulness Trainings," *Brain and Behavior*, Vol. 9, September 2019, article e01390.

Wu, Ran, Lin-Lin Liu, Hong Zhu, Wen-Jun Su, Zhi-Yong Cao, Shi-Yang Zhong, Xing-Hua Liu, and Chun-Lei Jiang, "Brief Mindfulness Meditation Improves Emotion Processing," *Frontiers in Neuroscience*, Vol. 13, October 10, 2019, article 1074.

Zanesco, Anthony P., Ekaterina Denkova, Scott L. Rogers, William K. MacNulty, and Amishi P. Jha, "Mindfulness Training as Cognitive Training in High-Demand Cohorts: An Initial Study in Elite Military Servicemembers," *Progress in Brain Research*, Vol. 244, 2019, pp. 323–354.

Zelenski, John M., Steven A. Murphy, and David A. Jenkins, "The Happy-Productive Worker Thesis Revisited," *Journal of Happiness Studies: An Interdisciplinary Forum on Subjective Well-Being*, Vol. 9, No. 4, 2008, pp. 521–537.

Zhang, Qiuxiang, Heng Zhao, and Yaning Zheng, "Effectiveness of Mindfulness-Based Stress Reduction (MBSR) on Symptom Variables and Health-Related Quality of Life in Breast Cancer Patients—A Systematic Review and Meta-Analysis," *Supportive Care in Cancer*, Vol. 27, No. 3, March 2019, pp. 771–781.

Zwilling, Christopher E., Ana M. Daugherty, Charles H. Hillman, Arthur F. Kramer, Neal J. Cohen, and Aron K. Barbey, "Enhanced Decision-Making Through Multimodal Training," *NPJ Science of Learning*, Vol. 4, No. 11, 2019, pp. 1–10.

Systematic Review Publications

Adhikari, Kishor, Farida Kothari, and Anjana Khadka, "The Effect of Short-Term Training of Vipassana's Body-Scan on Select Cognitive Functions," *Psychological Studies*, Vol. 63, No. 3, 2018, pp. 228–235.

Ainsworth, B., H. Bolderston, and M. Garner, "Testing the Differential Effects of Acceptance and Attention-Based Psychological Interventions on Intrusive Thoughts and Worry," *Behaviour Research and Therapy*, Vol. 91, April 1, 2017, pp. 72–77.

Ainsworth, Ben, Rachael Eddershaw, Daniel Meron, David S. Baldwin, and Matthew Garner, "The Effect of Focused Attention and Open Monitoring Meditation on Attention Network Function in Healthy Volunteers," *Psychiatry Research*, Vol. 210, No. 3, December 30, 2013, pp. 1226–1231.

Alkoby, Alon, Ruthie Pliskin, Eran Halperin, and Nava Levit-Binnun, "An Eight-Week Mindfulness-Based Stress Reduction (MBSR) Workshop Increases Regulatory Choice Flexibility," *Emotion*, Vol. 19, No. 4, June 1, 2019, pp. 593–604.

Allen, Micah, Martin Dietz, Karina S. Blair, Martijn van Beek, Geraint Rees, Peter Vestergaard-Poulsen, Antoine Lutz, and Andreas Roepstorff, "Cognitive-Affective Neural Plasticity Following Active-Controlled Mindfulness Intervention," *Journal of Neuroscience*, Vol. 32, No. 44, October 31, 2012, pp. 15601–15610.

Allexandre, Didier, Adam M. Bernstein, Esteban Walker, Jennifer Hunter, Michael F. Roizen, and Thomas J. Morledge, "A Web-Based Mindfulness Stress Management Program in a Corporate Call Center: A Randomized Clinical Trial to Evaluate the Added Benefit of Onsite Group Support," *Journal of Occupational and Environmental Medicine*, Vol. 58, No. 3, March 1, 2016, pp. 254–264.

Anderson, Nicole D., Mark A. Lau, Zindel V. Segal, and Scott R. Bishop, "Mindfulness-Based Stress Reduction and Attentional Control," *Clinical Psychology & Psychotherapy*, Vol. 14, No. 6, 2007, pp. 449–463.

Arch, Joanna J., and Michelle G. Craske, "Mechanisms of Mindfulness: Emotion Regulation Following a Focused Breathing Induction," *Behaviour Research and Therapy*, Vol. 44, No. 12, December 1, 2006, pp. 1849–1858.

Baby, Maria, Christopher Gale, and Nicola Swain, "A Communication Skills Intervention to Minimise Patient Perpetrated Aggression for Healthcare Support Workers in New Zealand: A Cluster Randomised Controlled Trial," *Health and Social Care in the Community*, Vol. 27, No. 1, January 2019, pp. 170–181.

Balconi, Michela, Davide Crivelli, and Laura Angioletti, "Efficacy of a Neurofeedback Training on Attention and Driving Performance: Physiological and Behavioral Measures," *Frontiers in Neuroscience*, Vol. 13, September 18, 2019, article 996.

Baltar, Yago Carioca, and Alberto Filgueiras, "The Effects of Mindfulness Meditation on Attentional Control During Off-Season Among Football Players," *Sage Open*, Vol. 8, No. 2, June 1, 2018, pp. 1–9.

Banks, Jonathan B., Amishi P. Jha, Audrey V. B. Hood, Haley G. Goller, and Lindsay L. Craig, "Reducing the TUTs that Hurt: The Impact of a Brief Mindfulness Induction on Emotionally Valenced Mind Wandering," *Journal of Cognitive Psychology*, Vol. 31, No. 8, 2019, pp. 785–799.

Barattucci, Massimiliano, Anna M. Padovan, Ermanno Vitale, Venerando Rapisarda, Tiziana Ramaci, and Andrea De Giorgio, "Mindfulness-Based IARA Model® Proves Effective to Reduce Stress and Anxiety in Health Care Professionals. A Six-Month Follow-Up Study," *International Journal of Environmental Research and Public Health*, Vol. 16, No. 22, November 12, 2019.

Basso, Julia C., Alexandra McHale, Victoria Ende, Douglas J. Oberlin, and Wendy A. Suzuki, "Brief, Daily Meditation Enhances Attention, Memory, Mood, and Emotional Regulation in Non-Experienced Meditators," *Behavioural Brain Research*, Vol. 356, January 1, 2019, pp. 208–220.

Becerra, Rodrigo, Coralyn Dandrade, and Craig Harms, "Can Specific Attentional Skills Be Modified with Mindfulness Training for Novice Practitioners?" *Current Psychology: A Journal for Diverse Perspectives on Diverse Psychological Issues*, Vol. 36, No. 3, 2017, pp. 657–664.

Bhayee, Sheffy, Patricia Tomaszewski, Daniel H. Lee, Graeme Moffat, Lou Pino, Sylvain Moreno, and Norman A. S. Farb, "Attentional and Affective Consequences of Technology Supported Mindfulness Training: A Randomised, Active Control, Efficacy Trial," *BMC Psychology*, Vol. 4, No. 60, 2016, pp. 1–14.

Bostock, Sophie, Alexandra D. Crosswell, Aric A. Prather, and Andrew Steptoe, "Mindfulness On-the-Go: Effects of a Mindfulness Meditation App on Work Stress and Well-Being," *Journal of Occupational Health Psychology*, Vol. 24, No. 1, February 1, 2019, pp. 127–138.

Broderick, Patricia C., "Mindfulness and Coping with Dysphoric Mood: Contrasts with Rumination and Distraction," *Cognitive Therapy and Research*, Vol. 29, No. 5, 2005, pp. 501–510.

Burger, Kathleen G., and Joan Such Lockhart, "Meditation's Effect on Attentional Efficiency, Stress, and Mindfulness Characteristics of Nursing Students," *Journal of Nursing Education*, Vol. 56, No. 7, July 1, 2017, pp. 430–434.

Cerna, Cristian, Felipe E. García, and Arnoldo Téllez, "Brief Mindfulness, Mental Health, and Cognitive Processes: A Randomized Controlled Trial," *PsyCh Journal*, Vol. 9, No. 3, June 2020, pp. 359–369.

Ching, Ho-Hoi, Malcolm Koo, Tsung-Huang Tsai, and Chiu-Yuan Chen, "Effects of a Mindfulness Meditation Course on Learning and Cognitive Performance Among University Students in Taiwan," *Evidence-Based Complementary and Alternative Medicine*, Vol. 2015, 2015, article 254358.

Chow, Theodore, Tanaz Javan, Tomas Ros, and Paul Frewen, "EEG Dynamics of Mindfulness Meditation Versus Alpha Neurofeedback: A Sham-Controlled Study," *Mindfulness*, Vol. 8, No. 3, June 2017, pp. 572–584.

Coo, Cristián, and Marisa Salanova, "Mindfulness Can Make You Happy-and-Productive: A Mindfulness Controlled Trial and Its Effects on Happiness, Work Engagement and Performance," *Journal of Happiness Studies: An Interdisciplinary Forum on Subjective Well-Being*, Vol. 19, No. 6, 2018, pp. 1691–1711.

Course-Choi, Jenna, Harry Saville, and Nazanin Derakshan, "The Effects of Adaptive Working Memory Training and Mindfulness Meditation Training on Processing Efficiency and Worry in High Worriers," *Behaviour Research and Therapy*, Vol. 89, February 1, 2017, pp. 1–13.

de Bruin, Esther I., J. Esi van der Zwan, and Susan M. Bögels, "A RCT Comparing Daily Mindfulness Meditations, Biofeedback Exercises, and Daily Physical Exercise on Attention Control, Executive Functioning, Mindful Awareness, Self-Compassion, and Worrying in Stressed Young Adults," *Mindfulness*, Vol. 7, No. 5, July 2, 2016, pp. 1182–1192.

Deady, Mark, Nicholas Glozier, Rafael Calvo, David Johnston, Andrew Mackinnon, David Milne, Isabella Choi, Aimee Gayed, Dorian Peters, Richard Bryant, Helen Christensen, and Samuel B. Harvey, "Preventing Depression Using a Smartphone App: A Randomized Controlled Trial," *Psychological Medicine*, July 6, 2020, pp. 1–10.

Denkova, Ekaterina, Anthony P. Zanesco, Scott L. Rogers, and Amishi P. Jha, "Is Resilience Trainable? An Initial Study Comparing Mindfulness and Relaxation Training in Firefighters," *Psychiatry Research*, Vol. 285, January 16, 2020, article 112794.

DeSteno, David, Daniel Lim, Fred Duong, and Paul Condon, "Meditation Inhibits Aggressive Responses to Provocations," *Mindfulness*, Vol. 9, No. 4, 2018, pp. 1117–1122.

Diaz, Frank M., "Mindfulness, Attention, and Flow During Music Listening: An Empirical Investigation," *Psychology of Music*, Vol. 41, No. 1, 2013, pp. 42–58.

Dixon, Mark R., Dana Paliliunas, Jordan Belisle, Ryan C. Speelman, Karl F. Gunnarsson, and Jordan L. Shaffer, "The Effect of Brief Mindfulness Training on Momentary Impulsivity," *Journal of Contextual Behavioral Science*, Vol. 11, January 2019, pp. 15–20.

Dundas, Ingrid, Per-Einar Binder, Tia G. B. Hansen, and Signe Hjelen Stige, "Does a Short Self-Compassion Intervention for Students Increase Healthy Self-Regulation? A Randomized Control Trial," *Scandinavian Journal of Psychology*, Vol. 58, October 1, 2017, pp. 443–450.

Eisenbeck, Nikolett, Carmen Luciano, and Sonsoles Valdivia-Salas, "Effects of a Focused Breathing Mindfulness Exercise on Attention, Memory, and Mood: The Importance of Task Characteristics," *Behaviour Change*, Vol. 35, No. 1, 2018, pp. 54–70.

Esch, Tobias, Jeremy Winkler, Volker Auwärter, Heike Gnann, Roman Huber, and Stefan Schmidt, "Neurobiological Aspects of Mindfulness in Pain Autoregulation: Unexpected Results from a Randomized-Controlled Trial and Possible Implications for Meditation Research," *Frontiers in Human Neuroscience*, Vol. 10, No. 674, 2016, pp. 1–15.

Fan, Yaxin, Yi-Yuan Tang, Rongxiang Tang, and Michael I. Posner, "Short Term Integrative Meditation Improves Resting Alpha Activity and Stroop Performance," *Applied Psychophysiology and Biofeedback*, Vol. 39, No. 3–4, 2014, pp. 213–217.

Flook, Lisa, Simon B. Goldberg, Laura Pinger, Katherine A. Bonus, and Richard J. Davidson, "Mindfulness for Teachers: A Pilot Study to Assess Effects on Stress, Burnout, and Teaching Efficacy," *Mind, Brain, and Education*, Vol. 7, No. 3, December 7, 2013.

Garland, Eric L., Adam Hanley, Norman A. Farb, and Brett E. Froeliger, "State Mindfulness During Meditation Predicts Enhanced Cognitive Reappraisal," *Mindfulness*, Vol. 6, No. 2, April 1, 2015, pp. 234–242.

Ghawadra, Sajed F., Khatijah Lim Abdullah, Wan Yuen Choo, Mahmoud Danaee, and Cheng Kar Phang, "The Effect of Mindfulness-Based Training on Stress, Anxiety, Depression and Job Satisfaction Among Ward Nurses: A Randomized Control Trial," *Journal of Nursing Management*, Vol. 28, No. 5, July 2020, pp. 1088–1097.

Giannandrea, Alessandro, Luca Simione, Bianca Pescatori, Katie Ferrell, Marta Olivetti Belardinelli, Steven D. Hickman, and Antonino Raffone, "Effects of the Mindfulness-Based Stress Reduction Program on Mind Wandering and Dispositional Mindfulness Facets," *Mindfulness*, Vol. 10, No. 1, 2019, pp. 185–195.

Glück, Tobias M., and Andreas Maercker, "A Randomized Controlled Pilot Study of a Brief Web-Based Mindfulness Training," *BMC Psychiatry*, Vol. 11, No. 175, 2011, pp. 1–12.

Green, Joseph P., and Katharine N. Black, "Meditation-Focused Attention with the MBAS and Solving Anagrams," *Psychology of Consciousness: Theory, Research, and Practice*, Vol. 4, No. 4, 2017, pp. 348–366.

Grégoire, Simon, Lise Lachance, and Geneviève Taylor, "Mindfulness, Mental Health and Emotion Regulation Among Workers," *International Journal of Wellbeing*, Vol. 5, No. 4, 2015, pp. 96–119.

Hafenbrack, Andrew. C., Lindsey D. Cameron, Gretchen M. Spreitzer, Chen Zhang, Laura J. Noval, and Samah Shaffakat, "Helping People by Being in the Present: Mindfulness Increases Prosocial Behavior," *Organizational Behavior and Human Decision Processes*, Vol. 159, July 2020, pp. 21–38.

Hildebrandt, Lea K., Cade McCall, and Tania Singer, "Socioaffective Versus Sociocognitive Mental Trainings Differentially Affect Emotion Regulation Strategies," *Emotion*, Vol. 19, No. 8, December 2019, pp. 1329–1342.

Hülsheger, Ute R., Hugo J. E. M. Alberts, Alina Feinholdt, and Jonas W. B. Lang, "Benefits of Mindfulness at Work: The Role of Mindfulness in Emotion Regulation, Emotional Exhaustion, and Job Satisfaction," *Journal of Applied Psychology*, Vol. 98, No. 2, March 1, 2013, pp. 310–325.

Hunsinger, Matthew, Michael Christopher, and Andi M. Schmidt, "Mindfulness Training, Implicit Bias, and Force Response Decision-Making," *Mindfulness*, Vol. 10, No. 12, December 1, 2019, pp. 2555–2566.

Hwang, Yoon-Suk, Harvey Goldstein, Oleg N. Medvedev, Nirbhay N. Singh, Jae-Eun Noh, and Kirstine Hand, "Mindfulness-Based Intervention for Educators: Effects of a School-Based Cluster Randomized Controlled Study," *Mindfulness*, Vol. 10, No. 7, 2019, pp. 1417–1436.

Jankowski, Tomasz, and Pawel Holas, "Effects of Brief Mindfulness Meditation on Attention Switching," *Mindfulness*, Vol. 11, No. 5, May 1, 2020, pp. 1150–1158.

Jennings, Patricia A., Sebrina Doyle, Yoonkyung Oh, Damira Rasheed, Jennifer L. Frank, and Joshua L. Brown, "Long-Term Impacts of the CARE Program on Teachers' Self-Reported Social and Emotional Competence and Well-Being," *Journal of School Psychology*, Vol. 76, October 2019, pp. 186–202.

Jensen, Andrew E., Jake R. Bernards, Jameson T. Jameson, Douglas C. Johnson, and Karen R. Kelly, "The Benefit of Mental Skills Training on Performance and Stress Response in Military Personnel," *Frontiers in Psychology*, Vol. 10, January 14, 2020, article 2964.

Jensen, Christian G., Signe Vangkilde, Vibe Frokjaer, and Steen G. Hasselbalch, "Mindfulness Training Affects Attention—or Is It Attentional Effort?" *Journal of Experimental Psychology: General*, Vol. 141, No. 1, February 2012, pp. 106–123.

Jha, Amishi P., Jason Krompinger, and Michael J. Baime, "Mindfulness Training Modifies Subsystems of Attention," *Cognitive Affective Behavioral Neuroscience*, Vol. 7, No. 2, June 2007, pp. 109–119.

Jha, Amishi P., Alexandra B. Morrison, Justin Dainer-Best, Suzanne Parker, Nina Rostrup, and Elizabeth A. Stanley, "Minds 'at Attention': Mindfulness Training Curbs Attentional Lapses in Military Cohorts," *PLOS ONE*, Vol. 10, No. 2, 2015, article e0116889.

Jha, Amishi P., Alexandra B. Morrison, Suzanne C. Parker, and Elizabeth A. Stanley, "Practice Is Protective: Mindfulness Training Promotes Cognitive Resilience in High-Stress Cohorts," *Mindfulness*, Vol. 8, No. 1, 2017, pp. 46–58.

Jha, Amishi P., Anthony P. Zanesco, Ekaterina Denkova, Alexandra B. Morrison, Nicolas Ramos, Keith Chichester, John W. Gaddy, and Scott L. Rogers, "Bolstering Cognitive Resilience via Train-the-Trainer Delivery of Mindfulness Training in Applied High-Demand Settings," *Mindfulness*, Vol. 11, No. 3, March 1, 2019, pp. 683–697.

Jha, Amishi P., Anthony P. Zanesco, Ekaterina Denkova, Joshua Rooks, Alexandra B. Morrison, and Elizabeth A. Stanley, "Comparing Mindfulness and Positivity Trainings in High-Demand Cohorts," *Cognitive Therapy and Research*, Vol. 44, No. 2, April 1, 2020, pp. 311–326.

Johnson, Susan, Ravid Moses Gur, Zhanna David, and Elise Currier, "One-Session Mindfulness Meditation: A Randomized Controlled Study of Effects on Cognition and Mood," *Mindfulness*, Vol. 6, No. 1, 2015, pp. 88–98.

Keng, Shian-Ling, Elysia Li Yan Tan, Tory A. Eisenlohr-Moul, and Moria J. Smoski, "Effects of Mindfulness, Reappraisal, and Suppression on Sad Mood and Cognitive Resources," *Behaviour Research and Therapy*, Vol. 91, April 1, 2017, pp. 33–42.

Klatt, Maryanna, Chris Norre, Brenda Reader, Laura Yodice, and Susan White, "Mindfulness in Motion: A Mindfulness-Based Intervention to Reduce Stress and Enhance Quality of Sleep in Scandinavian Employees," *Mindfulness*, Vol. 8, No. 2, 2017, pp. 481–488.

Kral, Tamira R. A., Ted Imhoff-Smith, Douglas C. Dean, Dan Grupe, Nagesh Adluru, Elena Patsenko, Jeanette A. Mumford, Robin Goldman, Melissa A. Rosenkranz, and Richard J. Davidson, "Mindfulness-Based Stress Reduction-Related Changes in Posterior Cingulate Resting Brain Connectivity," *Social Cognitive Affective Neuroscience*, Vol. 14, No. 7, July 31, 2019, pp. 777–787.

Kuo, Chun-Yu, and Yei-Yu Yeh, "Reset a Task Set After Five Minutes of Mindfulness Practice," *Consciousness and Cognition*, Vol. 35, September 1, 2015, pp. 98–109.

Kwak, Seoyeon, So-Yeon Kim, Dahye Bae, Wu-Jeong Hwang, Kang Ik Kevin Cho, Kyung-Ok Lim, Hye-Yoon Park Park, Tae Young Lee, and Jun Soo Kwon, "Enhanced Attentional Network by Short-Term Intensive Meditation," *Frontiers in Psychology*, Vol. 10, February 7, 2020, article 3073.

Lacerda, Shirley S., Stephen W. Little, and Elisa H. Kozasa, "A Stress Reduction Program Adapted for the Work Environment: A Randomized Controlled Trial with a Follow-Up," *Frontiers in Psychology*, Vol. 9, May 1, 2018, article 668.

Lai, Constantine, Benjamin MacNeil, and Paul Frewen, "A Comparison of the Attentional Effects of Single-Session Mindfulness Meditation and Fp-HEG Neurofeedback in Novices," *Mindfulness*, Vol. 6, No. 5, 2015, pp. 1012–1020.

Larson, Michael J., Patrick R. Steffen, and Mark Primosch, "The Impact of a Brief Mindfulness Meditation Intervention on Cognitive Control and Error-Related Performance Monitoring," *Frontiers in Human Neuroscience*, Vol. 7, July 9, 2013, article 308.

Li, Yunyun, Fang Liu, Qin Zhang, Xinghua Liu, and Ping Wei, "The Effect of Mindfulness Training on Proactive and Reactive Cognitive Control," *Frontiers in Psychology*, Vol. 9, June 1, 2018, article 1002.

Lin, Lin, Guoping He, Jin Yan, Can Gu, and Jianfei Xie, "The Effects of a Modified Mindfulness-Based Stress Reduction Program for Nurses: A Randomized Controlled Trial," *Workplace Health & Safety*, Vol. 67, No. 3, March 1, 2019, pp. 111–122.

Ma, Ying, Zhaozhuo She, Angela Fung-Ying Siu, Xianlong Zeng, and Xinghua Liu, "Effectiveness of Online Mindfulness-Based Interventions on Psychological Distress and the Mediating Role of Emotion Regulation," *Frontiers in Psychology*, Vol. 9, October 2018, article 2090.

Menezes, Carolina Baptista, and Lisiane Bizarro, "Effects of a Brief Meditation Training on Negative Affect, Trait Anxiety and Concentrated Attention," *Paidéia*, Vol. 25, No. 62, 2015, pp. 393–401.

Menezes, Carolina Baptista, Maria Clara de Paula Couto, Luciano G. Buratto, Fatima Erthal, Mirtes G. Pereira, and Lisiane Bizarro, "The Improvement of Emotion and Attention Regulation After a 6-Week Training of Focused Meditation: A Randomized Controlled Trial," *Evidence-Based Complementary and Alternative Medicine*, Vol. 2013, 2013, article 984678.

Menezes, Carolina Baptista, Mirtes G. Pereira, Izabela Mocaiber, and Lisiane Bizarro, "Brief Meditation and the Interaction Between Emotional Interference and Anxiety," *Psicologia: Teoria e Pesquisa*, Vol. 32, No. 2, 2016, pp. 1–8.

Molek-Winiarska, Dorota, and Dorota Żołnierczyk-Zreda, "Application of Mindfulness-Based Stress Reduction to a Stress Management Intervention in a Study of a Mining Sector Company," *International Journal of Occupational Safety and Ergonomics*, Vol. 24, No. 4, December 1, 2018, pp. 546–556.

Morrison, Alexandra B., Merissa Goolsarran, Scott L. Rogers, and Amishi P. Jha, "Taming a Wandering Attention: Short-Form Mindfulness Training in Student Cohorts," *Frontiers in Human Neuroscience*, Vol. 7, January 6, 2014, article 897.

Mrazek, Michael D., Michael S. Franklin, Dawa Tarchin Phillips, Benjamin Baird, and Jonathan W. Schooler, "Mindfulness Training Improves Working Memory Capacity and GRE Performance While Reducing Mind Wandering," *Psychological Science*, Vol. 24, No. 5, May 1, 2013, pp. 776–781.

Norris, Catherine J., Daniel Creem, Reuben Hendler, and Hedy Kober, "Brief Mindfulness Meditation Improves Attention in Novices: Evidence from ERPs and Moderation by Neuroticism," *Frontiers in Human Neuroscience*, Vol. 12, August 1, 2018, article 315.

Ortner, Catherine N. M., Sachne J. Kilner, and Philip David Zelazo, "Mindfulness Meditation and Reduced Emotional Interference on a Cognitive Task," *Motivation and Emotion*, Vol. 31, No. 4, 2007, pp. 271–283.

Pang, Dandan, and Willibald Ruch, "Fusing Character Strengths and Mindfulness Interventions: Benefits for Job Satisfaction and Performance," *Journal of Occupational Health Psychology*, Vol. 24, No. 1, February 1, 2019, pp. 150–162.

Prätzlich, Martin, Joe Kossowsky, Jens Gaab, and Peter Krummenacher, "Impact of Short-Term Meditation and Expectation on Executive Brain Functions," *Behavioural Brain Research*, Vol. 297, January 15, 2016, pp. 268–276.

Quaglia, Jordan T., Fadel Zeidan, Peter G. Grossenbacher, Sara P. Freeman, Sarah E. Braun, Alexandra Martelli, Robert J. Goodman, and Kirk Warren Brown, "Brief Mindfulness Training Enhances Cognitive Control in Socioemotional Contexts: Behavioral and Neural Evidence," *PLOS ONE*, Vol. 14, No. 7, July 19, 2019, article e0219862.

Quan, Peng, Wenna Wang, Chengjin Chu, and Lingfeng Zhou, "Seven Days of Mindfulness-Based Cognitive Therapy Improves Attention and Coping Style," *Social Behavior and Personality: An International Journal*, Vol. 46, No. 3, 2018, pp. 421–430.

Rahl, Hayley A., Emily K. Lindsay, Laura E. Pacilio, Kirk W. Brown, and J. David Creswell, "Brief Mindfulness Meditation Training Reduces Mind Wandering: The Critical Role of Acceptance," *Emotion*, Vol. 17, No. 2, March 1, 2017, pp. 224–230.

Rodriguez Vega, Beatriz, Javier Melero-Llorente, Carmen Bayon Perez, Susana Cebolla, Jorge Mira, Carla Valverde, and Alberto Fernández-Liria, "Impact of Mindfulness Training on Attentional Control and Anger Regulation Processes for Psychotherapists in Training," *Psychotherapy Research*, Vol. 24, No. 2, 2014, pp. 202–213.

Rooks, Joshua D., Alexandra B. Morrison, Merissa Goolsarran, Scott L. Rogers, and Amishi P. Jha, "'We Are Talking About Practice': The Influence of Mindfulness vs. Relaxation Training on Athletes' Attention and Well-Being over High-Demand Intervals," *Journal of Cognitive Enhancement*, Vol. 1, 2017, pp. 141–153.

Rothschild, Sarit, Gilat Kaplan, Tomer Golan, and Yoram Barak, "Mindfulness Meditation in the Israel Defense Forces: Effect on Cognition and Satisfaction with Life—A Randomized Controlled Trial," *European Journal of Integrative Medicine*, Vol. 10, February 1, 2017, pp. 71–74.

Schofield, Timothy P., J. David Creswell, and Thomas F. Denson, "Brief Mindfulness Induction Reduces Inattentional Blindness," *Consciousness and Cognition*, Vol. 37, December 1, 2015, pp. 63–70.

Semple, Randye J., "Does Mindfulness Meditation Enhance Attention? A Randomized Controlled Trial," *Mindfulness*, Vol. 1, No. 2, 2010, pp. 121–130.

Shonin, Edo, William Van Gordon, Thomas J. Dunn, Nirbhay N. Singh, and Mark D. Griffiths, "Meditation Awareness Training (MAT) for Work-Related Wellbeing and Job Performance: A Randomised Controlled Trial," *International Journal of Mental Health and Addiction*, Vol. 12, No. 6, December 2014, pp. 806–823.

Steinberg, Beth A., Maryanna Klatt, and Anne-Marie Duchemin, "Feasibility of a Mindfulness-Based Intervention for Surgical Intensive Care Unit Personnel," *American Journal of Critical Care*, Vol. 26, No. 1, December 1, 2016, pp. 10–18.

Tang, Yi-Yuan, Yinghua Ma, Junhong Wang, Yaxin Fan, Shigang Feng, Qilin Lu, Qingbao Yu, Danni Sui, Mary K. Rothbart, Ming Fan, and Michael I. Posner, "Short-Term Meditation Training Improves Attention and Self-Regulation," *Proceedings of the National Academy of Sciences of the United States of America*, Vol. 104, No. 43, October 23, 2007, pp. 17152–17156.

Throuvala, Melina A., Mark D. Griffiths, Mike Rennoldson, and Daria J. Kuss, "Mind over Matter: Testing the Efficacy of an Online Randomized Controlled Trial to Reduce Distraction from Smartphone Use," *International Journal of Environmental Research and Public Health*, Vol. 17, No. 13, July 5, 2020.

Upton, Shelley R., and Tyler L. Renshaw, "Immediate Effects of the Mindful Body Scan Practice on Risk-Taking Behavior," *Mindfulness*, Vol. 10, No. 1, May 16, 2018, pp. 78–88.

Van Gordon, William, Edo Shonin, Thomas J. Dunn, Javier Garcia-Campayo, Marcelo M. P. Demarzo, and Mark D. Griffiths, "Meditation Awareness Training for the Treatment of Workaholism: A Controlled Trial," *Journal of Behavioral Addictions*, Vol. 6, No. 2, June 1, 2017, pp. 212–220.

Walsh, Kathleen Marie, Bechara J. Saab, and Norman A. S. Farb, "Effects of a Mindfulness Meditation App on Subjective Well-Being: Active Randomized Controlled Trial and Experience Sampling Study," *JMIR Mental Health*, Vol. 6, No. 1, January 8, 2019, article e10844.

Watford, Tanya S., and Jane Stafford, "The Impact of Mindfulness on Emotion Dysregulation and Psychophysiological Reactivity Under Emotional Provocation," *Psychology of Consciousness: Theory, Research, and Practice*, Vol. 2, No. 1, 2015, pp. 90–109.

Watier, Nicholas, and Michael Dubois, "The Effects of a Brief Mindfulness Exercise on Executive Attention and Recognition Memory," *Mindfulness*, Vol. 7, No. 3, 2016, pp. 745–753.

Wenzel, Mario, Zarah Rowland, and Thomas Kubiak, "How Mindfulness Shapes the Situational Use of Emotion Regulation Strategies in Daily Life," *Cognition and Emotion*, Vol. 34, No. 7, May 6, 2020, pp. 1408–1422.

Wimmer, Lena, Lisa von Stockhausen, and Silja Bellingrath, "Improving Emotion Regulation and Mood in Teacher Trainees: Effectiveness of Two Mindfulness Trainings," *Brain and Behavior*, Vol. 9, September 2019, article e01390.

Wingert, Jason R., Jeffrey C. Jones, Robert A. Swoap, and Heather M. Wingert, "Mindfulness-Based Strengths Practice Improves Well-Being and Retention in Undergraduates: A Preliminary Randomized Controlled Trial," *Journal of American College Health*, May 20, 2020, pp. 1–8.

Wolever, Ruth Q., Kyra J. Bobinet, Kelley McCabe, Elizabeth R. Mackenzie, Erin Fekete, Catherine A. Kusnick, and Michael Baime, "Effective and Viable Mind-Body Stress Reduction in the Workplace: A Randomized Controlled Trial," *Journal of Occupational Health Psychology*, Vol. 17, No. 2, April 1, 2012, pp. 246–258.

Wu, Ran, Lin-Lin Liu, Hong Zhu, Wen-Jun Su, Zhi-Yong Cao, Shi-Yang Zhong, Xing-Hua Liu, and Chun-Lei Jiang, "Brief Mindfulness Meditation Improves Emotion Processing," *Frontiers in Neuroscience*, Vol. 13, October 10, 2019, article 1074.

Zanesco, Anthony P., Ekaterina Denkova, Scott L. Rogers, William K. MacNulty, and Amishi P. Jha, "Mindfulness Training as Cognitive Training in High-Demand Cohorts: An Initial Study in Elite Military Servicemembers," *Progress in Brain Research*, Vol. 244, 2019, pp. 323–354.

Zeidan, Fadel, Susan K. Johnson, Bruce J. Diamond, Zhanna David, and Paula Goolkasian, "Mindfulness Meditation Improves Cognition: Evidence of Brief Mental Training," *Consciousness and Cognition*, Vol. 19, No. 2, June 2010, pp. 597–605.

Zhang, Qin, Zheng Wang, Xinqiang Wang, Lei Liu, Jing Zhang, and Renlai Zhou, "The Effects of Different Stages of Mindfulness Meditation Training on Emotion Regulation," *Frontiers in Human Neuroscience*, Vol. 13, June 2019, article 208.

Zhu, Tingfei, Jiang Xue, Astrid Montuclard, Yuxing Jiang, Wenqi Weng, and Shulin Chen, "Can Mindfulness-Based Training Improve Positive Emotion and Cognitive Ability in Chinese Non-Clinical Population? A Pilot Study," *Frontiers in Psychology*, Vol. 10, July 3, 2019, article 1549.

Zwilling, Christopher E., Ana M. Daugherty, Charles H. Hillman, Arthur F. Kramer, Neal J. Cohen, and Aron K. Barbey, "Enhanced Decision-Making Through Multimodal Training," *NPJ Science of Learning*, Vol. 4, No. 11, 2019, pp. 1–10.